PROBLEMS AND PROSPECTS OF SUSTAINING DEMOCRACY IN NIGERIA

PROBLEMS AND PROSPECTS OF SUSTAINING DEMOCRACY IN NIGERIA

BAMIDELE A. OJO (ED.)

Nova Science Publishers, Inc.
Huntington, NY

Senior Editors: Susan Boriotti and Donna Dennis
Office Manager: Annette Hellinger
Graphics: Wanda Serrano and Dorothy Marczak
Information Editor: Tatiana Shohov
Book Production: Cathy DeGregory, Jennifer Vogt and Lynette Van Helden
Circulation: Ave Maria Gonzalez, Ron Hedges and Andre Tillman

Library of Congress Cataloging-in-Publication Data

Problems and Prospects of Sustaining Democracy in Nigeria: Voices of a generation /
edited by Bamidele A. Ojo
     p.cm.
  Includes bibliographical references and index.
  ISBN 1-56072-949-X.
  1. Democracy--Nigeria. 2. Nigeria--Politics and government--1993-. I. Ojo, Bamidele A.

JQ3096 .P755 2001
320.9669--dc21

                           2001031294

Printed in the United States of America

CONTENTS

PREFACE

The past few years have been very traumatic for many Nigerians. With the exception of those in power or close to the seat of power, the changes of 1998 were a welcome relief given the tyranny and repression that the country has suffered under General Abacha. With many people in prison and more in exile, the death of Abacha was received with a sigh of relief. The situation got even worse with the death of Chief M.K.O Abiola on the eve of his release from prison but as always the country must go on. Many observers saw in Nigeria, the resilience that has come to signify the strength and potential of this once "giant of Africa". Many have seen the destruction and the socio-political and economic decay of the past decades and as the whole world prepare for the new millennium, things could only get better in Nigeria. That is why the administration of President Obasanjo, even in the absence of anything significant, would still be preferable than the previous military administrations. Many Nigerians have seen the way the leadership has mishandled the Nigerian economy and abuse the rights of the people while exploiting and politicizing the ethnic diversity to satisfy their own individual agenda. It is with this in mind, and the renewed desire to begin to cultivate a Nigerian culture that appreciates the rule of law and sustains democratic governance as a means toward providing the best for all its people, that the aspiration and goals of a representative generation of Nigerians are put together in this volume. The call for Nigerians who want to make a difference received many responses and out of which the following has been selected to address some critical issues facing the new Nigerian political experiment. These opinions, sometimes academic and sometime less so, is considered a preliminary attempt to initiate a dialogue among Nigerians, in an attempt to foster better understanding of our need and identify what could bring us all together. This book is divided into four main parts: Constitutionalism and political reconstruction, social and economic issues, foreign policy issues and wither Nigeria? There are fourteen chapters in all and each representing the view of the authors as so noted. Many others responded to the call for contributions and due to inability to meet the deadline, set and extended several times, their essays cannot be included in this volume. The voice of a generation on democracy in Nigeria, I hope will constitute a renaissance of a more active role in the Nigerian political process by all Nigerians home and abroad.

In chapter I of this book, Victor Aikhionbare contends that Nigeria is at a cross road and the stage is set for a crucial struggle for the survival of this African "giant." Victor asserts that Nigeria must now come to grip with the ultimate question of whether to institute real democratic institutions that will sustain the nation for now and in the future and that more than ever, the political instrument of a constitution and the idea of constitutionalism becomes a very important part of any attempt to move the country beyond the praetorian regimes that have strangled Nigeria politically and economically for more than three decades since independence. In his excellent contribution, Dr. Aikhionbare underscores the importance of a constitution and prescribes how it can be used as a powerful tool to set Nigeria on a stable political course. He stresses the purpose of a constitution in any society, which is to create, organize, and distribute governmental power. And that it is put in place to assure that governmental power is exercised legitimately. This chapter also offers a lively new perspective on an old but timely argument about progressive constitutionalism and regressive authoritarianism by contending that Nigeria's future lies in a viable constitution.

The chapter further suggest that the constitution must represent the holy writ of Nigeria's civil religion, in which Nigerians expect to find the answers to their most troubling questions, especially the one of governance. And that the idea of constitutionalism and a constitution should therefore be a mirror that reflect the Nigerian history, a medium through which each generation of Nigerians turns its values, attitudes, and prejudices into law. Victor also emphasizes that it must serve as a myth that gains its power from a strong belief in it by all Nigerians. The chapter concludes by joining the voices of a generation of Nigerians in challenging all Nigerians to embrace and live by the idea of constitutionalism. This is followed by Adegboyega Somide. His piece on federalism, state creation and ethnic management in Nigeria addresses one of the major problems facing the Obasanjo administration today. He discusses the questions of state creation, federalism and ethnic management in Nigeria. According to him, State creation along ethnic lines in Nigeria has failed to produce desired results and that a powerful ethnic pull continues to prevent Nigerian federalism from functioning effectively. Utilizing John Kingdon's "multiple streams" model, Adegboyega pinpoints the origin of state creation policy in Nigeria, and the reasons for its persistence. It compares Nigerian federalism with older and more successful federal states such as the United States, and concludes that federalism is not necessarily a panacea to ethnic conflict. And that Nigeria does not possess the minimum requisites identified in the literature for a successful federalism, e.g. desire to federate, state autonomy in decision-making and financial independence from the federal government. But that state creation has served to expand the support bases of successive military governments, while failing to remove the structural imbalance in Nigerian federalism.

In chapter III, Bamidele Ojo examines the inadequacies of the 1999 constitution of the Federal Democratic Republic of Nigeria provision on federal -state relationship. He calls for a review that will facilitate a more independent component unit which will allow each state to develop its own agenda and promote its own goals within the general construct of the Nigerian polity. In this chapter he reiterates a common concern for the continued dependence of the Nigerian component states on the federal government, which is contrary to the true spirit of federalism. And also calls for a constitutional review which will allow for a more autonomous state structure and legitimate constitutional construction. This call is also premised on the notion that a far more independent sub-unit is indispensable for sustaining democratic governance and effective federal structure in Nigeria. Professor Layi Abegunrin in chapter IV proposes that the subject of federalism exerts a magnetic force among Nigerians. And that there was broad agreement that Nigerian federalism has been abused by military rule and that the way forward is to reconstitute our governance in such a manner as to avoid the over centralization of Nigeria's public affairs and governance imposed by military rule. The chapter examines and analyzes the tragedy of Nigeria's crisis of governance that has damaged inter-ethnic, inter-regional and other communal relationships. In conclusion, he gives some suggestions on how to restructure and sustain democratic culture and institutions that can lead to peace, political stability and long standing economic development in a democratic environment under a true federal system. Part II starts with Mark Okoronkwo's piece on leadership and elite politics in Nigeria. Mark identifies many major problem areas in the governance of Nigeria and according to him, the chaotic state of affairs in Nigeria is due mainly to the military and the failure of the leadership in general. He concludes the chapter on a strong note by making recommendation for a selfless, capable and patriotic leadership in the new Nigerian polity. In chapter VI, Zephyrinus C. Okonkwo, examines two ideas: Curriculum Innovations for the Nigerian Educational System, and Administrative Innovations for the Nigerian Educational System with emphasis on the tertiary level. Although these two ideas seen to be independent, they have a region of intersection which will be discussed in the sequel. Zephy discusses in some detail the needed curriculum innovations at all levels of the educational system and also deal with administrative innovations required at the colleges and universities in order to lay a strong foundation for a stable environment where students, professors, non-academic staff, and administrators can thrive as a community whose objective encompass teaching, research, and service. Dr. Okonkwo in this chapter affirms that like every educational system, the Nigerian Educational System must provide:

(i) An adequate, safe and secure environment for teaching and learning where the educated must imbibe adequate skills and knowledge to seek gainful employment within the society;

(ii) College level education, which must not only provide the student with enough basic skills but must also prepare the student for graduate education within and outside the country;

(ii) Responsive dynamic curriculum at all levels of education. Such curriculum, according to him, must respond to societal needs, and must include innovative methods of teaching and learning, innovative method of seeking knowledge, computer skills and information technology, strong emphasis on communications both in written and oral forms, reading and public speaking. The curriculum at all levels must be reviewed from time to time expunging irrelevant topics and courses and including new ones.

He also suggests that administrative innovations at the tertiary level must include:

(i) Tenure system at all tertiary institutions;

(ii) A method of checking the excesses of some professors and administrators through legislation and enforcement of the laws;

(iii) Provision of adequate funding for salaries and research for colleges and universities by the establishment of a stable method of funding including land-grant, Educational Tax, Luxury Tax, and Property Tax;

(iv)Streamlining teaching and research resources and reducing waste by eliminating redundancy and duplications in neighboring colleges and universities.

This chapter is followed by Adeolu Esho 's piece on the Nigerian elite wherein he takes a cursory look at the emergence of the Nigerian elites and their role in the systematic decimation of a country and the marginalization of a people. Adeolu also delve into the exodus of a generation of Nigerians in search of greener pastures, in need of self-preservation and filled with a burning desire to salvage their dignity and that of their families. The final portion of the chapter focus on issues that need to be addressed for a sustainable economic, political and societal development in Nigeria. This is followed by part III on foreign policy issues. This section is started by Professor Abegunrin's overview of Nigerian foreign policy since independence. In this excellent piece, he examines the foreign policy of each administration between 1960-1998. Based on the premise that the personality of each leader that has ruled Nigeria affected, and influenced the country's policy either negatively or positively, no matter how stable or unstable the political situations of the country have been under each regime, he emphasizes the dynamics of Nigeria's foreign policy and that the transfer of power to a capable, well disciplined, uncorrupted, and democratically elected civilian government in 1999 could provide fresh impetus to the economy, to human rights, to relations with the major industrial powers, and to better policy overall.

In chapter IX, Dr. Nowamagbe Omoigui discusses the Nigerian involvement in Sierra Leone. According to him, the notion of Africa as the centerpiece of Nigeria's foreign policy is romantic and admirable but needs to be vigorously reevaluated and placed in context. The centerpiece of Nigeria's foreign policy ought to be its citizens and their individual and collective interests outside the country insofar as it affects their quality of life inside the country. He asserts that Nigeria's sub-regional, regional and non-regional international ties need to be predicated on this basic framework and that Nigeria cannot afford to be naive enough to assume any permanent friends or enemies particularly when her presumptions are not reciprocated and her economic survival is in doubt. Nowamagbe also makes it clear that Nigeria is not the only country with a humanitarian or regional security interest in what was going on in Sierra Leone but that Nigeria needs to carefully reposition itself in the right orbit within the universe of other interested parties (bilaterally and multilaterally) and titrate her investments and risk-taking to the realities of her domestic situation and the current international environment. This is followed by Dr. Aderemi Ajibewa's chapter on Nigeria and Regional Security In West Africa. This chapter looks into the economic, military and socio-political clout of Nigeria in the sub-region as to determine if she could have the surplus to defend her neighbors in the West

African sub-region in line with her foreign policy posture. This chapter is also premised on the notion that Nigeria may become or act as the policeman of the sub-region or would seek accommodation with others through economic, political and defense alliances to defend the sub-region. The parameter that guides his analysis revolves around: What is the structure of Regional Security? In this respect, three criteria are examined to determine the adequacy of the regional intervention: a. Is there a Regional structure? b. How consensual or conflictual is West Africa? and c. Is there a structure of Regional leadership? 2. What is the 'diplomatic basis' / structure of the intervention? There are a number of variables which call for analysis, emphasis will be on the more critical ones.

In chapter XI, Dr. Kelechi Kalu undertakes a study of the political economy of Nigerian foreign policy with a focus on Economic Diplomacy within the Economic Community of West African States. Dr. Kalu asks the basic question: given the international system's constraints identified by Realism and Dependency theories, how much freedom do African countries have in designing their strategies for economic development? A basic analytic assumption here is that for African countries there is very little distinction between foreign and domestic economic policies. This assumption is based on the fact that domestic policy (e.g. taxation laws) affects how foreign countries and corporations perceive their relationship with a given country. And, that the structure and operation of the international economic system forms part of the structure and operation of the international political system where the concept of power, however defined, is central. For different reasons, both realism and dependency theories would agree that as a less developed country, Nigeria's external and/or domestic economic policies would be constrained by the international system.

The international system's constraints argument presupposes the absence of freedom or options for Nigeria to design an independent foreign policy and economic strategies for development outside of the rules determined by powerful political and economic actors in the international system. A systematic exploration and analysis of the relationship between Nigeria and the member states of ECOWAS yields insights for understanding regional and internal constraints on Nigeria as well as opportunities for its foreign and domestic economic policies. Section three of the book is focused on which way forward for Nigeria. And here, Dr. Tope Omoniyi in chapter XII, reaffirm the consensus of opinion that Nigeria has spent enough time in the doldrums during which it was confined to the margins of global economics and politics. According to him, internally, Nigerian citizens have suffered depredations and degradation brought on by embarrassingly high levels of mismanagement in spite of an abundance of both human and natural resources. And while the current new experiment at democratic governance is expected to go through a teething period with all the attendant problems associated with such a stage of development, the nation possesses the wherewithal to avoid some of the pitfalls that the post-industrial world experienced. To Tope, the despondency that has attended the last years of military 'occupation' must now transform into the positive rage that galvanizes the nation into 'action for development'. It is against this background that this chapter examines some of the relevant factors in designing a workable framework for national development. Dr. Omoniyi's emphasis is on the media and mass education in the democratic process, information technology and the global economy and a reappraisal of attitudes to class, culture and civic responsibility. This is followed by Dr. Nwuke's piece on managing multi-ethnicity. Kasirim Nwuke claims that the instruments that Nigeria has used to manage her multi-ethnicity have themselves become a factor responsible for the increase in the number and intensity of conflict and that efforts aimed at reducing the incidence and intensity of ethnic and inter-ethnic conflict must of necessity include a complete overhaul of these instruments. In this chapter, Kasirim review the emerging economics literature on the growth effects of ethnic fragmentation and provides a historical background to the management of ethnic conflict in Nigeria. It also examines three instruments of state creation, the Federal character principle, and the system of revenue allocation - used in Nigeria to manage the country's multiethnicity. This exercise end with Bamidele Ojo's chapter on constructive incorporation of traditional institutions into the new Nigerian experiment. According to him, Nigerian polity is an artificial British creation, which for obvious reasons was created while ignoring domestic variables, which is one of the many reasons for the socio-political and economic decay we are witnessing today. In this chapter he calls for a constructive incorporation of traditional institutions as a means of establishing political legitimacy and sustaining the new Nigerian political experiment.

Bamidele A Ojo PhD,
December 18th. 2000
Stroudsburg, Pennsylvania, United States.

INTRODUCTION :
A MISSION WITH A VISION

I was in the office that morning preparing for an 11 o'clock class when the telephone rang and a colleague informed me about the death of General Sanni Abacha. I immediately contacted the Nigeria Consulate in New York City and the news was confirmed. My feeling was that of amazement at the recent turn of event and as a political scientist and out of instinct, began to ponder possible political scenario, including whither Nigeria?, who takes over, what will happen to Chief Abiola and whether this is the turning point in Nigeria history. The following days confirmed my fears and raised many questions, many of which remain unanswered even almost two years to the day.

The assumption of power of General Abubakar and the death of Chief Abiola and the transition program followed by the election of Olusegun Obasanjo, were trend that will continue to baffle Nigerian historians and political scientist alike. With the transition and the democratic election of Olusegun Obasanjo, albeit a former military leader, came another opportunity for socio-political and economic rebirth in the life of a people. The task of nation building as well as state building therefore became the most important agenda for the leadership in Nigeria. I therefore put together a collection of issues that need to be addressed by the new leaders in an open letter to the newly elected president, calling for a responsible and accountable leadership in the country because one of the most important problem facing this country since independence and probably since its existence is the lack of effective and responsible leadership. The letter was also published by the Guardian Newspaper(Lagos) on the 22nd. of April 1999 as New Leadership In Nigeria. This piece is presented below as a forward to this collection of essays by a generation of Nigerians, who have been observing the Nigerian dilemma for decades now.

New Leadership in Nigeria

As a student of politics and democratic process, I have no doubt that we as a people are capable of reaching greater heights with the right leadership capable of promoting the human rights, the welfare and the prosperity of its people. While we celebrate this renewed opportunity to do something positive by our people since independence, we must understand that no domestic peace can exist and no prosperity will be attainable without social justice and the commitment to the promotion of and the defense of human rights. This is very much within our reach if we as a people are committed to it especially if we can eliminate the indifference on the part of the entire leadership. Yours is an opportunity to set a good example and I hope you will take this second chance to do just that. I also hope your government will endeavor to exploit to its limits the tremendous human assets that the country is endowed. We also need to bridge the gap between the government and the governed, between the elite and the mass, between the north and the south, within the north and within the south and within the groups and among our people.

A Popular Constitution

The first step toward achieving a viable democratic governance revolves around a legitimate and popularly accepted constitution. Your government must find a way to put in place a constitution but which is embraced by all Nigerians. There is a need to remove the military fingerprints that seems to soil all democratic experiments since independence.

The new constitution(the 1979 constitution was the best we have ever had) should be ratified by the states and approved through a referendum because a legitimate constitution is imperative for both socio-political and economic development. It will reinforce the institutionalization of our democratic experiment and the future of our polity. We must find a way to prevent the suspension of our constitution. Every Nigerian must be able to rise up and resist any attempt to violate a popularly accepted constitution. There is the need to end ruling Nigeria through decrees. This may dissuade future coup attempts.

An Identifiable Citizenry

One important step toward achieving any growth and prosperity in Nigeria is for our government to know and be able to respond to every Nigerian through an effective identification process. We need an identification card or social security card that would help the government in directly focusing its policy initiatives on the citizenry. This would help in monitoring social and economic welfare of Nigerians and facilitate effective taxation.

STATE AUTONOMY

To strengthen our federal system and sustain the process of nation building, there is a need for state autonomy. Additional resources need to be allocated to the states and they should have more control over education, health, transportation and other significant aspects of governance with direct and immediate impact on our people. The states should be allowed to define their respective agenda and to embody in their respective state constitutions and legitimate administrative structures from which to promote their domestic agenda and aspirations. It is at this level that I think we should involve our traditional institutions in this democratic experiment. Our traditional leaders/rulers because of their continued pseudo-political and spiritual role and as a link to our pre-colonial past should be allowed to provide a far reaching legitimacy for our new institutions and democratic engagements. We can no longer ignore their gradual irrelevance in our societal structure when they remain the only viable remnant of our authentic but forgotten traditions and identity.

DOMESTIC AGENDA

Obviously, you will be preoccupied with problems such as food and fuel shortages, unemployment, unpaid salaries, hyperinflation, sluggish economic growth and foreign debts but these are the problems that our leaders must resolve and many more. The mark of a good leader is not in the amount in foreign accounts nor is it in the disdain shown towards criticism nor the imprisonment of those who dare challenge their position or the desire to cater to ones personal needs. But a great leader is known for his courage and efforts to resolve the variants ills that befalls his nation. All that Nigerians ask for, is for you to do your best. Give it all and you shall be remembered as one of the few if any we have seen in our country. Many before you if not all have failed the nation and you have the unique opportunity of a second chance. The new leadership, you must end the endemic nature of the fuel shortages that suffocates our nation by privatizing oil refineries while taking firm control of foreign monopolies and at the same time ridden this sector of its paralyzing corruption.

Our tax system needs to be overhauled. We are a nation in need of an equitable tax system. We need all, not the civil servants alone, to pay their taxes. We call for a system capable of generating revenue necessary for our social and economic growth. It is time, to improve government ability to collect internal revenue effectively. To encourage investment and small business as well as to promote entrepreneurial spirit, our banking system need to be liberalized. A renewed life need to be injected into our economy.

THE MILITARY

This country must find a way to end military intervention in politics. A commission should be set up including both civilians and military personnel (retired and active) to find a way to restructure the military and provide them a more viable and constructive role to play in our society especially when we are not in dare need of them to defend our country. A civilian control of the military is indispensable in a democratic society and an effort should made to de-politicized the entire armed forces. The Nigerian police need to be retrained and provided necessary hardware in order to perform effectively. They remain a far more important agent in sustaining stability in a society riddled with corruption and criminal activities. I implore you to do all that is necessary to turn this around. Our law enforcement institutions need to be reformed and our prisons updated, equipped and reoriented towards rehabilitation and positively impacting on those that it serves.

ETHICAL LEADERSHIP

An ethical and accountable leadership is a means toward establishing the public trust in government and in this spirit, I hope your government and the entire elected representatives should declare their assets within three months of assuming office. The public must be brought along to realize that public office is not a means to accumulate wealth but an avenue to provide public service in the interest of all Nigerians. We must begin to change our public persona and the prevailing culture of corruption through a systematic and radical purging of our entire governmental structures and service system, of dishonesty, inefficiency and ineptitude. All contracts involving over a million naira should be made public and all information regarding the award and contractors should be disclosed and in pubic domain. We need good communication and adequately funded and equipped medical facilities in Nigeria. It is about time the government focus on the epidemic and the destructive impact of AIDS and HIV. It is time to provide effective preventive and quality health care for people. A healthy population is a productive population. Your government should respond with vigor and focus in addressing these issues. The mark of your leadership should be felt in the rural as well as in the urban Nigeria. Considering that, agriculture accounts for 40% of our gross domestic product but employs over 65% of our people, I think its about time to do something about this. We need to redistribute our wealth and provide capital to our farmers in order to engage in large scale agriculture. The farmers should be helped as well as protected so that we can be able to feed ourselves again. I call on you to privatize all agencies providing basic social services in order to generate competition and better services for our people.

We do not need our government spending our hard earn revenues in supporting unprofitable ventures and ineffective services such as NEPA, NITEL, Nigeria Airways, to mention a few. Privatization should not mean preserving the domination of these agencies, it must include choices and the opportunity for other capable entrepreneur to establish competition and as such provide better services for our people. It is time to revamp our economy and make it work for all Nigerians.

VISIONARY LEADERSHIP

We need a visionary leadership with an agenda. You government needs to develop a **national agenda** which should include a plan to reduce our dependence on oil and compulsory savings from revenues generated from it. The people in those areas where these resources are extracted should be protected and guaranteed a healthy and save environment. A domestic agenda should center on the promotion of socio-political and economic well being of all Nigerians. It should seek to exploit to the maximum our industrial capacity. Your government should undertake the review of budgetary allocation to ministries and parastatals and the reduction of our defense spending in order to reallocate funds towards those areas in needs such as education, health, communication, to mention just a few. We need to prepare our country to compete in the next millennium because a self-critical leadership with a viable domestic agenda will promote a stable foreign policy. We also need an immediate and structured payment plan that will eliminate our foreign debts within a period of time and there should be a moratorium on any loan or other form of indebtedness. Nigeria has lost her place in the region and on the world stage. You can reclaim our moral and political leadership in Africa and beyond. Our embassies abroad should be responsive to our citizens and engage in promoting the image and well being of Nigeria. We need a strong Nigeria capable of leading Africa through its present woes. Not only do we all as Africans need to work together on such problems as AIDS and the prevailing wars in many parts of the continent but also to generate enough market and economic interdependence that would make this continent the envy of the world. We are lagging behind in technology and the computer age is already passing us by. What we need is an action plan champion by a group of countries already making necessary strides within their own society. If you lead Nigeria well, Africa will respect your leadership.

Finally, I call on the President and the new leadership, to promote a culture of accommodation in our country. Your leadership should transcend regions and parties. The interests of all Nigerians should be the main stay of your administration. Appointments to federal positions and offices should equitably reflect the diversity of our nation. Your administration must support an independent labor system. To help your administration to focus on this agenda, you need a free press. The freedom of the press is indispensable to the sustenance of our political life and this political experiment. Your government must also promote a free and independent judiciary without which a domestic agenda will fail. A disciplined leadership must provide the much needed direction through bipartisan governmental appointments which should lay the foundation for a stronger and united Nigeria because our nation is in need of all that are capable of making a difference.

This is not the time for some to be prevented from or some to refuse to participate in our political experiment. We are all Nigerians whose birthright is to participate in promoting a common agenda for the best of all Nigerians. I am happy to be a Nigerian, the fact that I was born a Yoruba or Christian is nothing but an accident at birth and removes nothing from the fact that I am a human being whose interests like others should be protected and whose well being should be assured in a polity like ours. We all should be proud of being a Nigerian. The experience of the past years is nothing to write home about but we are encouraged that here is a renewed opportunity to attain our God given potential as all Nigerians have dreamt in those dark days. It is about time to begin to develop within all Nigerians the sense of nationhood. This is our future and this is our road toward bringing together a committed people embarking on a journey to building a great nation- Nigeria.

Bamidele A Ojo PhD
Stroudsburg. PA USA

PART I: CONSTITUTIONAL AND POLITICAL RECONSTRUCTION

One of the most fundamental issues facing the current democratic experiment in Nigeria is that of the question surrounding the 1999 federal constitution. As the main stay of the new Nigerian democracy, it is seen not only as a legacy of the Nigerian military incursion into politics but as devoid of any popular acceptability whatsoever. And as a result of which there have been calls for its review and an eventual referendum on it by the Nigerian people. That is the reason why, we begin this book by taking a critical look at this most important source of our nation in the next six chapters which are devoted to the examination of the various aspect of the 1999 Nigerian constitution.

Chapter I

Constitutionalism and the Future of Nigeria

Edo-Aikhionbare

Nigeria has arrived at a constitutional crossroad. Everyday, the country grows more impotent and her people more discontent. There are those both at home and abroad who prophecy her downfall as a nation. Why? Because since independence, the country has been plagued with a crisis of governance, lacking statesmanship and any deep commitment by successive regimes to simply do the right thing. The stage is now set for a crucial struggle for the political survival of this African "giant." As we approach the dawn of a new millennium, Nigeria must now come to grip with the ultimate question of whether to institute real democratic institutions that will sustain the nation for now and the future. More than ever, the political instrument of a constitution and the idea of constitutionalism becomes a very important part of any attempt to move the country beyond the praetorian regimes that have strangled Nigeria politically and economically for more than three decades since her independence.

As former American president Ronald Reagan once said, (a) constitution is an "impassioned and inspired vehicle by which (nations) travel through history."[1] Although, Nigeria has always had a constitution at one time or the other and at various interval since independence but what has been absent always been living, believing in, and being guided by the myth of a constitution. The earliest attempt at constitutionalism in Nigeria began with the Nigerian Order in Council, enacted as part of the Nigeria Independence Act of 1960 by the British Parliament which became effective on Nigerian Independence day, October 1, 1960. It was a statutory instrument made by the British queen on the advice of her Majesty's Privy Council.[2] The constitution embodied in this order remained in force until September 30, 1963 when it was revised to make Nigeria a republic. After a military coup in 1966, the army ran Nigeria until 1979 when civilians returned under a new constitution. But 1979 constitution was suspended in December 1983 following another military coup. In May 1999, Gen. Abdulsalami Abubakar handed over to a democratically elected civilian government headed by President Olusegun Obasanjo under a new constitution. The contention here is that having a constitution is one thing but accepting the idea of constitutionalism is another. It is not just having a constitution, but having a "honest" constitution that is not simply a facade but one that has a direct and formative relationship to the daily political life of the country. And also what has led to the absence of the principles of constitutionalism in Nigeria since independence. And can this country of great potentials embrace the idea of constitutionalism? Finally, what difference will this make politically, economically, and socially to Nigerians?

NIGERIA THE NATION

The moment has arrived which will decide whether the Nigerian experiment as a nation will survive and be a blessing to all Nigerians. There are those who question the very existence of a Nigerian state and have become emotionally disconnected from the very concept of a "Nigeria" because of the way the country was created and the difficulties of governing the country since independence. In order to adequately account for this frame of mind among some Nigerians, it is imperative that we recapture our past for the purpose of understanding the present and planning for the future in this new millennium. A review of Nigeria's historical background and the kind of arrangements that existed before the nation-state was born reveals that the seeds of political and legal problems were sowed long ago. In his eloquent attempt to underscore the enormous problem of building the Nigeria nation, Chief Frederick Rotimi Williams reminds us that Nigeria was a geographical unit created by the British imperialist expansion of the twentieth century. The peoples of Nigeria were never a nation, nor did they live together in one country before the advent of European imperialism. It was British imperialist expansion, through the forced amalgamation of Northern and Southern Protectorates in 1914, that brought the country now known as Nigeria into existence and the peoples for the first time under one government. An important aspect of the problem was that the various peoples speak different languages and have different cultural backgrounds. And the differences between the major ethnic groups in Nigeria, as he further contends, are much more greater than the differences between the nations of Europe.[3]

The fact is that almost every other country in the world was forged artificially like Nigeria for one reason or the other. This, by itself does not mean that Nigeria has failed to hold up as a nation, but it may have failed to carry out its legitimate functions as a state. Ali Mazrui described the six functions that are crucial to assessing the success or failure of a state as:

> "...sovereign control over territory; sovereign supervision (though not necessarily ownership) of the nation's resources; effective and rational revenue extraction from people, goods, and services; the capacity to build and maintain an adequate national infrastructure (roads, postal services, telephone systems, railways, and the like); the capacity to render such basic services as sanitation, education, housing, and health care; and the capacity for governance and the maintenance of law and order."[4]

Obviously, if there is anything that Nigeria as a nation has done well in from these criteria, is the maintenance of its sovereignty and independence within its borders. On almost all others, it can be said that Nigeria has been far from successful. But, this is more as a result of a crisis of governance than anything else. However, the consensus among many Nigerians is that they do want to live together as one country. And there are those who believe that the Nigerian Civil War of 1967-1970 was the true test of this desire for Nigeria to be kept as one nation.

There is no doubt that this new generations of Nigerians have the greatest respect for those Nigerians who contributed immensely to our nation building, particularly for making our independence a reality. Nation building and independence have been meaningless without a broad consensus about what the nation, the regime, institutional arrangements, and rules of the game should be. Many of Nigeria problems stem from the fact that agreement on these has been conspicuously absent. As a result, no government civilian or military - has been able to develop the authority or the legitimacy that would enable it to govern with the required degree of effectiveness but there is a simple remedy which is as bold as the times require which is through constitutional arrangements and the belief in constitutionalism wherein the peoples who have been brought together by the chance of history stay together.

PROSPECT FOR DEMOCRACY AND POLITICAL CHANGE

The growth of modern democracies around the world is heavily documented in the existing literature. as was predicted as far back as 1835 by Alexis de Tocqueville and some scholars contend that democracy is an irreversible trend for mankind- a "natural phenomenon" As Myron Weiner argued, "few issues are more likely to seize world attention...than the question of whether authoritarian countries in the third world will make a transition to democracy."[5] The question therefore become what are the prospect for real democratic changes in Nigeria in the next millennium?

Politics is about change - change in the laws and policies that guide a nation, change in the desires of the people, change in the ranks of government officials, and change in the very structures of government. Some of this dynamism is inherent in the nature of politics as a struggle for a better society. In the early 1980s, democratic governments were rare in the developing countries but in recent years, the world has witnessed tremendous changes in the way that many nations are governed. There has been a wave of democratization around the world. For example, the once monolithic Soviet Union dissolved into a federation of separate states. The most important of the successor states, Russia, has approved a constitution with has an elected parliament and president. The same kind of institutional change have taken place in all of the Eastern European nations that used to be part of the Soviet bloc, as well as a number of Caribbean and Central American states. In 1990 and 1991, every country south of Mexico had a democratically elected government and a popular democratic uprising overthrew the Marcos government in the Philippines.

At the same time, however, several other countries, including Liberia and Yugoslavia, literally have come apart through ethnic struggles and civil war. For the most part, Africa has lagged behind, but some movement towards democratization is becoming more and more popular everyday. None of these countries in Africa is being more closely watched than Nigeria. This is rather due to its share size and potential influence on the continent. The hope of many Nigerians and others around the world is that Nigeria will change for the better, at a time when great nations of the world courageously move towards democracy, the rule of law and human rights, Nigeria cannot afford to be left out. She, too, must change and change in a positive direction.

Virtually everyone in Nigeria seems to want democracy, but no one yet has determined how to make it work. But there is also widespread agreement in Nigeria that a civilian government is much more desirable than a military one and to equates civilian rule with democratic rule, as it provides a better chance of guaranteeing basic rights and it gives the citizenry a chance to determine their leaders through competitive elections. The fact Nigeria is experimenting with a new constitution, signifies this change which is not unique to Nigeria. Constitution writing is a common political phenomenon of modern times. There are about 160 nations in the world that are governed by a written constitution and more than half of these constitutions were written since 1974. On average, in the last few decades, more than 5 new national constitutions have come into effect every year. Some of these constitutions, are, of course, for new nations, but the surprising fact is that most were written for very old nations, such as Spain, Portugal, Turkey, and Greece. According to Robert Goldwin and Art Kaufman, the frequency of constitution writing in the world tells us at least two things: "first, constitutions are considered very important,...; second, it is very difficult and rare to write a constitution that lasts,"[6] which help to explain why there are so many new constitutions every year.

Making a constitution is a special and rare political activity which is only possible at certain extraordinary moments in a nation's history. It has been described as "one of the highest, if not the highest, form of political activity."[7] In a significant way, it is unlike any other political action, though the differences are neither sufficiently studied nor well understood. Its success or failure can have profound and lasting consequences for the nation and its people. Studies show that modern constitutionalism in the western democracies has generally involved the idea of a civil society organized and governed on the basis of a written body of "constitutional" law.[8] A "constitution" may simply refer to a nation's "basic law." It may seek official legitimation of the actual unlimited power of a nation's policymakers as demonstrated by the Supreme Soviet in the former USSR.[9] It may be a nation's "ideological manifesto"; an existing government's attempt to legitimize itself; or a nation's birth certificate.[10] In the case of Nigeria, however, the Nigeria Order in Council of 1960 and the subsequent 1963 revised version represented the nation's birth certificate, while the 1979 and the 1999 constitutions were intended to transform an authoritarian political system into a constitutional democracy. Hence, the quest for democracy has assumed the form of constitutionalism in countries with long, nondemocratic traditions like Nigeria, Korea, Nicaragua, and the Philippines, for example.

The old but timely argument about progressive constitutionalism and regressive authoritarianism is of significance to the argument raised here. Throughout the nineteenth century and into the first years of the twentieth century, a great many liberals held the view that only constitutional regimes can be politically, socially, and economically progressive. John Stuart Mill, for example, never abandoned the standard of utility because he was convinced that nations governed autocratically can only be regressive and stagnant. He was secured in his belief that constitutional government is useful, autocratic government is useless. Montesquieu, for instance, had noted that Protestant, tolerant, and constitutional countries, such as Holland and England, were economically powerful whereas Catholic, intolerant, and authoritarian Portugal, Spain, and Italy were economically regressive.

As a result, Montesquieu and the other philosophers pleaded for the reform of France, a Catholic country with an absolutist political regime. Therefore, the "Whig interpretation of history,"[11] as Mill's viewpoint came to be called performed an important mission in Montesquieu's days and France's progressive movement as a country. There is no doubt that this thinking was heavily influenced by the eighteenth-century enlightenment which set forth the dream of reason. Taking the scientific discoveries of the seventeenth and eighteenth centuries as their model and inspiration, the enlightenment philosophers claimed that the application of reason could remove all the social and political evils that stood in the way of human happiness and progress. They proclaimed that reason can light the minds of men and women, freeing them from ignorance and superstition.[12] Of particular interest to the suggested direction Nigeria must take is the progressivist premise that was part of the enlightenment. It is the idea that human history is the story of progress, or improvement - perhaps even inevitable improvement - in the human condition. Once the shackles of ignorance and superstition have been broken, human reason will be free to order society in a rational way, and life will steadily and rapidly become better for all. One by one, we have seen how societies around the world have proven this idea of progressive constitutionalism and regressive authoritarianism over the years. While some have argued that this has degenerated into shallow liberal self-congratulations, the fact is that, the progress that constitutional democracies continue to exhibit today far surpass the regressive features of authoritarian societies. It may sound as if this is the only way but so far, Nigeria and other countries plagued by a crisis of governance must take the same well-traveled road to establish a mechanism that will set them on a progressive foundation.

HOPE IN THE NEW MILLENNIUM

A new constitutional beginning in Nigeria must avoid repeating the mistakes of the past, as the philosopher George Santayana remarked, those who forget the past may be doomed to repeat its mistakes. The release of a new Nigerian constitution and the restoration of civilian rule just before the dawn of a new millennium is an historic opportunity for Nigeria. As Nosa Omoigui describes this, it is "another chance at

fulfilling its immense potential... inspir(ing) some hopes in many Nigerians."[13] The hope
is that this will mark the re-emergence of Nigeria as a democracy, with a clear sense of
direction and accountable leadership. For this hope to be truly realized, Nigeria must
embrace and live by the idea of constitutionalism. Whether a constitution will be able to
fulfill its purpose depends on accepting the idea of constitutionalism in the first place.
This will serve as the bedrock that will set Nigeria on a stable political course.

Constitutionalism simply entails the theory and practice of conducting politics in
accordance with a constitution. It has evolved, as Alan Rosenbaum contends, to mean the
legal limitations placed upon the rightful power of government in its relationship to
citizens. In his view, "it includes the doctrine of official accountability to the people or to
its legitimate representatives within the framework of fundamental law for better securing
citizens' rights. Behind this thinking lies the axiom that the people as a whole are the best
judges about what is and what is not in their best interest.[14]

Constitutionalism, therefore, provides solid guarantees for the individual by explicitly
limiting governmental powers, while providing clear procedures for the implementation
of the functions of government. It should establish a watchdog, in the form of a judicial
body, to safeguard the constitution and all the restraints written into it. In addition, it
provides procedures through which the responsibility of those who govern to the
governed is maintained by free and fair periodic elections. As such, the government is not
only limited but responsible and made responsive to those it serves. For all practical
purposes, politics and governance have not been conducted in accordance with the
available constitutions in Nigeria. The absence of legal limitations on the rightful power
of government in its relationship to the Nigerian citizenry both during the civilian
administrations and military regimes has led to this mind set that is responsible for the
current state of affairs in Nigeria. Instead of democracy for the many, it has always been
democracy for the few. This is not because the Nigerian mass population is not interested
in politics and are therefore willing to let the so-called elite make the decisions that affect
their lives, but because they have never really been presented with any other choice. As a
result, constitutions meant for Nigerians may have been valid but have lacked legitimacy.
Julius Ihonvbere has argued that "for constitutions to have value and legitimacy, the
enabling environment for constitutionalism must first be established."[15] By this he means
that a constitution should be process-led, involving wide ranging consultation and debates
among the people. Therefore, it is possible that a constitution can be legal, yet lacks
legitimacy. A clear distinction between the validity and legitimacy of a constitution is
also raised by Evod Mmanda when he contends that the basis of the validity of a
constitution lies in those who implements it, but its legitimacy rests on "the way it is
accepted by those it is targeting...the result of the way they consciously participated or
involved in making it."[16] Commenting on the new Nigeria constitution, John Mbaku
argues that the process by which a constitution is created is vital to its legitimacy. In his
opinion, many of Africa's post independence problems arise from the fact that during
decolonization, the transformation process was dominated by technocrats from the
colonial state and a few indigenous elites. Accordingly, the bulk of the African people,
especially the historically marginalized groups and communities - women, rural
inhabitants, those who had been relegated to the urban periphery, etc. - were not

enfranchised and provided the facilities to participate fully and effectively in the process. As a result, he asserts, many of Africa's national constitutions were alien instruments and seen by the majority as such. He also believe that engaging the people in constitution making serves another important purpose similar to the way people give birth in his village; "it is a community affair and afterwards, the child belongs to the village,...owned by the village and cared for with pride by the village. If the child turns out to be a rascal, it is no longer just a vagabond, but the village's vagabond."[17]

The question of legitimacy is a difficult problem in African nations and others around the world where constitutional rule has not been really democratic in the past, where the constitution has existed in form but the people have not seen their interest or their aspirations reflected in its implementation. This is why there is so much cynicism and alienation among the ordinary Nigerian citizen.

The primary purpose of a constitution in democratic societies is to create, organize, and distribute governmental power on behalf of the people. Constitutions are designed in democratic societies to guarantee that governmental power is not abused and that it is exercised legitimately.[18] It is obvious that there has been an absence of the idea of constitutionalism in Nigeria because none of the Nigerian constitutions so far have been able to serve as a stumbling block to tyrants, monarchs, military adventurists, and passionate power seekers. It is not surprising, therefore, that Nigeria has witnessed what Samuel Huntington called the "cyclical" nature of alternating between military despotism and civilian passionate power seekers that can care less about what the people want? If Nigeria in the new millennium is to move beyond the praetorian regimes of the past, the rules of the game in the form of a viable and an enduring constitution must clearly relegate the Nigerian military to its proper role.

PROPER ROLE FOR THE MILITARY

The absence of a Nigerian constitutional mind set and lack of democratic governance since independence can be easily traced to the on-again and off-again interference in the political process by the military. Up until now, the military have had control of the Nigerian governance for more than three decades since independence. Even though the Nigerian constitutions have clearly stated that the Federal Republic of Nigeria shall not be governed, nor shall any person or group of persons gain control of government or any part of it, except in accordance with the provisions of the constitution, remains ineffective so far. The Nigerian military has ignored their constitutional duties and instead, take pleasure in subverting the constitution by imposing their will on the society. The Clausewitzian principle that holds that the military is bound to the service of the nation that created it guides contemporary societies around the world. The tradition in civilized societies for centuries now has been and continues to be, one of civil supremacy over the military. The role of the soldier and the statesman have been clearly defined since the beginning of the nineteenth century, whereby the military is subordinated to civil, constituted authority. Painful as this may be, the soldier has reluctantly accepted that the statesman and the citizenry are the master. Not so in Nigeria. The constant coups and counter -coups that has plagued Nigeria since independence point to the reverse. The soldier has become the master and the people their servants.

Modern societies have identified three important roles that the military ought to play in civilized societies: (1) to protect the establishing nation against any outside threat to its sovereignty; (2) to maintain domestic order when necessary; and (3) to help manage ethnic violence. The political instrument of a constitution eliminates the danger of usurpation or the formal suppression of civil authority by the military because the military cannot become a state within the state that created it.

It is not in the realms of civilized societies for the military to claim the right to define what is or is not in the national interest. Chief Williams alludes to this role when he argued that "the role of the military is to carry out the policies of the civil government and to subject itself to the will of the people...," categorically rejecting any independent role for the military in Nigeria.[19] The acceptance of a civilian supremacy over the military, whereby the latter willingly execute the policies of the former and only influence policy-making in relevant areas through normative, group, or institutional processes, is crucial to the idea of constitutionalism in Nigeria. A Nigeria with a constitutional mind set will relegate the military to providing advice without challenging the authority of the civilian political leadership even if the decision of the civilian authorities is contrary to the advice provided by the military.[20] This is what is found in countries like the United States, for example, where the constitution made the democratically elected president the civilian head of the military by making him Commander in Chief of the Armed Forces. This political act made possible by a belief in, and an acceptance of, a constitution confirms the Clausewitzian idea that "war is a continuation of politics by other means."[21] Simply translated, all military decisions and actions are made within the political context. This generation of Nigerians categorically demand an effective military instrument bound to the service of the state in a firm obligation under a constitution for the sake of future generations of Nigerians. All Nigerians demand loud and clear that a system that compels the military to be checked through the political means be instituted now. All Nigerians demand unequivocally that Nigeria should be define by a sense of ideal, purpose or direction, so as not to be transformed into a cameo of military personalities by coups and counter coups. After all, a citizenry that is aware of its constitutional rights can certainly serve as a great defense against coups.[22]

FINDING THE RIGHT CONSTITUTIONAL MIX

All of Nigeria's constitutions since independence have failed to impose a certain pattern of government on the polity, therefore failing to mold the nation in that image. Nigeria has experimented with both the parliamentary and presidential models of democracy and found neither was strong enough to overcome its deeply rooted social and political divisions. To be sure, one is clearly a democratic alternative to the other.

Choosing between these will certainly have profound significance in terms of how the country is governed, particularly in the executive and legislative branches. In a parliamentary system, the chief executive, called a prime minister, is chosen not directly by the voters but by the legislature. The prime minister, in turn, selects the other cabinet ministers from the members of parliament. This system encourages a multi party state because it requires a majority in parliament to control the executive. The prime minister remains in power as long as his or her party maintains the majority of the seats in the legislature or as long as the majority coalition formed holds together. In a presidential system, the president is elected by the people and derives his or her powers from a written constitution. The separation of powers between the executive and the legislative branches, the distinguished feature of the American political system, means that the president must deal with a competitor, the legislative branch, in setting policy and even managing the executive agencies.

Whether Nigeria goes presidential or parliamentary will also affect two important aspects of how laws are made: how one becomes a member and what one does as a member. In a parliamentary system, ordinarily a person becomes a member of parliament by persuading a political party to put his or her name on the ballot. Though usually a local party committee selects a person to be its candidate, that committee often takes suggestions from national party headquarters. In any case the local party committee selects as its candidate someone willing to support the national party program and leadership. Voters in the district choose not between two or three personalities running for office but between two or three national parties in the election. By contrast, a person becomes a candidate for representative or senator in a presidential form by running as an individual but usually with a party label. As a result of these different systems, a parliament tends to be made up of people loyal to the national party leadership who meets to debate and vote on party issues. In a presidential system, however, the legislature is made up of people who think of themselves as independent representatives of their districts or states and who, while willing to support their party on many issues, expect to vote as their constituents' beliefs and interests require.

The right constitutional mix must be carefully guided by the notion of restraints on political authority. To prevent arbitrary and absolute power in government, a Nigerian constitution must reject any concentration of power in the hands of any one body. Such a document must find a way to make it impossible for any single organ or government to become truly sovereign and overwhelm the others. Therefore, the emphasis should be how to restrain political power, as well as how to make it effective. To this end lies the necessity to establish a watchdog, in form of an independent, apolitical judicial body, that will safeguard the constitution and all the restraints written into it. The Nigerian judiciary must be the keeper, the arbiter of the constitution and the glue that holds the society together. Only through an apolitical judiciary can the faith of the Nigerian people be kept, because not only will this institution be expected to protect us against our government, but to protect us against each other. It is only the judiciary that will broker the fight between the executive and the legislative branches, as well as between the central government and the constituent governments.

The difficulty of finding the right constitutional mix is made even worse by the lack of a clearly define relationship between the different levels of government in Nigeria. While Nigeria claims now and in the past to be practicing federalism, the so-called Federal Republic of Nigeria has been anything but federal.[23] Since independence, the reality is that these intergovernmental activities have resembled a unitary system where the central government dominated and continues to dominate. Charles Hauss has described the nature of Nigerian federalism as "a kind of ping-pong ball" which has had a destabilizing implications.[24] Since independence, there has been attempts to create sub-national political units that will aid in the governance of the nation. Still, there remains considerable uncertainty about what the respective responsibilities of the central and constituent governments should be. It is our contention here that only through constitutional and institutional reforms can federalism work in Nigeria. The tug of war that continues to rare its ugly head in Nigeria between the different levels of government can only be resolved through a constitutional federal structure.

Federalism is a system of government in which power is divided by a written constitution between a central government and regional, or sub-divisional governments. It is a system deeply rooted in the belief and practice that issues that are not national in scope are most appropriately addressed by the level of government closest to the people. Each level must have some domain in which its policies are dominant and some genuine political or constitutional guarantee of its authority. As a result, it serves as a balancing act between the central government and the states in which power is balanced with power, authority with authority, responsibility with responsibility, independence with independence, and sovereignty with sovereignty. As Jide Ajani noted in a recent report, "it would do Nigerians a lot of good if the spirit of federalism is allowed to permeate every aspect of the Nigerian life."[25] The constitutional relationship among sovereign governments, state and national, is inherent in the very structure of the constitution and is formalized in, and protected by it. The people of the states are therefore free, subject only to restrictions in the constitution itself or in constitutionally authorized Acts of the national legislature, to define the moral, political, and legal character of their lives. It is predicated on the premise that the states posses unique authorities, qualities, and abilities to meet the needs of the people and should undoubtedly function as laboratories of democracy.

Certainly, in a large, pluralistic society like Nigeria, a true federal structure will allow many functions to be "farmed out" by the central government to the constituent governments. The lower levels of government, accepting these responsibilities, can become the focus of political dissatisfaction rather than the national authorities. In reality, the inadequate transportation and communications system, the sheer geographical or population size of Nigeria makes it impracticable to locate all political authority in one place. What is the meaning of true federalism without allowing the states to carry out functions it is better equipped to do? Of great importance, therefore, is the need for a Nigerian constitution to begin to dismantle the central hold on some key areas of governance, starting with the police force. The Nigerian Police Force as presently constituted, has been described as a "bundle of disappointment, discomfiture, discouragement and failure."[26] There is an urgent need to establish state police forces that will cater to the needs and aspirations of the different states, because the Nigerian Police of today and in the past, does not typify the quintessential police force any country would desire, or even keep. A decentralized police force will certainly meet the need to have state police that is very much at home with the idiosyncrasies of the people it is meant to serve and protect.

Also, a true federalism will bring government closer to the people, allowing more direct access to, and influence on, government agencies and policies, rather than leaving the population restive and dissatisfied with a remote, faceless, all-powerful central authority. A true federalism will provide an opportunity for states and local governments to serve as training grounds for future national leaders, while becoming testing grounds for new national initiatives. The nature of the Nigerian constitutional system must encourage a healthy diversity in the public policies adopted by the people of the several states according to their own conditions, needs, and desires. In the search for enlightened public policy, individual states and communities must be free to experiment with a variety of approaches to public issues.

One-size-fits-all approaches to public policy problems can inhibit the creation of effective solutions to those problems because what is good for Imo state may not be good for Benue state. Further, there should be strict adherence to constitutional principles. National action limiting the policymaking discretion of the states shall be taken only where there is constitutional and statutory authority for the action and the national activity is appropriate in light of the presence of a problem of national significance. With respect to federal statutes and regulations administered by the states, the national government would grant the states the maximum administrative discretion possible. Intrusive federal oversight of state administration will neither be necessary nor desirable.

In retrospect, the Nigerian way of life always has been characterized by a number of political subcultures, which divide along ethnic, religious, regional, language, wealth, and educational lines. Such obvious reality would appear to be at odds with a political authority concentrated solely in a central government. With a unitary system, the various political subcultures certainly will be less able to influence government behavior relative to their own regions and interests. A reliance on constitutional federalism will prevent the constituent governments from being mere appendages of the central government, as this has been in the past. As Omoigui warned recently, "federalism is not guaranteed to work in a country where constitutionalism, to a fair number of its people, is an alien concept."[27]

A VIRTUOUS NIGERIA IN THE NEW MILLENNIUM

The success of any new Nigerian constitution will also depend on the document reflecting and encouraging a new Nigerian political culture. For a nation like Nigeria with different cultures, social tensions, and distinctive configurations of political power, a constitution should serve an additional purpose; specifically, to promote certain ideas and aspirations. It must take into account the socio-cultural and historical backgrounds while building the kind of structures that will promote the ideals and aspirations of democracy.[28] Despite the diverse nature of the Nigerian society and the wide range of ethnic groups, language, economic classes, and other interests, the Nigerian constitution must reflect a patterned set of ideas, values, and ways of thinking about government and politics in the new millennium. This should include some democratic values like equality, fairness, liberty, the right to own property, no matter how abstract some of these may be. Usually, the homogenous a population, the easier it is to have a political culture that is based on consensus. Even in a nation that is heterogenous in geography and ethnic background like in Nigeria, it is possible for shared cultural ideas to develop.

Nigeria needs a constitution that will create a system of governance in which no single class rules; one in which all Nigerians share political power as each checks the potential excesses of the others. We must accept the philosopher David Hume's contention that only a constitutional government can best control the unholy mix of personal ambition and political power.[29] Such a system requires citizens to be vigilant and to jealously guide their liberties against encroachment by would-be tyrants in their midst. As Chinua Achebe recently warned, "in a democracy, the tendency is for people to drop their guards and relax that everything is okay. One mistake we must not make as a people is to drop our guards. We are to be watchful of the process.[30]

Nigerians will need to be vigilant more than ever, because if they become complacent and indifferent to public affairs, they will find a tyrant as ever before, waiting to relieve them of the burden of self-government and deprive them of their liberty. According to Niccolo Machiavelli, the greatest enemies of free government are complacent and self-interested citizens.Nigerians must learn to care for the "common good" rather than themselves, for we have seen how the love of wealth, luxury, and ease, together with a corresponding indifference to public affairs lead to corruption. The greatest danger that Nigeria faces is that it will be destroyed from within by corruption. Therefore, to keep corruption at bay, Nigerians must practice "virtue." We must be attentive and alert to public affairs, always striving to do what is best not for ourselves, but for the interest of the entire citizenry. One way to promote civic virtue is through participation in public affairs and cooperation among all. Nigerians who join with their neighbors to settle common problems and disputes will learn the importance of cooperation, while feeling a sense of attachment to their own welfare with the welfare of the community as a whole. By offering all Nigerians the opportunity to participate, the resulting constitutional democracy should promise to cultivate a widespread and deeply rooted devotion to the common good. But if Nigerians are to be "virtuous," then, they must be free to assemble, to argue among themselves on the best course of action to take as a nation, to expose corruption and criticize their leaders and one another. As Rosenbaum argued, "in a constitutional democracy, the dissent and conflicts that inevitably arise, owing to the premium publicly placed on independence of thought and action, require a continual reexamination of the 'constitutional' foundations of society which foster competing visions of the ideal society."[31] If any Nigerian constitution fails to guarantee Nigerians the right to enjoy and exercise these essential liberties, the republic is doomed to an early death.

Only through lasting constitutional and institutional reform can the personalization of political power be eliminated in Nigeria. Since independence, there has been a tendency to identify policies or problems with the individuals who are in power at the time, followed by an exaggeration of their importance in the process. A good example is giving retired Generals Obasanjo and Abubakar so much credit for democratic progress and blaming retired General Babamgida and late despot Abacha for democratic stagnation in the country. This type of politics of personality can only take place in a country like Nigeria in which most institutions are very weak and lacking constitutionalism, making the person who occupies an office more important than the formal responsibilities and rules for the office itself. Such emphasis on the individual may well work out when the individual in power is someone of integrity and virtue, but it also opens the door even wider for the abuse of power when such individual lacks either the ethical principles that is needed without clearly define rules of the game. A free government and its citizenry must be ruled not by the whim or caprice of any person or persons, nor even of the majority of citizens, but by law. It is the rule of law that separates a free society from the abyss of anarchy and wanton destruction. Any constitutional arrangement in Nigeria must be based on laws, not of men, for such is most consistent, more concerned with fairness.

A dependence on the laws will further guarantee the peoples independence because the laws are impersonal. When citizens depend upon individual people or even a majority of people, the entire citizenry can be subjected to their will and be easily robbed of their liberty.

CONCLUSION

There is little reason to assume that anything will change in the next millennium unless there is a way to reconcile any regime's constitutional provisions with the realities of the Nigerian society. Simply, in the absence of commonly accepted rules of the game that place limits on what political leaders can do and not do, it will be hard to limit, less eliminate, some of the most dangerous aspects of the elite culture that exit in Nigeria today. The fact is that there is an irresistible force that is overwhelming the ranks, orders, and the elitist privileges of the old way of life in Nigeria. The voices are chanting for a change, not just any change, but a change for the better, if not the best. They are calling for Nigerians to be freed from the political and economic stagnation of the past, a chance to do things differently and right. No one assumes naively that the road to democracy will be easy, but there are a number of economic and socio-political developments that lead us to believe that this will grow and thrive in twenty-first century Nigeria. As Nigerians continue to be educated and become informed of what their state of public affairs is and what it ought to be, their interest in political matters will contribute to the growing faith in the ordinary Nigerian's ability to participate knowledgeably in public affairs.

Ultimately, as Rosenbaum contends, any final evaluation of a nation's constitution must be made with respect to how effective the document will be in guiding society toward fulfillment of its constitutional ends.[32] Any Nigerian constitution must represent the holy writ of Nigeria's civil religion, in which Nigerians expect to find the answers to their most troubling questions, especially the one of governance. The idea of constitutionalism and a constitution should therefore be a mirror that reflect the Nigerian history, a medium through which each generation of Nigerians turns its values, attitudes, and prejudices into law. It must serve as a myth that gains its power from a strong belief in it by all Nigerians.

We are at a special moment in our history, not just because we are on the eve of a new millennium, but because the world in which we are part and parcel of is changing at a dazzling rate. We, too, must change with the changing world. In so many ways we have failed to use our nation and our independence to assume our proper role in the world. We have failed to transform our natural blessings to improve the well-being of our citizens. Shouldn't we be fixing our roof while the sun is still shining? Shouldn't we be shoring up our foundation before the rain gets in? Now, above all, is no time for complacency. This generation of Nigerians feels a sense of urgency to seize this moment in our history, to strengthen the weak and to challenge the strong among us to lead us into our full greatness as a nation. We, too, believe that the values of life, liberty and the pursuit of happiness are not just for some human beings, but for Nigerians as well.

Isn't it just common sense that we, as Nigerians, make sure that the political instability of the past remains just that? Isn't it just common sense that we can learn to live together as one and avoid the politics of ethnic destruction?

Isn't it common sense that the irresponsibility of those who govern us must be arrested now and forever? What others may call idealism is a common sense reality I know we can achieve through constitutionalism. It is certainly time for us to unleash the potential of Nigerians as public citizens, for only then will Nigeria be the place that it can be. We must put every Nigerian on the train of that deeper, broader common good, for only then will all Nigerians get to the promised land of glory in peace and plenty. All Nigerians must resolve not to allow the problems of the past becloud our sense of responsibility to the country now. Our duty to this nation must surpass all other things.

True, government cannot be all things to all the people all the time. Nor should it do trifling things much of the time for some people. But it should do some large and essential things all of the time for the whole of the nation within a constitutional framework. It will be naive for anyone to simply assume that the prospect for a good government in Nigeria will depend entirely on a good constitution. Our view now and forever is that the will of the people of Nigeria is perhaps most important in making any constitution work. The choice between optimism and pessimism regarding the future of Nigeria is one that individual Nigerians have to make. In the opinion of this author, it is better to ere on the side of hope rather than despair. There are abundant reasons to justify this position.

This chapter represents one of the voices of a generation of Nigerians, challenging all to embrace and live by the idea of constitutionalism, because as Paul Dunn contends, "even a divine constitution requires something further; it demands a kind of people who will, by their very natures, receive and respect such a constitution and function well within the conditions it establishes."[33] This generation of Nigerians urges all Nigerians to bridge the divide of ethnicity, region, religion, and language so that the Nigeria of the new millennium sees deeper than these differences. While we believe that Nigeria should be made whole, we do not want to erase our differences because it is those differences that should give us our common energy to be virtuous in our approach to the future. The beautiful paradox of Nigeria is that we are many, that we are individual, that we are different, but that we are also one - one people, one family, one nation. That has been our faith and our destiny together. We may be at the end of a millennium, at the end of four decades of our independence, but we still have it in our power, as Thomas Paine said, "to begin the world (all) over again,"[34] for, only the best is good enough for "our own dear native land," Nigeria.

Chapter II

FEDERALISM, STATE CREATION AND ETHNIC MANAGEMENT IN NIGERIA

Adegboyega Somide

INTRODUCTION[1]

The search for a workable constitutional framework has preoccupied Nigerian leaders since the amalgamation of three British protectorates in West Africa in 1914 to form the nucleus of the modern-day Nigerian state. Although Nigeria is comprised of an estimated 250 distinct ethnic groups, making it one of the most culturally diverse states in the world, the biggest threat to its unified existence emanates from the blistering rivalries among its three dominant groups--Hausa-Fulani, Yoruba, and Ibo. The ethno-linguistic disparateness of the three largest groups has been reinforced further by religious and regional divisions. The northern half of the country, home to the Hausa-Fulani group, is predominantly Muslim.[2] In the south, adherents of the Christian faith comprise the majority of the Ibo and the Yoruba who are located in the southeast and the southwest, respectively.[3] The dissolution of the First Republic in 1966 by a *coup d'etat* and the ensuing thirty-month civil war that claimed an estimated one million lives between 1967 and 1970 were triggered by unresolvable ethnic competition. Subsequently, there have been five successful ethnically inspired military coups. Three attempts at democratic rule have failed. The last, in 1993, was abrogated abruptly by the Hausa-Fulani dominated military government when the election results appeared to favor a southerner from the Yoruba ethnic group. The ethnic tensions that engulfed the country following the cancellation of the 12 June 1993 election was deepened by the execution of Ken Saro-Wiwa and eight other activists in the Movement for the Salvation of the Ogoni people (MOSOP) in the oil-producing region of southern Nigeria. In the aftermath of that execution, Nigerian Nobel laureate, Wole Soyinka, described the military occupation and killings of the Ogonis as Aonly the first Nigerian experiment with ethnic cleansing...a mere prelude to the far more thorough subjugation that is planned for other parts of southern Nigeria.[4]

Despite strong demands for alternative constitutional forms such as unitarism or consociationalism[5], Nigeria has remained a federal state. Its official name is the Federal Republic of Nigeria and succeeding military governments have referred to themselves as the Federal Military Government.[6] The fateful attempt in 1966 by Major-General Aguyi-Ironsi to abolish Nigeria's federal structure by decree engendered stiff opposition, ethnic killings, and ultimately a civil war. Affirmation of Nigeria's faith in federalism was echoed in the 1987 report of the Political Bureau, established by the Babangida regime to conduct a national debate and make recommendations on Nigeria's political future. The Political Bureau wrote: "Nigeria should continue with a federal system of government... the present three-tier arrangement of government namely, federal, state, and local, should continue."[7] Therefore, a near consensus could be said to exist among the political class (military or civilian) and the intellectuals that a federal constitutional system offers the most viable solution to Nigeria's multiethnic character. The implicit assumption is that a federal system, by "disaggregating constitutional authority between two levels of government," can better regulate political and ethnic conflict.[8] My goal in this chapter is twofold. First, utilizing John Kingdon's multiple steams model for agenda setting, I attempt to explain the sources and persistence of state creation as a policy to correct structural imbalances in Nigerian federalism and to reduce ethnic conflict. Second, I assess the extent to which this policy has achieved its designed objectives. The constituent units of Nigerian federalism have metamorphosed six times, from 3 regions in 1960 to the present 36 states. (See tables 1 & 2). I argue that a powerful ethnic pull has prevented Nigerian federalism from functioning effectively. State creation as a means of dismantling ethno-regional solidarity suffers from two inherent contradictions. First, the process of state creation encourages politicization of ethnicity. The result has been a Nigerian state in which ethno-regional identity continues to be a matter of great concern at the federal or central government level. Thus, while state creation can be said to have brought government closer to the local peoples and communities, and to have removed some minorities from the domination of larger groups, it has failed to crack the primordial ethnic solidarity "of indigenous Nigerian society."[9]

Second, a major source of instability and disunity--domination and control of the federal government by one of the original three regions--has not been removed by the creation of more states. Rather, state creation has proved an effective tool in maintaining northern hegemonic rule. The north dominated the federal government before the state creation exercises began and has continued to dominate it. By decentralizing the structure of societal conflicts, other avenues for resource competition and political ascendancy have been created for would-be challengers to the federal machinery of control. State creation in Nigeria has all the trappings of divide and rule. It has successfully reduced, but by no means eliminated, the type of ethnic rivalries that earlier threatened the nation's unity under a three-state federal structure.[10]

DEFINITIONS AND CONCEPTS

Federalism as a modern constitutional arrangement of government structure has its origin in the 1787 American constitution.[11] Nwabueze defines it as:

an arrangement whereby powers of government within a country are shared between a national, country-wide government and a number of regionalized (*i.e.* territorially localised) governments in such a way that each exists as a government separately and independently from the others operating directly on persons and property within its territorial area, with a will of its own and its own apparatus for the conduct of its affairs, and with an authority in some matters exclusive of all the others.[12]

Elazar has maintained that the main organizational feature of federalism is "non-centralization--the constitutional diffusion and sharing of powers among many centers. Its logical outcome is the construction of the body politic out of diverse entities that retain their respective integrity within the common framework."[13] The above explains why multiethnic states, such as Nigeria, tend to resort to a federal arrangement. First, a federal arrangement potentially can guarantee the autonomy of its constituent units. Second, its emphasis on non-centralization of power promises to remove dominance of one ethnic group over the others. These reasons persuaded Nigeria to adopt federalism.

As noted by Uma Eleazu, Nigerian leaders "thought that through federalism, they will maintain unity in diversity, that within the federal structure the diverse ethnic groups can be welded into a modern nation."[14] The following section examines the literature of federalism as it relates to ethnic conflicts. An examination of all the approaches to the study of ethnicity is beyond the scope of this chapter. Thus, only aspects of ethnicity considered relevant to federalism are considered. Section 2 lays out the theoretical model employed in this study and section 3 provides historical background on Nigerian federalism. Section 4 applies the multiple streams model to Nigerian federalism. Section 5 further explores the use of state creation as a policy to resolve ethnic conflict, and the role of the military in this effort.

1. FEDERALISM AND ETHNIC GROUPS

What are favorable conditions for successful federalism? This has been a perennial question in the federalism literature and the debate can provide insight into Nigerian federalism. K. C. Wheare has argued that the desire by the constituent units to federate and the existence of administrative and institutional capacities to run a federal system are essential to successful federalism.[15]

According to Wheare, factors ranging from military insecurity, geographical contiguity, and economic advantage to shared cultural affinities and similarity of socio-political institutions can influence the desire to federate.[16] Without the "desire to be united," federalism probably will result in failure.[17] The above conditions for successful federalism were largely absent in Nigeria. In fact, federalism was Hobson's choice at Nigeria's independence. The colonial administrative structure inflamed the natural distinctiveness of the three territories by erecting separate administrative traditions. The Nigerian regional leaders were neither keen about unitary nor federal arrangement. At the pre-independence constitutional conference held in Ibadan in 1950, there was a consensus that the country's social and political diversity are worth preserving.[18] The only other alternative, short of a breakup, was a consociational arrangement, an idea not favored by the British and which could only have delayed Nigerian independence. Any compromise between the three Nigerian delegations ultimately had to satisfy the Imperial Government's position which unmistakably supported a federal Nigeria.[19]

In Thomas Franck's conceptualization, federalism stands a better chance of surviving when the following three conditions are present: 1) there is an ideological commitment among the constituent units to establish a federation; that is, the leaders and the people must "feel federal." Federalism must be considered an end in itself rather than a means to an end; 2) there exist historical, cultural and linguistic sameness, and physical and economic complementarity ; and 3) there is an acknowledged need to solve ethnic imbalance or to secure independence from foreign rule.[20] In Franck's typology, the first category consists of primary motivating factors. These factors are the most accurate predictors of successful federalism. The second set of factors is said to be necessary but not sufficient reason for successful federalism. The third set of conditions is comprised of tertiary factors, that is, when a federation is formed as a result of bargain-striking rather than a genuine mutuality of interest. When federalism arises as a result of secondary or tertiary factors, they must be transformed quickly into primary factors which is often difficult, if not impossible, in developing nations because they often lack broadly shared values and charismatic leaders that could galvanize ideological commitment to federalism.[21]

Nigerian federalism provides a good illustration of Franck's contention that a federal system based on tertiary factors alone will be difficult to sustain.[22] Nigerian federalism is based on tertiary factors. The need to preserve cultural pluralities of the three constituent units, coupled with the British disposition for a federal structure as a condition for independence made federalism a *fait accompli*. The subsequent divisions of the original three units were also based on ethnic considerations. It is clear the Nigerian setting was not conducive to a long-term federal arrangement. The unresolved issues of the frenetic pre-independence negotiations have been haunting the country ever since. One of the most daunting has been how to resolve the ethnic imbalance. Invariably, the burning questions revolve around the number of states needed and whether or not ethnic boundaries should coincide with those of the states. Federalism is not necessarily a response to ethnic diversity.[23] In many successful federations (United States, Brazil, Mexico , Germany, Argentina, Venezuela, and Australia), racial and cultural cleavages are not territorial in nature, and thus are not a consideration in setting the boundaries of the constituent units.[24] In cases where federalism has been adopted to deal with ethnic conflicts, two general patterns are discernible. The first pattern is when no attempt is made to make ethnic territories coincide with the constituent units of the federation which is generally the case in Malaysia where the major ethnic groups (Malays, Chinese, and

Indians) are spread across the 12 states. This principle is also apparent in Spain and Canada where ethnic minorities, while retaining autonomy, are spread across state boundaries.[25] The second pattern includes those states in which the constituent units of a federation correspond with ethnic group territories. Examples are the former Soviet Union (FSU), Yugoslavia, and Czechoslovakia.[26] At least in theory, Nigeria falls into this category since the creation of its present constituent units was based on the principle of ethnic autonomy. The recent experiences of FSU, Yugoslavia, and Czechoslovakia would seem to suggest that stable federal system thrives in countries that are either culturally homogeneous or where ethnic group distribution is not the basis for territorial division.

But the application of the federal principle to multiethnic states such as Nigeria has ignored several principles of federalism. Power sharing in a federal arrangement requires a "proper territorial base." Thus, in ethnic federalism such as Nigeria, state creation has resulted in ethnic enclaves which ossify rather than dissolve allegiances. In short, ethnic-based federalism is very difficult to sustain because it tends to magnify ethnic separateness which is antithetical to the principle of federalism. Federalism is about negotiation, cooperation, compromise, and mutual tolerance which are more difficult to achieve because of the uncompromising nature of ethnic rivalry.[27]

But why have some nations been more successful in creating an overarching national loyalty despite their multiethnic character? Why is the assimilationist approach more problematic in third world settings? Is there a correlation between states' economic performance and perhaps the level of ethnic conflict or political stability?

The great variation in per capita incomes of the world's federal states and the continuing ethnic tensions in prosperous countries such as Belgium and Canada would seem to suggest that economic prosperity as a cause of stability is at best inconclusive. It may well be that the manner in which federalism was acquired, whether it was through a broad-based consensus or was imposed, matters a great deal in predicting failure or success. Furthermore, the historical particularities shaping and conditioning the nature of conflicts among the ethnic components determines the trajectory of the federation and whether certain options are open or foreclosed.

2.   THE MULTIPLE STREAMS MODEL

I utilize a modified version of the broader multiple stream[28] model in this chapter to identify the factors explaining the adoption and persistence of state creation policy in Nigeria. John Kingdon conceives the policy process as consisting of three streams--problems, policies, and politics. Each stream is separate from the others and driven by its own dynamics.[29] Adoption of specific policies is more apt to occur when the three streams are joined at critical times referred to as policy windows.[30] In other words, a specific proposal to a problem will likely be adopted when Aa political change makes it the right time for policy change, and potential constraints are not severe."[31] According to Kingdon, specific issues come to the attention of policy-makers as problems when they are revealed as such either by "systematic indicators" or by "a focusing event like a crisis or disaster." [32] Systematic indicators, such as research or routine monitoring within governmental agencies, non-governmental organizations (NGOs), or the academe could reveal an issue as a problem, thus capturing the attention of "governmental decision makers." [33] For example, research on households without adequate health care coverage or sexual harassment in the workplace may help confirm the magnitude of these problems. But focusing events such as crises and disasters tend to establish the magnitude of a problem with greater conviction. For instance, a rash of school bus accidents or "bridge collapses" may focus attention on school bus drivers' qualification and "highway infrastructure deterioration."[34]

The policy stream consists of alternative solutions to a problem generated by policy communities of specialists in a given policy area such as health or housing. Specialists often have a shared interest in certain policy domains for different reasons. Congressional staffers, academics, interest groups analysts, planning and evaluation officers, and budget officers, frequently form communities on a wide variety of issues. To any given problem, various ideas in the form of possible solutions are floated around in manners akin to how molecules floated around in the "primeval soup" before life was formed.[35] As ideas are tried out in speeches, "as bills introduced" and so on, some disappear while others survive. In this policy "primeval soup," criteria for selection are technical feasibility, value acceptability, and future constraints.[36] Technical feasibility is said to be concerned with implementation, that is, whether a proposal will accomplish the goal for which it is designed and whether or not it can be administered. In order for a specific proposal to survive, it must be "compatible with the values of the specialists."[37] For instance, a conservative-dominated Congress probably will resist a proposal that seeks to expand the size and role of the government at the expense of the private sector while a liberal government may be more receptive to such an idea. Additionally, feasibility deals with the "anticipation of future constraints." Policy-makers will be more inclined to consider proposals whose budgetary costs are deemed acceptable, and which the public is likely to support.[38] The third stream--the political stream--consists of three components. The first is the national mood, the notion that a rather high percentage of the population of a given country usually thinks along the same lines and that a change in the national mood will be reflected in policy agendas and policy outcomes.[39] The second component is the perception, attitude, and calculations of organized political forces. According to Kingdon, proposals tend to be supported by politicians if they sense a consensus among interest groups. When an issue is conflictual, political leaders will formulate their image of the balance between support for, and opposition to, a specific proposal. The politicians' perception of this balance ultimately determines whether a proposal will rise to prominence. The third element of the political stream is a change in the government ideological complexion occasioned by elections or other means. This sort of turnover often precipitates profound changes in policy agendas.[40] The coming together of the three streams or coupling at critical moments is made possible by policy windows. Kingdon argues policy windows usually open by dramatic events and provide opportunities for policy entrepreneurs to push for their proposals. Policy entrepreneurs are individuals who have invested time, energy, and money to promote a specific proposal in anticipation of future benefits. Kingdon maintains that successful policy entrepreneurs join problems, policies, and politics at that opportune moment when windows open. Any crisis or a change in the political stream is seized upon as a chance to push their pet solution. When problems, solutions (policies), and politics are joined at that critical moment, the idea will gain prominence and will likely be adopted.[41] A brief discussion of Nigeria's historical background and constitutional history should enhance the reader's understanding of the application of the multiple streams model.

3.   NIGERIA'S PRE-COLONIAL SETTING

Modern Nigeria is comprised of three major previously autonomous groups--Hausa-Fulani, Yoruba, and Ibo--and numerous other smaller groups with close historical and traditional ties to one of the major groups. The Hausa-Fulani are the dominant group in the northern half of the country. The Yoruba occupy the southwest while the Ibo inhabit the southeast. A fourth distinct region, referred to as the Middle Belt, has played and continues to play a key role in the ethnic power balance in Nigeria. This area lies between the northern and southern regions and extends east/west across Nigeria from the Cameroonian border to the border of Republic of Benin. Although regarded as within the northern region in the tripartite division of the country, the people of this area (Tiv, Idoma, etc) are neither culturally Hausa nor is Islam their dominant religion.[42] In the pre-colonial times, the three dominant ethnic groups had a well-defined territorial, political, and social organizations. In the north, Islam, which was first introduced around the eleventh century A.D. had become wide-spread by the fourteenth century. The organization of the emirate system by the Hausa-Fulani group further contributed to the cultural and religious integration of the north. However, despite the Islamic Revolution of the nineteenth century, vast areas of the north such as the Middle Belt are heavily Christian. Even in the far north, Zaria and Bornu have always had sizeable Christian representations.[43] Beginning around the 11th century, the Yoruba Kingdoms in the southwest had established a strong political and military organization. Notable were the Oyo, Ife, and Benin Kingdoms. All the Yoruba Kingdoms accepted the primacy of the secular authority of the Alafin (ruler) of Oyo, while the spiritual leadership of the Oni of Ife also provided unity. All Yorubas claimed a common ancestry in Oduduwa. However, by the late nineteenth century, the Yoruba Kingdoms had experienced political disintegration as a result of the European intrusion and the effects of the slave trade.[44] The Ibos in the southeast were the only group lacking an elaborate political and military cohesion perhaps due to the physical environment of thick forest precluding easy interaction among people. As a result, "village democracies" primarily consisting of the elders within the village "formulated rules and standards of social behavior" in the name of the spirits of the village's ancestors.[45]

3.1   Colonialism and the Evolution of a Federal Constitution

The manner in which the British exploited the cultural and territorial solidarity of these three major groups laid the foundation for the Nigerian federal structure. Administrative convenience and commercial gains were the primary considerations of the British and no serious attempt was made at nation-building. If any thing, gulfs were created between groups to achieve efficiency.[46] It is generally acknowledged among scholars of Nigerian federalism that the colonial administration set Nigeria up for ethno-regional confrontation, thus necessitating a three-state federation at independence.[47] While this may be true, Nigerian politicians (military and civilian) and ethnic entrepreneurs have helped to perpetuate that feature by exploiting it for political gains despite claims to the contrary. The importance of the 1884 Berlin Conference in the evolution of the Nigerian state could not be overestimated. Prior to 1884, Britain had not crystallized plans for political control of the northern half of what was destined to become Nigeria. But when the Berlin Conference stipulated effective political control must be maintained in African colonies in order for them to be internationally recognized, Britain hastily designed an occupation plan that would later turn into a nightmare for the Nigerian state. At issue was how to achieve effective governance. By 1900, three British protectorates had been established in the area now called Nigeria. The Northern Protectorate (1900) was administered by the Royal Niger Company, headquartered in Asaba, under Foreign-Office supervision; administration of the Lagos Colony (1862) and Yorubaland Protectorate (1900) was carried out by the Colonial Office; and the southeast territory was organized as the Niger Coast Protectorate (1893) ruled through a British consul-general in Calabar. In essence, the establishment of three separate colonial administrations set Nigeria on an irreversible course to a federation. The colonial administrative tradition reinforced the pre-existing economic, geographic and ethnic pluralities of Nigeria. As pointed out by Afigbo, the rivalries among the three administrative units at times gave the impression they belonged to rival imperial powers, not one.[48] Far removed from the intricacies and realities of the enormously diverse areas it had acquired, the British government relied on its administrators in the three protectorates to determine future administrative arrangements for Nigeria. In 1898, the imperial government in London established a committee chaired by Earl Selborne to study and report on the future administrative plan for the three regions. The committee's recommendation that the status quo be maintained was not surprising. The key members--Sir Henry McCallum, Sir Ralph Moor, and Sir George Goldie--had been the administrators of Lagos, Niger Coast, and Northern protectorates, respectively. The preservation and furtherance of the political careers of the three men, rather than the future of a Nigerian state, appear to have been the motivating factors in the committee's reluctance to opt for unification. The justification for the Selborne Committee's decision was that a central administration of the vast area would be impossible given the limited network of communications available at the time.[49] The committee recommended a division of the territory into two--the Soudan Province (northern Nigeria) and the Maritime Province (southern Nigeria) with unification set for a future date contingent on administrative feasibility and efficiency.[50] The result was that while the north retained its cultural distinctiveness as a region, the two southern protectorates (Lagos/Yorubaland and the Niger Coast) became one in 1906. This served to intensify the conflict in two ways. First, the regional distinctiveness and disparities now acquired administrative character. Second, the colonial policy of indirect rule, utilized in northern Nigeria by Lord Lugard, helped to preserve and strengthen the existing northern socio-political structure. When this system was extended to the south, there was the irony of its having destroyed the existing political and social institutions, even though it purportedly utilized the indigenous leaders in administering the area.[51] As far as Lugard was concerned, indirect rule was a *sine qua non* in northern Nigeria. It was a vast territory and the cost of British civil administrators would have been prohibitive. The centuries-old political and religious cohesiveness in the north was to be the vehicle for effective British control, albeit with significant concessions to northern rulers. For example, the British administration agreed not to interfere with the religious needs and practices, and Christian missionaries, unlike in southern Nigeria, would be kept out of the north.[52] In addition, there would be a recognition of Islamic educational institutions, not Western education, in the north. And unlike the south, where English was the language of administration, the Hausa language would be adopted as the official language in the north.[53] Following the unification of the three protectorates in 1914, their distinct administrative features were reinforced as they continued to be administered as autonomous regions with divergent political and social characteristics. In essence, it was a union only in name. Here too, Lugard's contempt for the southern educated elite was evident. His recommendation that the seat of the central government be moved from Lagos in the south to Kaduna in the north was reversed by Hugh Clifford whose vision for a truly unified Nigeria had entailed a plan to do away with indirect rule by promoting Western education throughout Nigeria. But his recommendation was rejected by the Colonial Office. Consequently, his 1922 constitution was modified to retain indirect rule in northern Nigeria while electoral government was introduced in southern Nigeria.[54]

Therefore, it came as no surprise that the north would insist on political supremacy in an independent Nigerian state. The introduction of the Richard's Constitution in 1947 was significant in the constitutional development of Nigeria for two important reasons. First, it introduced regional assemblies in the three regions--the north, the east, and the west--and legislative politics to northern Nigeria for the first time. Second, the new Nigerian legislative council had a Nigerian majority, 28 out of 44 members, even though only 4 were elected. The remaining 24 were nominated by the assemblies in the three regions.[55] But while the Richard's constitution might appear to have relaxed some imperial control, there was very little difference in the *modus operandi* of the British administration of Nigeria. For instance, a provision allowed the Governor to bypass the Legislative Council for the enactment of laws if the latter refused to pass such laws. The franchise was still restricted and only four members of the Council, as in 1922, were elected. The author of the constitution, Sir Arthur Richard, would later admit that the constitution was designed to seek Nigerians' discussion rather than management "of their own affairs."[56] The MacPherson constitution of 1951 (named for the then Governor of Nigeria, Sir John MacPherson) was the third in Nigeria's constitutional development and ushered in an era of Nigerian majorities in the regional and central legislatures with restricted legislative powers. But the franchise still was restricted and indirect elections and official appointees determined the composition of the legislatures which were encumbered as the Governor exercised considerable discretionary power in executive and legislative matters. There were important differences between the regions. First, on the eve of independence, whereas the franchise was universal in the regions of the southern Nigeria, women in the north were disenfranchised. Until four days before independence, indirect elections were still in use in the north and official and special members were seated in the legislature. These practices had been eliminated in the southeast and southwest by 1958.[57] If there had been any fears among the regions of being subordinated to the central government in which their influence could be constrained, the 1951 constitution was a confirmation of such trepidation. Approval by the central legislature for regional appropriations was required. The cabinet ministers, divided equally among the three regions, were subordinated to the administrative head of the ministry who might or might not be from the ministers' region.[58]

The feverish pace toward independence had meant equally frenetic efforts by the elite not only to consolidate their respective regions, but also to be poised to assume power in the central government. The above constraints led to increasing demands for regional autonomy which was conferred by the Lyttelton constitution of 1954. This constitution could thus be said to have legalized ethno-regional particularism. It established a Nigerian federation with three separate regional governments empowered to determine their own internal matters with respect to taxation, appropriation, bureaucracy, etc. It was, therefore, not surprising that each region moved quickly toward indigenization of their civil service, public corporations, and parastatal. Employment in the public service was determined by region of origin and civil servants who had been working outside of their region of origin lost their jobs and had to move back home.[59]

The federal elections of 1954 were clear evidence of ethno-regional politics. The political parties--the Northern People's Congress (NPC), the National Council of Nigeria and the Cameroon (NCNC), and The Action Group (AG)--were formed in the north, east, and west, respectively. Aside from in the West, where NCNC won the majority of seats due to a splintering within the AG, voting was along ethno-regional lines. Where outside parties won some seats, no time was wasted in using coercion to bring the district in line.

Two other factors were to enter the picture which would figure prominently at the constitutional conference held in London in 1958. First, the minorities within each region began clamoring for the creation of more states in order to avoid being subordinated to the ethnic majority in their respective regions. Second, the north wanted its seat in the federal legislature to reflect a population which it claimed was more than the two southern regions combined.[60] In response to these problems, The Willink Commission was set up by the British government in 1957 to evaluate and make recommendations on state creation as a means to alleviate the minority problem.[61] In the end, the Willink Commission recommended against the creation of more states. The British Government had taken the attitude that if more regions were going to be created, Nigeria's independence would have to be postponed to give the new states "at least two years to settle down."[62] This, unfortunately, was not palatable in an atmosphere of anticolonialism in Nigeria and the world.[63] The Imperial Government's decision not to create states before granting independence meant that the conspicuous imbalance in Nigerian federal structure would be left unresolved, a fatal mistake as evidenced by the political crisis of the first republic (1962-1966) which culminated in a civil war in 1967.[64] By accepting the Willink Commission's recommendations against state creation, Nigerian leaders missed an opportunity to resolve the ethno-regional question before independence.[65] In what is now regarded as a gross miscalculation, southern leaders, in the hope differences with the north would be addressed in the post-independence period, gave in to the north's demand for proportional representation (by quota) which gave the latter 174 of the total 312 seats in the federal assembly in Lagos. According to Dudley, the overwhelming imagery of independence had made southern leadership accept completely "Nkrumah's dictum to: seek ye first the political kingdom and everything else shall be added unto you."[66]

4. MULTIPLE STREAMS AND STATE CREATION POLICY IN NIGERIA

Kingdon's multiple stream approach provides a useful analytic lens to explain the division of Nigeria into a twelve-state federal structure in 1967. In other words, how did an idea that had been rejected earlier--state creation--suddenly become an acceptable policy option shortly before the civil war in 1967? In addition, this approach also helps explain the persistence of the policy over the past three decades. In other words, why has it remained on the agenda of successive regimes despite its many flaws? Several proposals were floated as possible solutions to ethnic rivalry in Nigeria before and after independence. At a pre-independence conference held at Ibadan to consider the division of power between different levels of government and whether more regions should be created based on ethno-linguistic sameness, each region took a sharply divergent position.[67] The north proposed a federal structure with a weak center in which the federal authority would emanate from the constituent units and argued the existing boundaries should be left unaltered.[68] The Western region wanted a federal structure in which boundaries were adjusted as much as possible along ethno-linguistic lines.[69] The Eastern region's proposal was diametrically opposed to that of the north since it was essentially a unitary formula that would have downgraded the existing regional authorities to a local government status.[70] The Eastern region's plan would have provided the central government with the power of disallowance, by being able to intervene to block or appeal initiatives from the regional legislatures."[71] Although proposals to create more states were advocated by ethnic minorities and politicians before independence, they were rejected. The Willink Commission in rejected all proposals to reconstitute the Nigerian federation.[72] Thus, at independence in 1960, Nigerian federalism faced, among others, two major problems. First, there was an imbalance in its federal structure in which the north was bigger than the east and west combined. The second problem was the growing ethnic minority agitation for states of their own. Those opposed to the creation of more states, including the Willink Commission, based their argument on four factors. First, it was feared the creation of new states might create fresh minority situations. Second, creation of states along ethnic lines was thought to be impossible since ethnic lines could not be made coterminous with state boundaries. The third problem was economic and cultural viability of the units. Finally, there was a concern that once begun, the process of state creation would be difficult to stop.[73] During the First Republic (1962-1966), attempts to correct the structural imbalance by breaking up the north had been opposed strenuously by the NPC. Similarly, the minority question was given little attention by the political parties in the other two regions. Championing the cause of minorities could mean a reduction in population and territorial size and, consequently, a diminution of power *vis-a-vis* the other two regions.State creation as a means to restructure Nigerian federalism became possible when three factors coupled at a critical moment in time. First, there was the problem stream. Nigerian federalism was collapsing under a political crisis brought on by ethnic hatred. The territorial integrity of the Nigerian state had been challenged openly by secessionist threats. The focus event was the secession of Biafra in 1967. The imminent breakup of the country thus made boundary adjustment an attractive policy option. Once this view gained currency among the political and policy elites, the second stream--policy stream--crystallized. It became clear that only by weakening the three units could the threat of secession be eliminated. Furthermore, creating states was both a feasible and acceptable option to the policy community. A military leadership predisposed to the idea could carry it out without concern for the electoral consequences. In the political stream, the new leadership after the coup which overthrew Aguiyi Ironsi in 1967 was ideologically committed to a united Nigeria.[74] They were receptive to the idea of creating more states because it was the only way in which their vision of a united Nigeria could be attained.But, why did subsequent administrations continue the process of state creation if the threat of secession had been removed in the first exercise in 1967? Once again, the multiple streams model can be fruitfully applied here.

4.1   Federalism Under Strain: The Post-Independence Period

At independence, Nigeria inherited a tripartite federal structure which soon degenerated into a civil war. Deep-seated antagonisms among the three ethno-regional units were exacerbated by several important factors. The first was the structural imbalance in which the north was physically and demographically larger in area and population than the east and west combined. The north encompassed 79 percent of Nigeria's land area while the west and east had, respectively, 12.7 and 8.3 percent. Although hotly contested, the 1963 census figures put the north's population at 53.5 percent of the total population of Nigeria, the west was 23 percent, and the east was 22.[75] This asymmetry in Nigeria's federal structure was further compounded by the fact that the south (east and west) was wealthier than the north, and had benefited far more from Western educational system.

One of the consequences of these differentials was that the north and the south viewed each other with great fear and mistrust. The south feared that the north could rule indefinitely by virtue of its size. The north, on the other hand, believed it needed to have control of political power to ensure a timely squaring of the economic and educational imbalance.[76] In addition, because revenue allocation was derivative, it created disparities in regional financial health and hence varied "degrees of autonomy *vis-a-vis* the federal center's financial grants."[77] This helped to foster an attitude of separatism. The fear of domination of one ethnic group by another, whether real or putative, have been given strong political expression by ethnic entrepreneurs and has kept the issue of state creation on the agendas of Nigerian regimes. Nigerian governments began to view state creation as an ever-ready solution to the twin problems of ethnic tension and the legitimacy crisis.(See table 1). State creation also accorded nicely with the political objectives of the northern ruling elite. First, territorial fragmentation was likely to be more disruptive in the south than in the north. Religious and linguistic uniformity, coupled with the hierarchical socio-political structure in the north, was expected to counteract the effect of state creation there. Conversely, challenge to the north's hegemony would be weakened with territorial fragmentation of the southern regions. Second, competition for scarce resources at the state level would probably shift the focus of ethnic leaders away from the federal government. From the foregoing, it is clear that the problem for which the policy was initially designed ceased to be the primary motive in the subsequent decades (*i.e.*, the four state creation exercises from 1976 to 1996). Therefore, regimes political survival and hegemonic domination of the north have become major driving forces behind state creation policy.

Table 1. Attitude Toward State Creation in Nigeria, 1960-1996

Year	Ruling elite/head of government	Major problems	Attitude of ruling ethnic group	Attitude of non-ruling ethnic groups	Additional states created	Number of states
1960	Northern-based NPC. PM: Balewa	Regional rivalries	Unfavorable, against the goal of keeping the north as a unified region	Favorable due to apprehensions about northern domination	0	3
1963	Northern-based NPC. PM: Balewa	Regional rivalries, crisis in western region	Favorable only toward western region	Unfavorable	1, from western region	4
1967	Northern military	Biafra secession	Favorable, to weaken ethno-	Favorable, except in Biafra	8	12

	elite\Gen Gowon		regionalism			
1976	Northern military elite\Gen Mohammed	Recent coup, increased minority agitation	Favorable, possibly to broaden regime's support base	Favorable, to attract economic development & federal distributable resources	7	19
1987	Northern military elite\ Gen Babangida	Recent coup, economic crisis, minority lobbying	Favorable, possibly to increase regime's legitimacy	Favorable, possibly to attract federal resources	2	21
1991	Northern military elite\ Gen Babangida	Economic crisis, transition program, minority agitation	Favorable, probably to reward regime's supporters	Favorable. Same as in 1987	9	30
1996	Northern military elite\ Gen Abacha	Annulment of 1993 elections, execution of the Ogoni 9, sanctions	Favorable, to consolidate power and broaden support base	Favorable. Same as in 1987, 1991	6	36

Source: Based on various sources dealing with the subject of state creation in Nigeria. See references.

Table 2. Evolution of Nigeria's 36 States, 1960-1996

Region 1960	Region 1963	State 1967	State 1976	State 1987	State 1991	State 1996
Northern	Northern	Benue-Plateau	Benue	Benue	Benue	Benue
						Gombe
					Kogi*	Kogi*
			Plateau	Plateau	Plateau	Plateau
						Nasarawa
		Kano	Kano	Kano	Kano	Kano
					Jigawa	Jigawa
		Kwara	Kwara	Kwara	Kwara	Kwara
					Kogi*	Kogi*
		North-Central	Kaduna	Kaduna	Kaduna	Kaduna
				Kastina	Kastina	Kastina
		North-Eastern	Bauchi	Bauchi	Bauchi	Bauchi
			Borno	Borno	Borno	Borno

					Yobe	Yobe
			Gongola	Gongola	Adamawa	Adamawa
					Taraba	Taraba
		North-Western	Niger	Niger	Niger	Niger
			Sokoto	Sokoto	Sokoto	Sokoto
						Zamfara
Total					Kebbi	Kebbi
Northern: 1	1	6	10	11	16	19
Eastern	Eastern	East-Central	Anambra	Anambra	Anambra	Anambra
				Imo	Enugu	Enugu
		Rivers		Rivers	Imo	Ebonyi*
			Imo	Cross River	Abia	Imo
		South-Eastern	Rivers	Akwa Ibom	Rivers	Abia
			Cross-River		Cross River	Ebonyi*
					Akwa Ibom	Rivers
						Bayelsa
						Cross River
Total						Akwa Ibom
Eastern: 1	1	3	4	5	7	9
Western	Western	Western	Ogun	Ogun	Ogun	Ogun
			Ondo	Ondo	Ondo	Ondo
						Ekiti
			Oyo	Oyo	Oyo	Oyo
					Osun	Osun
		Lagos	Lagos	Lagos	Lagos	Lagos
	Mid-	Mid-Western	Bendel	Bendel	Delta	Delta
Total	Western				Edo	Edo
Western: 1		3	5	5	7	8
All States:	2					36

Source: Arthur S. Banks and Thomas C. Muller, eds., *Political Handbook of The World: 1998* (Binghamton: State University of New York, 1998, p. 685, and Eghosa E. Osaghae. *Crippled Giant: Nigeria since Independence* (Bloomington: Indiana University Press, 1998.

*Carved out from two states as shown.

**Lagos was Nigeria's federal capital territory (FTC)until 1991.

5.   STATE CREATION AS SOLUTION TO ETHNIC CONFLICT

During the First Republic, the three major political parties had been regionally based, with each drawing most of its support from one of the three dominant groups. Consequently, each political party had resisted any attempt to establish new states within its region. The logic was that a diminution of their territory and population correspondingly would weaken their leverage *vis-B-vis* the other major parties and in the national assembly. When the A.G.-controlled Western Region was plunged into a political crisis leading to a formation of a new party by a splinter group, the NPC-NCNC-coalition federal government quickly exploited the situation by carving out the Mid-western region from the Western region.[78] The creation of the Mid-western region in 1963 thus represented the first state creation exercise in post-independence Nigeria.

Tables 1 and 2 above show the shifting and differing attitudes of Nigerian groups toward state creation as well as the evolution of the present 36 units. The threat of Biafran secession marked the beginning of a serious attempt to restructure Nigerian federalism by breaking up the original three regions. The state creation exercise carried out by the Gowon administration on May 27, 1967 sought to correct the ethnic imbalance and to eliminate the threat of secession by the existing ethno-regional strongholds. The result was a twelve-state structure in which the north was divided into six states, the east into three, the west into two, while the mid-west was left intact. [79](See table 2). On February 3, 1976, the Murtala Mohammed administration (upon recommendation of the Irekefe Commission) further continued the process by creating seven more states, leading to a 19-state federation. General Babangida added two additional states in 1987 and 21 in 1991, making Nigeria a 30-state federal structure. The latest exercise in state creation was carried out by General Abacha who increased the number of states to 36 by adding 6 states in 1996. State creation policy since 1976 could thus be said to have been motivated by reasons other than those in the pre-civil war period. However, successive governments have continued to maintain that the fragmentation process was designed to stabilize Nigerian federalism. Among the rationale provided are the following: 1)to remove existing imbalance in Nigeria's federal structure, 2) to give state status to additional ethnic minorities, and 3)to broaden the base of political participation in national affairs.[80]

By creating states along ethnic lines, federalism in Nigeria has tended to reinforce ethnic identity thus negating the stability sought in federalism in the first place. In order for this contradiction to be resolved, and to end the demands for more states, Nigerian federalism would have to be based on a 250-state structure. Is this possible?

The other alternative to enhance stability is to de-emphasize ethnicity by ensuring that divergence exists "between the constituent units and ethnic divisions"[81] This alternative has been rendered impossible by the mutual antagonism of the Nigerian ethnic groups.

5.1   The Military in Nigerian Federalism

There is a considerable controversy as to whether democracy is indispensable in a federal system. Scholars also disagree on what constitutes acceptable power-sharing between the general government and the constituent units in a federation. Some authors maintained that Federal military government is a contradiction in terms since federalism is "basically incompatible with authoritarianism or military rule." [82] This view stresses the constitutional and institutional aspects of federalism such as electoral politics, a party system, separation of power, and checks and balances which do not exist in a military rule.[83] Therefore, power-sharing is taken very seriously by proponents of this view. There must be real autonomy which allows the constituent units freedom of action "in matters of resources, claims or control of institutions."[84] Others posit that federalism experiences have contradicted its stringent theoretical claims. The assumptions of broad division of power and authority with little overlap, assume federalism is a "static and rigid" system, unresponsive to the socio-economic dynamics.[85] The evolution of United States federalism has been used to illustrate that the "federal content" of that system was determined by the changing "structure of societal conflict, consensus and resources."[86]

Nigerian federalism is different from the American, Canadian, or German for several reasons, including the fact that it is military federalism. Federalism did not arise as a result of a compact between the people and government. In order words, there was no broad-based consent of the peoples of Nigeria to establish a federation as a constitutional form. Nor was federalism a result of a contract between previously independent states.[87] Federalism was an accident of history resulting from the 1914 amalgamation of three adjoining West African colonial territories of Britain. With the exception of one region (Mid-Western) created in 1963, all post-independence state creation exercises have been carried out by military rulers in response to "strong local demands."[88] One can make a counterfactual argument that Nigeria would not have been fragmented so easily had it remained under civilian rule. These characteristics of Nigerian federalism have led Sam Oyovbaire to argue that the tension between regions and central authorities which formed the basis for the establishment of "two communities of classical federalism" never has been a feature of Nigerian federalism.[89] Under the military government, state governors are appointed by the federal chief-executive and are therefore directly responsible to him. The Federal Military Government, in practice, exercises "full authority throughout the country"[90] in sharply contrasts with the requirements of federalism. As Elazar points out, if each government cannot "retain its own decision-making capacity and freedom to say no, [then] coercion by the federal government" is highly likely.[91] The source and sufficiency of revenue always have been considered crucial for successful federalism. Wheare points out that resource endowment in the units should be sufficient enough to ensure financial independence from the central government when he writes: "the regional governments will be unable to perform their functions or they will be able to perform them only at the price of financial dependence upon the general government, that is, at the price of financial unification.[92] This, in fact, has been the case in Nigeria. Most scholars of Nigerian federalism agree military rule and financial unification have turned Nigeria into a *de facto* unitary government. The military is by nature a centralized institution whose principle of chain of command does not accord with the concept of power decentralization in federalism.[93] The federal government, for instance generated seventy-five percent of total government revenue mainly from oil in 1987. In contrast, the figures were forty-nine percent in 1961, and fifty-three in 1965.[94]

CONCLUSION

It is hoped that this paper has enhanced understanding of the policy of state creation in Nigerian federalism by using the multiple streams approach to explain its origin and persistence. Furthermore, the dilemmas of federalism in Nigeria have been highlighted by probing the compatibility of the Nigerian historical, social, and political experience with the principles of federalism. I have argued the manifest function of state creation, removal of the imbalance in the Nigerian federal structure, has not been achieved. State creation for this purpose began on the eve of the 1967 civil war when General Yakubu Gowon divided the existing four regions into a twelve-state federal structure. Subsequently, the nature of Nigerian politics has changed. Unlike the pre-civil war period, when there was no consensus on state creation, the interests of politicians, ethnic entrepreneurs, the military and the northern ruling elites currently have all helped in the perpetuation of a policy of territorial fragmentation. So far, neither federalism nor state creation has been able to solve the problems of ethnic domination and regional imbalances in Nigeria. As Nwosu has correctly observed, "The North is still the north, and likewise the East, West, and the Middle Belt, in terms of their world view."[95] For instance, while the northern states of Kaduna and Kastina may be keen competitors on various distributive issues, their differences tend to vanish in affective matters such as religious and cultural independence. The legitimacy crisis of the military regimes has definitely expedited the process of fragmentation. State creation has become a useful instrument in expanding their support base. Creating states by decrees has proved to be a legitimizing act for each successive military government since the Gowon administration. Despite the purported consultation that usually preceded the exercises, there were no discernible criteria or rules for creating states, and the issue is forever open.

Chapter III

THE REHABILITATION OF 1999 NIGERIAN CONSTITUTION: THE FEDERAL GOVERNMENT AND THE INTEGRITY OF THE COMPONENT STATES

Bamidele A. Ojo

The 1999 constitution remain the most important document sustaining the Nigerian polity today. As a result of its relevance to the survival of our nation, it must be legitimized through its being popularly accepted and be recognized for guaranteeing the rights of Nigerians and sustaining the political institutions in Nigeria. As it stands, this constitution suffer from the fact that, it was put into place by the military and represents a disconnect and flagrant disregard that the military had for the citizenry by involving it(the citizenry) in the decision making infrastructure under their otherwise illegal and undemocratic regimes. The component of such documents therefore display the inadequacies that are very characteristic of such a political landscape. The question of legitimacy is very paramount in the process of democratization(Ojo, B.A.,1999). The society and all its infrastructure must exist under the presumption that they are legal and be respected because of the trust within which they were created in the first place. This is not assumable but must be earned and earning it starts with the peoples perception of its construction. Its construction must meet peoples expectation which should involve (equal) peoples participation under free and fair representation and expression of desires, needs and purpose. The environment within which it is constructed should be perceived as being free of any form of oppression. The question therefore is whether the 1999 Nigerian constitution was constructed under these conditions and if not what are the process in place to facilitate its rehabilitation and the restoration of legitimacy. This then becomes the driving point for the rehabilitation of this constitution.

The legitimacy of the constitution and any institution created from it must be derived from the people. This constitution in essence must be supported by the majority of Nigerians and the steps toward its rehabilitation should involve a review by a specially constituted authority, confirmed by elected representative and adopted through a referendum. A popularly accepted constitution is a needed conduit for sustaining our present political experiment in Nigeria. Different groups and individuals have different opinions on the constitution and what need to be done in order to rehabilitate it. In this piece however, the primary focus of challenge is its inadequacy in terms of the devolution of power between the different units constituting the Nigerian state. The power structure as recognized by the constitution is highly un-federal in nature and ill-federal in function. The component units remain largely dependent contrary to a federal notion demanding an autonomous and independent units in reality. The sense of autonomy can best be guaranteed by a requisite desire for an individual states (or units) constitution, which although subservient to the federal constitution, but reflects the aims and aspiration of the people resident in those units(states). This will afford the state the opportunity to create a lasting agenda and promote those agendas within the Nigeria polity. This could effectively be used to develop in those component units the sense of Nigerianess and common sense of identity(brotherhood) within Nigeria.

These units must therefore develop a sense of independence in all aspect of governance including revenue generation, so as to demonstrate less reliance on federal support and effective judicious use of federally allocated funds.

The 1999 Nigerian Constitution in recognizing the states in chapter 1 Part I, 2(2) describe Nigeria as a federation consisting of states and a federal capital territory and in 3(1) of the same chapter and part, listed the names of the composing states while in the following Part II, recognized the division of legislative power between the national legislature and the state assemblies(1999 Federal Constitution of Nigeria). These explicit delineation of authority and power between the federal government and those of the states, was no doubt an attempt to redress the points of possible conflict between these units, which implicitly recognized their existence but should not have been done as a means to reduce the power of these component states vis-a-vis the federal government, if infact, the constitution effectively recognizes these units as component units of this federation. There is an apparent micro-management of power between the units and the federal government which stems from the fact that for many years the federal government is more else the national government in a unitary rather than in a federal state structure. The distribution of power in this manner is one of many legacy of the militarist framework within which the constitution was framed and constructed. The states should have been given the autonomy to develop their representative local government infrastructure which should remain independent of the god fatherist or patronizing supervision of the federal government. The ultimate governing body should be the constitution which in reality recognizes these units and component units while affirming the unifying role of the federal power in cases of conflict between the former and the latter. Another troubling aspect of this constitution is the attempt in section 7 to define the local government authority is unnecessary and undermines the very essence of democracy and grass root participation. It reduces the ability or freedom of the people themselves to organize, determine and promote their respective agenda. Or that should have been necessary is to categorically affirm the fact that the interest and agenda so promoted within this units, when so created should not in conflict with the federal constitution. Why should a federal constitution delineate precisely the number of local government s in each states when there is a possibility that within a given period of time, there might be a movement requesting new local governments. And if and when this happens, the resources of the local government so created is shared with the original local government from which it has been created. For example, let us assume that there are 10 local governments and from these 5 new local governments were created from local government A, B, C, D and E (as A1, B1, C1,D1, E1), which means that local government A,B,C,D,E will have to share their revenues and federal allocations with A1,B1,C1,D1 and E1. This is unfair and violate the principle of fairness, justice and equality that is the bedrock of any democracy. And again, every single demand for new local government will always most likely results in constitutional changes and such an incessant amendments to a constitution will surely undermines its credibility and effective legitimacy. The descriptive dictation of what should be and who should be doing what is extra democratic in a constitutional democracy.

A clear adoption of the Nigerian constitution is necessary as a means toward legitimizing this construct and to rid it of its military stigma. It should be reviewed to reflect the basic need of a democratic Nigeria, reflecting the will and the aspiration of the Nigerian populace irrespective of their ethnicity, belief, gender or stature. An important aspect of constitutional making is the nature of the support for it. If the 1999 Nigerian constitution, as it is perceived, is seen as unrepresentative of the entire national ideal, it is should be the prerogative of the contemporary leadership to facilitate its legitimate rehabilitation. The current debate on national sovereign conference is inevitable considering the Nigerian political culture. A culture dominated by sense of deprivation resulting from colonial legacy which is not only reflected by the inter-ethnic tension but also years of military domination(Ojo, B.A.1998). The Ibos as well as the Yorubas and many other minority groups have seen the Hausa/Fulani led north dominated the Nigerian political scene since independence and one cannot be surprised that the north has been blamed for the country socio-political and economic malaise that has plagued the country since then. It is therefore important that President Obasanjo's presidency survives its present travails to lay the foundation for sustaining the present democratic experiment. The fear of the north, however unrealistic it might seem to the south, must be allayed as a means towards building some level of trust among the Nigerians. The call for a national conference is well founded given Nigerian tenuous socio-political and economic situation. It will allow the different ethnic groups to bear their fear and aspirations in a national dialogue that might eventually help to rehabilitate the Nigerian nationhood. We need to engage in a national dialogue as a means towards establishing a national sense of common duty and identity. Such a dialogue will help establish a national response to many questions including that of the sharia.

The adoption of the sharia law in Zamfara and followed by some other northern states remain one of the most immediate challenge to the 1999 constitution of the Democratic Republic of Nigeria(other problems include ethnic crisis both in the Delta, Ife-Modakeke, the OPC problems in Lagos, among others). The response and the resolution of this critical issue will go a long way t sustaining the democratization process in the country. First, we should not be so eagerly dismissive of the issue by concluding that it signifies the end of the new Nigeria. In fact, it should serve as a clarion call for an immediate address of some of the issues that continue to dog the development of nationhood and independence. We must accept that this is a diverse nation and as a result of which there exist many conflicting issues across the country. Religion is one of these issues and a recognition of this will provide the first step toward its resolution. Anybody, according to the constitution, has the right to profess any religion and should not be denied such a wish. The one limiting factor is that the constitution is supreme and in cases of conflict, the federal law will superceed any state or local ordinance. The sharia law proclamation is limited by the constitutional provision and especially runs contrary to the principle of secular statehood, which gives priority to federal laws over local or religious laws. The essence of democracy is the protection of the fundamental human rights of the citizenry which in effect guarantee fair trial and equal justice for all and the introduction of sharia law violates the rights of non-muslims to a fair trial and equal justice. This is the same reason why many would opine against the institution of some traditional belief as the law of the land. For example, believers of shango or ifa divination may want to define access to justice as being judged under the jurisdiction of the shango of ifa high priest and if an Hausa lives in such a jurisdiction as they do now in many southern states, should they be subject to such a traditional religious law?

The question is if we are ready to permit the different units in the country to declare any type of religious law, which might jeopardize the individual and collective rights of our people. If we allow sharia in the north we must be ready to allow peoples in the south like the Ibos or and the Yorubas, to adopt unique religious laws as well. The sharia crisis makes it more imperative for Nigeria to rehabilitate the new constitution through establishing a new national consensus for it and also for the different states to adopt their state-centered constitution, reflecting their choices, goals, history and strategies for development. But they must all acknowledged the primacy of the federal constitution, from whence they derive their legitimacy and authority. The will form the basis of an effective constitutional federal structure which is lacking in the federal-state-local governments relationships in Nigeria. Regional identities are very important but should not be seen as a means toward fragmentation of the Nigerian state. This is were the leadership plays an important role. Nigerian leaders should desist from exploiting ethnic and religious differences for their individual political goals.

The state constitution should reflect the same principle of separation of power that is present in the federal constitution. The Governor remain the chief executive with each state determining if it want to adopt a bicameral or unicameral legislature. In many of the states, a second assembly, in addition to the lower or first assembly, should incorporate the traditional rulers as they deem fit because it is the only traditional and authentic political institution in Nigeria today. People who have made viable contribution to their states could also be elected into the second house. The legitimizing role of the traditional rulership should be exploited in order to sustain the democratization process. Each state must also determine its local government structure which must be designed within the provision of the federal constitutional. The local government should be structured into township and ward administrative structure. It facilitates effective democratic participation at the grassroot level. The Township should be administered by an elected council headed by a supervisor as the chief executive and assisted by a Township treasurer, Police Chief, Building and sanitory Officer and a Fire Chief. The ceremonial power of political leadership should rest with the traditional ruler or in case of a township of appropriate population in a town or city of a larger community, the ceremonial power should reside with an appropriately charged senior chief. The township treasurer would be responsible for tax issues and budgetary allocation of the township, while the police chief will be responsible for policing and security of the community and the fire chief, for the emergency responsibility. The building and sanitary officer will be responsible for town planning and health and sanitation functions. The state constitution should also make provision for the ward administration.

At the ward level and depending on the size of such a community, the traditional ruler within the units should also have ceremonial executive power. And at the local government level, the ceremonial executive power should reside with the ruler elected among the most senior rulers in the area. Each ward should, like with the case of the chairman at the local government level, directly elect a ward supervisor for a term of office. The rest of the governing executive at the ward level could be the ward treasurer, planning officer, an health /sanitation officer, a ward chief of police and fire chief. The sub-local government structures therefore gives the people more control over their lives and provides for more accountable and responsible governance.

The new Nigerian experiment is a map toward an effective and responsive governance. It is not an end in itself and it should tap into the need and desire of the population as means of establishing a credible and lasting and stable polity. It is unrealistic to expect an effective functioning of the new infrastructure because it is not the structures that matters but the extent to which they help to develop a mind set and culture with which we are able to inculcate a pattern of socio-political interaction capable of sustaining common sense of nationhood. Democracy is a state of mind which need to be nurtured and sustain through a consistent and stable application of the rule of law and respect for the constitutional infrastructure. In the Nigerian situation, the inclusion of the traditional political infrastructure provide the necessary legitimacy for nation-building and the bases for sustaining the current political experiment. That is why a constitutional review becomes paramount as a means of rehabilitating this construct and sustaining our polity.

Chapter IV

FEDERALISM, POLITICAL INSTABILITY AND THE STRUGGLE FOR DEMOCRACY IN NIGERIA

Olayiwola Abegunrin

INTRODUCTION

The problem of building a nation from a collection of ethnic groups is one of which all nations of Africa have faced since their independence in the 1960s, and still face today. By her very size, Nigeria has a greater problem than many of the African states. Nigeria with a population of about 110 million, the most populous nation in Africa, and it has been estimated that one out of five Africans is a Nigerian(Olayiwola Abegunrin, 1993). The British are the sole creators of the political entity known as Nigeria. This elementary truth has been put most forcefully by two of Nigeria's leading statesmen. In 1947, Chief Obafemi Awolowo, wrote that:

Nigeria is not a nation. It is a mere geographical expression. There are no "Nigerians" in the same sense as there are "English", "Welsh" or "French". The word "Nigerian" is merely a distinctive appellation to distinguish those who live within the boundaries of Nigeria from those who do not. On top of all this the country is made up of a large number of small, unintegrated tribal and clannish unit, who live in political isolation from one another. The Yoruba, for instance, belong to the same racial stock. But they are divided into a number of tribes and clans, each of which claims and strives to be independent of the other.(Obafemi Awolowo, 1947).

To confirm Chief Awolowo's statement, the first Prime Minister of the Federal Republic of Nigeria, Alhaji Abubakar Tafawa Balewa, affirmed during the Legislative Council debates in 1948, that, ASince 1914 the British Government has been trying to make Nigeria into one country, but the Nigerian people themselves are historically different in their backgrounds, in their religious beliefs and customs and do not show themselves any sign of willingness to unite.... Nigerian unity is only a British intention for the country(Abubakar Tafawa Balewa, 1948). Therefore, given, Nigeria is not a nation but an historical accident.Pre-independence and post-independence Nigeria was deliberately designed to fail by the British colonialists for reasons to promote the economic interests of Britain during and after (beyond)the time of the creation of Nigeria through the amalgamation of three distinct nations into one country called Nigeria in 1914 by the imperial Governor Frederick Lugard. The first official recognition of the name "Nigeria" appeared in the debate in the British House of Commons on the Royal Niger Company Bill in July 1899.(Margery Perham, 1937).

As a proconsul from 1897 till 1919(apart from five years as Governor of Hong Kong), Frederick Lugard had encouraged the isolation of the north from the south by imposing a system of indirect rule in the north, using the Islamic emirs as the princes had been used in India. By contrast the originally culturally, and politically organized Yoruba Empires, and other ethnic nationalities in the South were well endowed with natural resources, and had moved faster towards democratic politics. The amalgamation of Western, Eastern and Northern territories to form the colony and protectorate of Nigeria, by the British was done to garner the economic wealths of the south to offset the money spent by the British to pacify the less endowed northern Nigeria, and to balance the budget of the Northern territories. Nigeria's problems of today are legion, both economic, social, political, education and health. Now every sector of our(Nigeria)society is collapsing or has already collapsed. Only a disciplined, committed, and nationally popular, acceptable and democratically elected leader can lead Nigeria. It is now a demonstrated fact that judging from the Nigeria experience of instability since its independence; peace, political stability, and long standing economic development can only be achieved in a democratic environment.

THE ECONOMY

In March 1992, for the first time in a rare show of candor, General Ibrahim Babangida said, "frankly I have kept asking my economists why is it that the economy of this country (Nigeria) has not collapsed up till now? What is it that keeps it up? Surely, it is not our knowledge, it is not anything we have read. I still have not found any answer"(The Daily Times, March 1992). But in reality the Nigerian economy has collapsed, Babangida was only deceiving the Nigerians, for his own survival. For example, the Central Bank of Nigeria's (CBN) report for the first half of 1992, gave a very grim economic picture of the country. In the report, the CBN raised an alarm over the "disturbing socio-economic conditions, characterized by a slow down of economic activity, a worsening inflation, higher unemployment, greater tension in the private and public sectors"(CBN, Annual Report 1992). The World Bank-International Monetary Fund(IMF), so-called Structural Adjustment Program(SAP), orchestrated by the Babangida administration, and imposed on Nigeria since 1986(Olukoshi, 1995) has not worked but instead the program had ruined Nigerian economy. The SAP as implemented did not create the base for a sustainable economic development for Nigeria. The

Structural Adjustment Program of the World Bank and the IMF has not worked anywhere(Mkandawire and Olukoshi, 1995). For examples, look the situations in Zambia, in Ghana, in Brazil or in Philippines, the economic improvements of these countries are very negligible if there is any improvements at all, after many years of imposition of the so-called structural adjustment conditionalities.

According to professor Dotun Philips, "SAP tended to have mainly the impact of a deflationary package, thus its most visible and widespread result to date is stagflation, characterized by hyperinflation, rising unemployment, serious capacity underutilization, decumulation of investment, degeneration of social services, and continued decline in general living standards."

Another Nigerian reknown economist, Adebayo Adedeji, an apostle of Africa's alternative to SAP, also has misgivings about the SAP program, by saying that:

> The objectives of Nigeria's structural adjustment paradigm is to perpetuate its mono-cultural economic system, its narrow base and the persistence of a high level of external dependence which renders it highly susceptible to external shocks. And that no one can honestly deny that the worst economic performance has been during the era of structural adjustment. the overarching objective of SAP is a fundamental realignment of the economies of developing countries along free market lines. This has involved reducing the role of the state, removing subsidies, liberalizing prices and opening economies to flows of international trade and finance. Nigeria must embark on a sustainable human centered holistic development paradigm...It is development that gives priority to the poor, enlarging their choices and opportunities and providing for their participation in decisions that affect their lives. It is development that it is pro-people and pro-women. African governments must resist wherever necessary all international pressure to join the global band-wagon(Africa Today, August, 1998).

One of the Nigerian's renowed technocrats, Chief Gamaliel Onosode, as far back as 1992, admitted that the Nigeria's economy has collapsed, and that Nigerians have been impoverished. He pointed out that, as for him, he has to manage torn carpets in his house, and has stopped eating eggs and drinking milk with his breakfast due to the Nigeria economic hard times(National Concord, July, 1992). We strongly believe that a sound national economy is the only durable basis for the nation's security, and political stability, and that democracy is in turn a prerequisite for economic development, and survival of the nation's citizens. Statisticians are yet to come up with the exact figure or the rate at which Nigeria's purchasing power have shrank since the military administrations of Generals Babangida and Abacha have taken over in August 1985. General Olusegun Obasanjo, Nigeria's vocal critic of the Babangida administration before the June 12, 1993 election, and now new Nigerian Head of State, and an avowed critic of SAP puts it at more than 500 per cent. General Obasanjo's calculation was based on the weak purchasing power of the Nigerian currency-the Naira (The Washington Post, April 6, 1999). Its rating alongside other convertible currencies particularly the dollar against which it exchanged for N85.30(as of January 1999), at the government sponsored foreign exchange market has remained a major source of embarrassment to both the government, the CBN and operators of the market.

The unenviable status of the naira as a currency with indeterminable value has turned an hydra-headed problem pushing high the rate of inflation, budget deficit and generally stagnating economic activities. The same factor increase Nigeria's deficit expenditure to about $10 billion in 1992, and about $30 billion as of January 1999, and paying $2.5 billion a year to service this debt, thereby over heating domestic economy. Nigeria's economy is troubled by chronic political instability since the 1979 elections, and made worst by the Babangida-Abacha labyrinth of political transitions, and the so-called structural adjustment programs (Osaghae, 1998).

Since the Babangida-Abacha military administrations have taken over, Nigeria's standard of living has fallen very drastically. The oil boom of the 1970s has turned to oil doom in the 1990s. Nigerian people are now hostage to their country's crumbling economy. Despite large oil reserves that rank Nigeria sixth in the World, and number one oil producer in Africa, and abundant other natural resources, Nigeria's per capital income of only $1,300 a year is one of the worst in the world, worse even than perennial pauper Haiti. None of the country's four oil refineries are operational as of December 1998, forcing Nigeria to import petroleum, and pricing it beyond the reach of most Nigerians. By 1960s when Nigeria became independence, its level of economic development was the same as that of some Asian countries, such as Singapore, South Korea, and Taiwan that are now emerging as Newly Industrializing Countries(NICs)[Abegunrin and Vivekananda, 1998]. Is an irony that after 40 years of independence, Nigeria is still at the bottom of the economic pie. It has been estimated that more than $280.00billion in oil revenues during the last 25 years (since 1974)have largely been squandered as one military dictator after another has helped him-self to the country's (Nigeria's) treasury. The late dictator General Sani Abacha pocketed $7.5billion during his five year joyride that ended with his death on June 8, 1998. With his thievery, Abacha "made his predecessor, Ibrahim Babangida, who was known for taking a 25 percent cut of major deals, look almost respectable."(BBC News Reports, June 1998)..Nevertheless, both of them(Babangida and Abacha) were rogues who deliberately destroyed the Nigerian economy. Abacha, in addition, was the most ruthless of Nigeria's recent military dictators. One Nigerian newspaper has labeled him and his wife "the looters of the century."

Nigeria is $30 billion in debt(January 1999 figures) to foreign investors, and in a country where its currency, the naira used to fetch one and a half U.S. dollar until 1983, but worth only a penny as of January 1999. Adding more difficulty, oil prices are half of what they used to be a few years ago. Despite its vast farmlands, and natural resources, the largely subsistence agricultural sector has failed to keep up with rapid population growth, and Nigeria, once a large net exporter of food, now must import food, especially rice and wheat from Thailand and United States(Reuters in The Washington Post, April 29, 1999). Agricultural production in 1996 suffered from severe shortages of fertilizer, and production of fertilizer fell even further in 1997. Unemployment has remained intractable since the Babangida administration took over in August 1985. As of 1998, about 15 percent of Nigeria's 40 million labor force was reportedly employed. Nigerian workers have lost confidence in their government. Many of them have left the country and relocated to foreign countries to earn decent living and enjoy improved working conditions. The impact of this is felt more in the education, and health care sectors where specialists, and academics needed more to contribute to development have massively left the country(West Africa, August 1998).

EDUCATION

The Military Government under Babangida closed down all the Universities in Nigeria, by a decree, titled Teaching Essential Services Decree of 1993. Under this decree university teachers are deemed to have resigned if they went on strike for more than one week. With this decree the military government under General Babangida, as of June 17, 1993 terminated the appointments of all the teachers in the Nigerian Universities with immediate effect(National Concord, June 18, 1993). In addition, the military government disbanded the Academic Staff Union of the Nigerian Universities(ASUU). The Labor Unions in the country were incapacitated at the same time. The very poor remuneration of the teachers in the Nigerian universities, had resulted in the "brain drain" syndrome in which thousands of(the university teachers), academic staff who are teaching in the universities, and whose researches are expected to propel the country forward for development are quitting the universities, or leaving for overseas universities, or to the private sectors in Nigeria, where the conditions of service are very much better. According to the recent available figures, Nigerian university teachers are the least paid, not only in Africa but in the World as a whole. For instance, the highest paid professor in the Nigerian university system is earning N80,000 ($1,000) per year, while in the private sector a senior manager(an equivalent of a university Lecturer grade 1-a newly graduate with a Ph.D. degree(an assistant professor in the American university system), earns N95,000 per annum with all other benefits and allowances attached.

The Nigerian universities are under-funded to the extent that government subventions in recent times have been decreasing in proportion to the increasing number of students in the university system. For instance, students enrollment has increased by 200 percent since 1987, while budgetary allocation has fallen from 2.26 percent in 1987 to 1.45 percent by 1998., even though in 1992, the naira's value was roughly 20 percent of its 1987 value. Presently most of the Nigerian university teachers who could not avoid to go to foreign countries to look for jobs are running around our big cities and towns looking for contracts, since they have nothing to do. In Nigeria of today, school teachers demand bribes to pass school children to the next grade, and to admit students into the schools. The whole society has been invested with corruption that even the store clerks often refuse to give customers their change.

Corruption has become a way of life for many Nigerians, especially the ruling class and their business partners. Since coming to power in 1985, the Babangida administration, and followed by Abacha regime had ruined not only the Nigerian university education system, but all our education system from elementary school to the university level. In Nigeria schools go on strikes nearly every three months. For the Nigerian university students, between 1990 and 1995, they have not stayed in the school for one full three consecutive months, as a result of on and off strikes. Thousands of these students are now on the streets of the Nigerian cities and towns roaming about doing nothing, while they are supposed to be in the class-rooms, and their schools libraries doing their studies. From the independence in 1960, Nigerian education system used to be the best in Africa, but since the military administration has taken over all schools in the 1980s, the whole education system had been ruined.

HEALTH CARE

Currently health care services in Nigeria are in shambles. There are no medications for patients in the government hospitals, and just like in the education system, the medical doctors in these hospitals are not well paid. The hospitals are without necessary, essential and modern medical equipment. It is very sad and very shameful that since Babangida-Abacha administrations patients are required to provide their own medicines at hospitals. The worst part is that those patients who could not provide their own medicines are turn away from the hospitals. From 1960s until the early 1980s, University Teaching Hospital, Ibadan, and the University of Lagos Teaching Hospital were the leading medical research center, and cancer research center respectively in Africa. Today, they are short of medical doctors, and just struggling to survive. As a result of all these inadequacies, many of the Nigerian best trained practitioners, both doctors and nurses have left the country for Saudi Arabia, other Middle-east countries, United States of America, Canada, and European countries to earn decent living, and enjoy better working conditions. Nigeria with a 57 percent literacy rate, poor health care, and life expectancy of a man is 53 years; and that of a woman is 56 years, one of the worst in the continent of Africa. The country's infrastructure is decaying, and corruption and squalor have turned the hope of common person in the society, and "the Nigerian idea" into a nightmare.

TRANSPORT AND COMMUNICATION SYSTEMS

Debilitating infrastructures, particularly bad roads, epileptic electricity supply, and inefficient telecommunications network is another legacy of woes of the dictatorship of Babangida-Abacha 15 years administrations(Agbese, 1991). Currently Nigerian Railway System which was the cheapest transport system in the country has been paralyzed. Since January 1993, workers of the Nigerian Railway Corporation have gone on strikes more than six times. And up till the death of Abacha there was no solution insight on their demands for going on strikes. The current state of the urban transport system in Nigeria is very shameful. Despite about N12 billion sunk into the so-called Federal Mass Transit Program since 1988, by the military regimes, transportation has remained an intractable problem. Just like the Babangida-Abacha military regimes themselves, the management of this Federal Agency is very corrupt, and inefficient. Even the State Transport Corporations are not doing better if not worst.

Because of the poor state of the transport system in the country, commuters now spend over one-third of their income on fares, as transport operators have increased charges to be able to maintain few available vehicles in the country. Despite abundant oil reserves that rank Nigeria as the sixth oil producer in the world, and four oil refineries in the country, oil is a very scarce commodity in Nigeria, especially since the nation-wide riots following the annulment by Babangida of the June 12, 1993 elections won by the late Chief M.K.O. Abiola(The Washington Post, July 7, 1993). Nigerian telecommunication system is a mess. It is very easier, better, and cheaper to call anywhere in Nigeria on telephone from outside the country than calling within the country. The fact of the situation is that most of the times Nigerian telephones never work.

POLITICAL SITUATION AND ITS PROBLEMS

After 40 years of independence, Nigeria still appear uncertain about its future. Apart from political instability, civil war and economic problems, there are still questions about the nation's identity, and its political system. The first political question for every African nation is whether it is a nation. Each country could be ripped apart by tribal jealousies, and military dictatorships, and all are weakened by them. Nigeria brings together more people, and more ethnic groups than any other African nation. Therefore, with 250 ethnic groups, Nigerian political situation is unique in the African setting(Frederick A. Schwartz, 1965). Politics is about influence and influential people; that is, about people who have influence and/or who achieve power. The fruits of power are economic advantage, social prestige, and security for those who possess it. Through the promulgation of laws, ordinances, and decrees, those in power apportion rights and privileges and enforce the apportionment by recognized sanctions. The institutions, rules, and customs according to which power is achieved and exercised form the constitution(the supreme law of the land)of a country, and in a sense these are the residue of past politics. The constitution is like a skeleton, which politics endows with flesh, blood, and the breath of life(Odegard & Helms, 1947).

When he took over power in August 1985, General Ibrahim Babangida said, that he wanted to create something new in Nigerian political history-a new political thinking for Nigeria. But in essence his actions, and all that he did particularly since June 12, 1993 presidential election which he annulled have created doubts not only in the minds of the majority of the Nigerian people, but even in the minds of many of his own advisors, and colleagues in the military. Babangida's legacies are assassination of his political opponents, particularly the Yoruba, Southern leaders; and those his death squad could not kill were thrown into jails. Corruption was at its peak during the Babangida-Abacha administrations(1985-1998). Their administration was morally bankrupt, consequently, this led to a threatening state of moral degradation of our entire society and expansion of the boundaries of kleptocracy and mismanagement. The citizens of Nigeria have interests in and concern for the unity, progress, economic growth and development, and political stability of the country. Nigeria had one civil war before, and they were lucky to keep Nigeria as one unified country after that civil war. But the whole international environment has changed in a very dramatic way since that civil war of 1967-1970(Ralph Uwechue, 1971). Today, there are so many forces and interests out there that may or will successfully militate against Nigeria surviving a second civil war, particularly this time around. No country has ever fought two civil wars, and survive it, and still stay together as one united country. If care is not taken, the situations in Rwanda and Yugoslavia will be a child's play from what Nigeria will go through if any crisis should broke out again in Nigeria.

The people of Nigeria spoke loudly, firmly, and clearly through the democratic decision of June 12, 1993, afterward, the military government was expected to be courageous enough to step down and hand over to a transitional civilian administration as demanded by all ethnic groups/nationalities in the country. All the progressives, and patriotic Nigerians demanded a "National Conference of all Nationalities" in Nigeria to be held before General Abdulsami Abubakar military administration rushed to hand over to civilian administration. It is very obvious that all the southern nationalities in Nigeria led by the Yoruba and the Igbo are united in demanding for the "National Conference of all Nigerian Nationalities in Nigeria," while the northerners led by Hausa-Fulani hegemony refused to go to conference. Going to any conference of all Nigerian Nationalities is like committing a political suicide as far as far as the northerners were concerned. For the southerners, Nigeria needs to be reorganized, and restructured without any further delay to a true federal system with complete autonomy for the states, and not the present unitary military dictatorship which the country has been operating since the Ironsi military regime in 1966, abolished the federal system of government, and imposed the unitary system. General Johnson Aguiyi Ironsi, Awithout formally consulting the Nigerians and without waiting for the submission of the report of the Constitutional Study Group in progress, which he himself instituted. He acted contrary to advice of the majority members of his Supreme Military Council, and influenced by the advice of his four, close Igbo advisers, his so-called experts, promulgated Decree No. 34 in April 1966.   By this decree, Ironsi Military Government abolished the federal system of government, and introduced the unitary system. "This was a unilateral act which arbitrarily jettisoned the fundamental basis of the Nigerian political union"(Nigeria Roundup, 1960).

The Ironsi's abolition of the federal system, and imposition of the unitary system of government, was the immediate cause of the May 1955, northern riots in which Igbos living in northern cities were massacred. These riots were organized by the alienated northern ex-politicians, civil servants, local government officials, and businessmen who had been deprived of their lucrative supply contracts by the change of regime. Also, there were massive popular feelings within the country that the Ironsi military administration was ethnically dominated, because most of his advisers were from his ethnic group. There were allegations that the Ironsi regime's "aim was to take over the country, exploiting, and colonizing the backward north", and putting Igbos in all the strategic positions in both the military and civilian in the government. With these allegations the northerners demanded that, "let there be secession, no unitary government without referendum"(West Africa, June 4, 1966). The consequence of all these riots was the Igbo(Easterners)secession and the civil war of 1967-1970 (John de st. Jorre, 1972).

British colonialism in Nigeria was formally installed, and completed by the defeat of the Sokoto caliphate in 1903(Frederick Schwartz, 1965). British colonial rule held the Jihadist aggression against other Nigeria nationalities in a state of permafrost till 1960 when independence was granted to the colony. From the constitutional conference to now, the Federation so created has been plagued by political instability rooted in the hegemonic pursuits of the caliphate rump in its varied forms. The caliphate remains committed to the exclusive hegemonic control of Nigeria and the permanent denial of the right of all other Nigerian nationalities to self-determination. This mission of domestic colonization by the caliphate has manifested itself over, and over in political sulking, threats of Northern secession from the Federation, religious bigotry, brazen anti-secularism, acculturation, political oppression of progrom on other nationalities, and the effective frustration of the emergence of a truly Nigerian armed forces, and security agencies.

According to The Houston Yoruba Declaration of 1997, what the Yoruba are saying is "regional autonomy, not national disintegration"(Isokan Yoruba Magazine, 1997). No domination of one ethnic group by another, either majority or minority, and each state wants its autonomy. In line with the Yoruba position, the whole of the Southern Nigeria nationalities, which includes the Igbos, and other ethnic groups from the southern Nigeria, including the people from the Middle Belt are demanding for state autonomy-- that is complete federalism and not unitary system as the military, and their civilian business partners have been ruling Nigeria since 1966. This unitary and centralized system of government, without any doubt is likely to lead to another major, and serious national crisis which the country cannot avoid, and nobody wants to go through such a crisis again.

For this reason all aspects of Nigerian society, and its institutions need to be restructured, and reorganized from the bottom to the top. No body wants secession, but if that is the path the military with their northern oligarchy chose they would have themselves to blame at the end, and nobody else. If Nigeria is going to remain as one united political entity, complete federalism will be the best approach. Therefore, the major issue that Nigerians should insist on from now on is the restoration of state autonomy which will restore complete federalism to the constituent states that make up the Nigerian state. The demilitarization of the Nigerian polity can only start with the actualization of the democratic will of the people. For this to be achieved, productive and sustainable, demilitarization has to include the return of power to the states. If today Britain, the former colonial power and the creator of Nigeria, is talking of autonomy with its constituent nationalities like the Welsh, Scottish and Irish on the eve of this 21st century, obviously, Nigeria needs to see the handwriting on the wall. With the current situation, Nigeria cannot survive as a quasi-federal nation, but complete federalism with full autonomy for the states. Nigeria's economic development and political stability depend on extending the freedom, benefits and choice of directions to the states. Indeed, for a sovereign conference of all nationalities to achieve a meaningful and political stability, the current atmosphere of the domination of several Nigerian nationalities by those with access to military power led by the north oligarchy must be replaced by a return of autonomy to the states which can lead to a true federation of Nigeria. Even under the federal arrangement(constitution) when the two Southern Regions demanded for self-government in 1956, the north, led by Alhaji Ahmadu Bello, the Sardauna of Sokoto, speaking for the north said, "the north does not intend to accept the invitation to commit suicide"(Ahmadu Bello, 1962). The Eastern region and Western Region went on and formally became self-governing regions in August 1957. The north was still reluctant to have a regional autonomy, but prefer to continue under the British colonial rule until March 115, 1959, just a year before the formal independence. Under the 1959 Nigerian constitution, each of the three regions was given constitutional power to regulate its education, agriculture, health care, judiciary and trade. Under this same 1959 constitution Nigeria was granted independence by Britain, and each region was empowered to develop, and modernize its economy, culture and society at its own pace.

REVENUE ALLOCATION

Once federalism is restored in Nigeria, the states should be given fiscal autonomy and be allowed to manage their finances within the limit of their resources. Every state at the present stage of development needs its revenue to carry out much-needed development projects. One of the Nigerian economists, P.N.C. Okigbo gave an insight to this problem, and warned that, "Any attempt to subsidize and give grants to each unit of the federation without due consultation with and approval of the so-called, well-to-do sections of the country will lead to abuse of power in the center, interstate animosities and feuds, as well as charges of favoritism(Okigbo, 1965)" The above statement is true and candid as far as Nigeria of today is concerned. While an American understood clearly why former president John F. Kennedy appointed his brother into his cabinet as the attorney general, a Nigerian cannot understand and will not accept for a Nigerian Chief Executive to do the same. The country has just not developed up to that standard yet. Finally, on this issue of revenue allocation, 10% of income from the natural resources should be return to the local government of derivation, 10% to the state of derivation, 50% to be shared on the basis of equality among the states, 20% for the federal government, 5% for internal loan to the states, and the remaining 5% for savings for emergency preparedness. It is also very important that each state should and must be given the power to levy tax on its own people for its own development projects as needed.

CONCLUSION

Only restructuring, tolerance, patience, and acceptance of one another, regardless of ethnic group or section of the country one might come from will make the country become a truly integrated nation. It will be very unrealistic to adopt or impose a constitution which pre-supposes the existence of an already integrated society. What the Nigerians need is states autonomy within the framework of a federation; one in which minority and all ethnic groups are effectively guaranteed equal opportunities, freedom, and their civil rights from the threat of domination by any of the three major ethnic groups, and especially from the Nigerian armed forces which has become a terror to the country. The subject of federalism exerts a magnetic force among Nigerians. There is broad agreement that Nigerian federalism has been abused by military rule, and that the way forward is to reconstitute our governance in such a manner as will avoid the over-centralization of Nigeria's public affairs, and governance imposed by military rule. Therefore, the way for Nigeria survival is a total reorganization, and restructuring of all governmental institutions, including the armed forces. A restoration of complete federal system of government which will give complete autonomy to the states is the best solution to the Nigerian political problems and instability if the country is to survive as a united political entity. Autonomy in this sense means that, for each state to be in control, and make the best use of its own resources, just like it was in the old west, east, and northern regions in the 1960s. A complete autonomy will encourage, and promote an effective state which is very vital, and essential for the provision of goods, and services- and the rules, and institutions that allow free markets to flourish, and people to lead healthier, happier, and better lives. Without this sustainable development, both economic, and social is impossible.

To achieve peace, political stability, and long standing economic development under a federal system, the following actions must be taking without further delay:

1. Immediate convocation of a conference of a democratically elected representatives, two each, of all Nigerian nationalities; all without exception. This conference is to work out a new structures, framework, system and procedures and all constitutional attributes of a new union in which human rights and democratic governance form the pillars of the state.
2. Commitment to the establishment and nurture of a democratic culture, good and transparent governance through rational socio-economic management.
3. Commitment to a rapid modernization of Nigeria through the market economy, greater accountability in public affairs, and guaranteed freedoms.
4. Commitment to emergence of state dedicated to unending progress in Nigeria, and in Africa in which both states and citizens achieve a much higher level of capacity to compete in the international community of the third millennium.

Bad political choices and decisions, economic mismanagement, corruption, lack of vision on the part of the leaders(both the military, and their civilian business partners), lack of open political discourse and accountability, explain Nigeria's sad story. In a country like Nigeria, where economy is staggering and corruption and neglect are rampant, it is doubtful and even cynical if the election of General Olusegun Obasanjo could bring about any meaningful change. The transition program implemented by Abdulsalami Abubakar although prone to all the dangers which led us to the edge of the abyss in the first place, will most likely reconfirm the hegemony and hasten the disintegration of the flag state Nigeria, if steps are not taken to redress the corruption and lack of accountable and responsive leadership.

PART II: SOCIAL AND ECONOMIC ISSUES

There are many contending social and economic issues that face the newly elected leadership in Nigeria and as we move into the new millennium, many of these issues will make and unmake the Nigerian democracy and polity as well as determine the direction of the country's attempt at nation building. For an effective state-building, the new Nigerian experiment must therefore address these and many other questions as well as these of leadership, probity, educational and social infrastructure.

Chapter V

AN ESSAY ON LEADERSHIP AND GOVERNANCE IN NIGERIA

M. A. Okoronkwo

INTRODUCTION

In management practice, we know that to solve a problem fully, the first approach is to identify the problem. Then we analyze it, studying all its components and ramifications. Lastly, we make appropriate recommendations or prescribe the solution. Similarly, if an abused child or woman does not open up and tell people in authority what has happened to them so that their problem can be identified, it will be absolutely difficult to understand their problem much less solving it. Also if a patient does not expose his problem or sickness to the doctor, the doctor cannot identify the nature of the sickness nor prescribe treatment to solve the problem. In other words, if we hide a problem out of shame, pride or protecting the culprits, we are lying to ourselves and will not be able to solve it. Denying the existence of the problem cannot bring a solution.

This essay takes the same approach; it aims at examining the problems of leadership and governance in Nigeria over the past 39 years of its political independence from Britain since 1960. I intend to briefly remind our leaders of the challenge facing them, in fact all of us, in the next millennium. I will identify some major problems, why they have remained intractable, and the failure of Nigerian leaders and the elite at proper governance of the country or management of its God-given resources. I will show how mismanagement of these resources, more than any other single factor, has led to massive unemployment and poverty in our country, contributed to unending inter-ethnic tension, lack of patriotism, brain drain, and the ongoing sabotage or vandalizing of our facilities. It is clear that political and economic instability has frightened investors. In this chapter we will show the way forward and make recommendations for turning things around.

This chapter will address substantive priority issues of particular concern, with a view to engaging the attention and commitment of our present and future leaders and all noble-minded Nigerians at home and abroad. The issues confronting Nigeria range from leadership, the management of the economy, basic infrastructures, utilities and resources, reforming or restructuring strategic institutions, including the army, police, revenue allocation policies. Other crucial areas are: mass unemployment, poverty, social justice and redefining the nation's value system, (self-discipline, standards and criteria, reward and punishment), security, investment and health care delivery. It is intended that the issues will form part of the agenda of our new President during his term into the next millennium.

VISION OF A COMPATRIOT

The transition from military rule to civilian rule of 29 May 1999, is an opportunity to lay a good foundation for the incoming third millennium if the leadership will show the courage and selfless service required to drastically turn things around for the better. Of course, it might be naïve to expect the President to achieve more than a fair proportion of the desired results within a short period of four years, taking into account the magnitude of the problems left behind from previous misgovernment.

However, the presidential term of four years could make a very big difference by making progress irreversible. My vision therefore for the next millennium which is less than nine months from the time of writing is, first, a Nigeria that all Nigerians at home and abroad will be proud of. Second, a Nigeria where there is peace, security of life and property, in which all citizens, no matter their tribe or religion, have equal opportunity to pursue their lawful vocation with dignity and decency; where our children and grandchildren wherever they may be will be happy to return to and live as comfortably as their means can provide. Third is a Nigeria where the law protects every innocent citizen and is enforced on all, including the leadership, the Police or the Army, and where police or army brutality is a thing of the past, confined to history. Fourth, a Nigeria where respect for human dignity and fundamental rights of the individual is observed religiously by all those in authority and the Police in the same way as mores or professional code of conduct. Fifth, a Nigeria in which the leadership in all walks of life is visibly accountable to the people or the public, where performance and merit are the main criteria for attaining and remaining in a high office and not primarily ethnic or tribal consideration. Sixth, a Nigeria where people are recognized for their selfless service to the country or humanity, magnanimity, decency, or integrity, and not where glorification of Money or millionaires ranks as high as the glorification of God. Seventh, a Nigeria of my vision in the next millennium is a progressive, political and economic entity banded together by common bonds, common goals, good network of properly macadamized, asphalt and regularly maintained motorable roads crisscrossing the country from North to South, from East to West and within or linking States as this will enhance economic development amongst communities. Like other amenities and utilities, roads are a uniting factor if evenly distributed. Eight, a Nigeria that is supplied with adequate and stable electric power day and night, 365/366 days a year, not only to the cities but also to thriving communities in Local Government areas.

In today's high-tech world, Nigeria cannot afford to deny its people and businesses regular, stable full current of electricity power supply. Nine, a Nigeria where cleanliness of our surroundings and environmental care are a strong part of our custom and practice, where our city streets, highways, home frontage, markets, motor-parks and side-walks are no longer used for garbage dump or litter. Ten, a Nigeria where clean potable water is regularly available and accessible to communities, where clothes which have weathered laundry services abroad and still retain their whiteness as snow will not turn yellowish when they come out of our country's laundry due to untreated water supply. Eleven, a Nigeria where the telephones function at all times to any part of the country or the world at large and thus spare the users a sudden rise in their blood pressure when they cannot get through to their destination numbers.

In addition, a Nigeria where the Internet is accessible to 21st century citizens in whichever part of the country we decide to live. Twelve, a Nigeria where our valuable mail and parcels will safely pass through the Post Office and delivered without missing no matter how attractive the item, even if officially opened and checked by the Customs Service.

Thirteen, a Nigeria where our business friends from the Orient domiciled in the country, especially Pakistanis, Indians Lebanese, Jordanians, Syrians, etc. will be welcome with an open hand but not at the expense of, nor preferred to, fellow Nigerians from other parts of the country on the basis of religion. Moreover, these people must operate within the law of the land without engaging in corrupting people in authority. Fourteen, a country where fellow Nigerians are free to take up residence in any city in the Federation without discrimination by indigenous people and city authorities due to most natives' obsession with the strong feeling that their State belongs only to them. Fifteen, a Nigeria where petroleum marketing companies are not allowed to collude with independent fuel marketers to hold consumers hostage at any time by hoarding petrol, diesel and kerosene and selling them at cut-throat, black-market prices of 600% rising to 900% above official market prices per liter. As of December 1998 fuel sold at 350-500% over and above official prices per liter due to fuel scarcity and has continued so since January 1999. This is a perennial problem to motorists and others who use petrol/diesel generators to light their homes and work their bore-holes. Sixteen, a Nigeria where our women, particularly innocent girls and ladies, are protected by law from the vices of men in our male-dominated culture and society. I envision a Nigeria where it is incumbent upon us, our leaders and legislators to bring about adequate Federal/State legislation to punish offenders and to stop the primitive behavior of consigning girls under 16 years of age, some of them as young as 10-12 years, to monogamous and polygamous men in the name of tribal marriage. In addition, it is the hope of this writer that there will be legislation in place by 1st January 2000 to protect all womenfolk from sexual harassment and abuse by macho men so that our womenfolk can look forward to the next millennium with dignity.

LEADERSHIP

Fellow countrymen, I see leadership as the most crucial factor in the governance of Nigeria and the management of its affairs. The success of a sea voyage depends on the alertness, skill, determination and commitment of the ship's captain, just as an air journey depends on the same qualities of a pilot. By the same token, whatever is envisioned here for the next millennium will depend on the leadership, its focus, commitment, self-discipline, and strong faith in itself to deliver. It will equally depend on courage. A leader who cannot control or discipline his subordinate staff or appointees will hardly achieve his mission. Leaders must be able to face up to challenge from business people and any person, no matter how big or important, whose activities are contrary to public interest. This is essentially true in politics as it is in management. The First Republic gave us hope. We had credible leaders who had the nationalist spirit. We had credible elite too, no matter how few, who took over the post-Colonial Civil Service upon the end of British Rule.

We had credible military, the much vaunted Sandhurst trained. Nigerians were confident of a prosperous and bright future. Recalling late K.O. Mbadiwe's vision of greater tomorrow for that country, this writer sincerely saw then in 1960 a greater tomorrow for Nigeria. The failure, however, came not from the earlier leaders who, in their various degrees of contribution, brought about Nigeria's Independence in 1960 to an ill-prepared, largely ignorant population.

The failure came with successive military rules. The military believed that they had a loyal civilian workforce to run the nation. However, what they appear to have got was a largely disillusioned workforce giving them lip service in exchange for favors. In such a situation, "Things fell apart, and the center could not hold; mere anarchy was loosened upon the earth" if I may quote from Chinua Achebe's Things Fall Apart. Leadership over the past 15 years leaves much to be desired. The military remained too long enough to lose their vision on what the people actually wanted.

Military rule threw the country's Constitution to the winds. By doing so, the leadership of the military regimes that ruled the country for so long changed the course of Nigerian history for the worse. With the negotiated, established Constitution of Nigeria, which was a Covenant of the Collective Will of Nigerian peoples, thrown asunder, the military changed the basis of our common value system. They may be experts in conquering territories, but in almost all cases their job ends there; they are ill-equiped to sincerely conquer minds. If our leaders in the past loved their country as nationalists do, they would have shown self-discipline and exemplary leadership so that the people will have trust in them. Military rule may rightly claim to have kept the country together as one country at certain points in time, but not necessarily as a sustainable united entity. I recall with great emotion our original national anthem reminding us all of our need of each other in staying together in peace, unity and progress even though tribes and tongues may differ. The Constitution is a contract between the Government and the governed, the leadership and the population at large. The singular act of suspending the Constitution and not abiding by it obviously killed the faith and trust the silent majority of Nigerians have with the military leadership. The military judges the civilian government, and rightly too, by the standards provided in the Constitution. But why do the same military not accept to be governed by the same Constitution when they take over political power by means of a coup d'etat? It defies reason why they consider themselves competent to impose a Constitution upon the population when they are leaving power!

The Second Republic seemed to offer Nigerians fresh hope for unity and progress as inscribed on the Federal Coat of Arms. This period coincided with the peak of the oil boom when Nigeria was ranked by output as the sixth oil power in the world, within the OPEC club. The leaders and the elite during this period of the greatest oil boom no longer saw themselves as serving the people. Rather they made themselves masters of the people. The masses watched their leadership, watched the sqandermania that went on and on. The ascendancy or worship of money, call it Naira, over and above every other thing has begun. The old Victorian values of prudery, self-discipline, patience, hard-work, merit, which were the bastion of social cohesion and stability during British Colonial rule were shunned.

The military people, known to be disciplined and well nurtured in the best Sandhurst tradition, unfrocked themselves of those sustaining values. The prevailing obsession of the leaders with power and money was passed on to the onlookers, the rest of society. As a result, people positioned themselves to get their share of the so-called national cake, by any means possible. The slogan of sharing the national cake amongst those who have access to it gripped everyone with connection to the leadership. In the moral chaos that ensued, the military struck again, supposedly to correct things and restore stability and unity.

It was one military regime after the other. Discipline in the management of affairs in the public and private sectors completely collapse in Nigeria, and with it the loss of faith in every Nigerian leader.

THE POLITICS OF THE ELITE

I am not sure who coined the phrase "If you can't beat them, join them". But it is the elite who propagated it as their defense mechanism. In times of national hopelessness and helplessness, the elite as leaders of thought were looked upon to assume the role of defenders of the Constitution, civil liberties and of fundamental freedoms. In times of national stress, their role in this respect becomes untenable due to the risks involved in opposing a dictatorial regime. But it was amazing how they could easily trade their criticism of military regimes for political office in the same military administration that they have consistently criticized. Who drafted those oppressive military decrees against the Nigerian people? It was the civilian elite. Who lent credibility to those military tribunals that tried civilians without the option of appeal to the Civil Courts in accordance with the law? It was the civilian elite. The elite of civil society so eagerly abandoned their respected positions to avail themselves of the little patronage the military regimes offered. The elite of civil society participated in all the dictatorial military regimes that ever ruled Nigeria. They helped sustain "militocracy" in that country by giving the military governments the credibility it badly needed from civil society at one time or the other.

The elite of civil society claim that they have to accept ministerial and other high positions in the military government in order to effect positive changes from the inside. From what we know, some of those civilian elite either got frustrated or were booted out sooner or later. Yet a good number stayed on by sacrificing the principles they stood for all of their lives. By so doing, they sacrificed the trust, hopes and aspirations of the rest of civil society who rely on them and their intellectual capacity in the unequal national battle between right and wrong in the governance of the country. Political convenience seems an ever-ready option at the back of the mind of our elite. The military may have a point that they have never had a pure military government in Nigeria. What they have had so far is a mixture of a military-civilian administration in which the interests of the military and civil society were represented but not actually served. There must be something rewarding in politics that makes almost everybody, from military people to the academics, from traditional rulers to businessmen, to want to be a leader.

All of them must have something in common that they desire – political power for its own sake or personal reasons but not to serve the people. "Give me political power and I will make the money" is their silent mission statement. If this is so, no wonder the population has since lost faith in everybody, leaders and the elite alike.

SOCIETY'S RESPONSE

Nigerian society, notably in the South, is eclectic but still it mirrors its leaders. After years of sitting on the fence and watching and praying for the country to get better to no avail, the masses, taking cue from their leaders, joined the bandwagon. One other slogan became common: If you can't beat them, join them! Voices of reason and criticism came from the academics for awhile.

Critics of bad government from academia sooner or later threw away their strong value judgement to join the club or were co-opted in order to silence their criticism. Appointed as ministers, advisers or chairmen of corporations, the academics have no more qualms joining the leadership club which they had consistently criticized. With their scruples gone, their well articulated position and guidance to the silent majority of the citizenry went with it. The population formed an opinion: The failure of our leaders is the result of the failure of the elite in Nigeria. The masses, equipped with a very strong opinion that all leaders are the same, and everybody is corrupt from top to down, are no longer in any mood to be convinced to the contrary. As an example, marketers of petroleum fuel seized upon every little opportunity to hoard fuel in order to worsen the fuel scarcity in the country so as to make their millions of Naira from the scarcity.

Petrol pumps in almost every gas station are corrupted, dismembered or disconnected in order to give false readings of the quantity of gas or petrol delivered from them. I recall that tampering with weights and measures sent people to prison in England during and after the Industrial Revolution! In Nigeria, this act is condone by those in authority if not by most Nigerian users of petroleum fuel. The picture is seen everywhere in one form or another. City tax and rates collectors printed their own receipts, using them to collect taxes and rates which they never accounted for to the City or Local Government Authorities. Their excuse, when caught, is that those in authority are "chopping" the money so they themselves want to "chop" small, not to be left out. The massive bank failure in Nigeria some time ago was the result of willful default on bank loans. I was shocked at the responses from some defaulters. One defaulter explained to his friends that he did not expect the loan to be repaid at all because everybody that matter in the country is doing the same business. He alleges that those in authority are taking loans without paying back. Another defaulter was urged by his friends and relations to sell one of his commercial buildings in town and make a lump sum repayment to the bank for the time being so that he could be released from police detention. This defaulter, who is reported later to have died in detention, told his interlocutors that he would not repay any money, that the matter would die down sooner or later because those in authority are in the same situation of not paying back. These are but a few examples of how bad or secretive leadership sends the wrong signal to the rest of society.

With the collapse of the willpower of academia to sustain the morale of the silent majority of Nigerians, the once critical society loses faith, becoming indifferent to how the country will end up. As a result, undiscipline in public and private life ruled supreme. Insatiable greed followed. Quite a number of the mass media people, the time-honored third estate of the realm, changed course. There were though a number of exceptions who stood strong as giants in the face of dictatorial terror. By getting the much taunted brown envelopes, a number of poor journalists became ready tools of selfish leaders. Greed gave rise to inordinate ambition for political power. To achieve their ambition, almost every other Nigerian would want to be a leader in one way or the other. He wants to enter politics. If he fails to get an office, he expects to get government or political party contracts for which he will make as much money as he can by inflating the bills. When they succeed, this type of leaders normally would appeal to the sentiments of their ethnic or tribal groups to support their political ambition.

To guarantee undiluted ethnic support and to reward such supporters, the political leader in waiting starts floating around the policy of reflecting the federal character in every Federal Government appointment. It looks like a one-time temporary measure so many people hardly see through it. It looks innocuous. To catch up with this policy of federal character in the Civil Service, federal institutions and corporations, the once enviable, competitive educational standards and entry levels to Nigerian universities have to be lowered for the North. That policy started an irreversible trend and has today been viewed to compromise the quality of Nigerian education when compared to European and North American standards. Our graduates and doctors trained at home are no longer held at par with their foreign-trained counterparts. They have to sit a test in other countries to support the credibility and quality of their Nigerian diplomas or degrees!

If selfish interests, greed or ethnicity is not to blame for our poor leadership condition and performance, then what is? It will serve our country better if once again this generation can witness the appointment of capable and courageous people without a tint of greed in their eyes to run the affairs of our country and to lead or manage our country's resources in the next millennium. In this connection, if Nigerians will continue to vote for the political party as distinct from the individual candidates at election time, the participating parties will have to submit their candidates to a Joint Clearance Panel for clearance as to their suitability to serve the public. The Joint Clearance Panel of Nigerians may comprise an equal number of senior officials of the political party concerned, the mass media, the human rights movement or organized labor and representatives of the Federal Electoral Commission. The names of the candidates shall be published not less than 90 days in advance to allow for an evaluation of each candidate's suitability for public office. At every level, it has been almost impossible for good persons, good leaders, to surface or survive intra-party politics. Due to their modesty, good persons hardly will survive in a Nigerian political power struggle environment.

MANAGEMENT OF THE ECONOMY

Mismanagement of the Nigerian economy is the most devastating to the population. It has virtually wiped out the middle class except, perhaps, in name only. The collapse of the Nigerian Naira proves this point. Nigerian leaders up to now seemed to be convinced by their financial advisers that with a weak Naira, achieved through gradual but steady devaluation normally prescribed by the IMF, Nigeria will earn more foreign currency by selling more volume abroad. One caveat: to sell more quantity does not mean selling profitably, nor does it mean obtaining higher prices. When our economy slumped, our leaders soon went borrowing, without comprehensive analysis of the cumulative effect. It is to give a large measure of independence to the Central Bank of Nigeria to manage the currency that prompted the Vision 2010 team of experts to recommend quite strongly complete independence for the Central Bank of Nigeria. By the Vision 2010 recommendations to Gen. A. Abubakar, the Ministry of Finance shall no longer interfere with the management of our currency. It is pertinent to mention here that the Governor of the Central Bank of Brazil whose economy is more than one and a half times that of Nigeria, not based on oil economy, resigned because the Brazilian currency was devalued from approximately 2.08 to about 2.14 to the US$1.00!

Sadly enough, the Naira slumped from N22 to about N55 per US$1.00 in less than 6 months during Gen. Babingida's reign and up to N80/US$1.00 during Gen. Abacha's rule without one token resignation from our money managers! The steady fall of the Naira in the face of increasing costs of living has dramatically reduced the ability of the ordinary Nigerian to maintain a decent life. Unless and until there is a decent, sustaining wage or salary for the Nigerian worker, big and small, there will be no end in sight for bribery and corruption in that country. In light of this observation, the inability of the Federal and State Governments, as claimed, to pay a minimum wage of 5,100 Naira per month is an unfortunate event. At current exchange rate, N5,100 is only worth approximately US$55.00 per month. The current basic minimum wage level of N3,000.00 per month is equivalent to US$32.25. How can we expect a civil servant earning this wage or salary to give the Civil Service/Government his absolute loyalty without cheating his employers or the public to make extra money? Well placed Nigerians may not know that some drivers employed by Local Governments receive about N1,200.00 per month which is equivalent to US$16.13 per month. How could such a civil servant be asked to go and buy you spare parts or petrol at the filling station or to take a government vehicle for servicing without expecting him to cheat a little in order to make ends meet? I see it will be a wasted effort to attempt to fight bribery and corruption in any shape or form, without first addressing and rectifying the low wages and salaries which will be paid to workers in our country in the next millennium. I recall that in the late 1950's and early 1960's, a civil servant at the Assistant Secretary level, holding a Bachelor's or Master's Degree, was on a starting salary of Nigerian £720 per annum. That was £60 per month. That time, the exchange rate was £0.52 to the US$1.00, thus £60 was equivalent to US$115.38 per month. That was 38 years ago. Without taking inflation in account and changes in other factors, US$115.38 per month (US$1,384.62 per annum) in 1960 will be worth $461.54 per month ($5,538.48 per annum) in1999.

In today's value that will be about N42,923.22 per month (515,078.64 per annum). (In arriving at these figures, I applied an estimated rate by which the basic wages portion of the emoluments of a particular category of staff of an international organization has appreciated over a 25 year period, which is approximately 4 times over 1970 basic wages.) I have not taken into account the inflation from 1970-1999, nor such allowances as housing, car, medical and dependent children. It is quite unlikely that an Assistant Secretary today in our Civil Service will be receiving a starting basic salary close to the above amounts. In this respect, I stand to be corrected if the facts prove otherwise. The purpose of this exercise is to see how far the Nigerian worker has fared over the past 38 years in comparison to the global trend.

It may now be understandable why it is impossible to eliminate bribery and corruption in that country unless the salary and wage structure is drastically revalued upward to afford the Nigerian worker a decent living standard above the subsistence level. In order to make the civil servant a loyal, reliable and productive worker, it is imperative to restructure the entire Federal, State and Local Government salary/wage structure. There is no doubt in my mind that the wastage of resources, the looting by officials and workers at large who have access to our treasury or material resources and the millions or billions tucked away in secret foreign bank accounts, can do the miracle of meeting the major domestic and international needs of Nigeria, including a decent, sustainable living wage for our workforce.

MASS UNEMPLOYMENT, JOB CREATION AND INVESTMENT

The potential of our human resources and the availability of abundant natural resources are sources for further wealth creation. If wisely and properly managed they will afford the economic and social miracle we have been dreaming of for years in vain.

Some time ago, immediately after the military regime of Buhari/Idiagbon, one of the movers and shakers of the Nigerian political scene, Chief Arthur Nzeribe (recently elected a Senator) who was on self-imposed temporary exile abroad, was credited by a London-based African magazine as saying that he had in his possession a list of about 1,000 names of Nigerian billionaires who could afford to lend the Federal Government the amount of one million US Dollars each. That is US$1 million x 1,000 lenders = $1,000 million or $1 billion. The only condition attached, according to the magazine, was that the military should allow the billionaires who lent the money a free hand to run the Federal Government for an unspecified term. Of course, the condition is suspect. Assuming that Chief Nzeribe's offer is true and credible, and that that amount is repatriated to fatherland, it would have helped to establish a medium size or giant factory, in partnership with foreign ventures, to give full employment to quite a large number of unemployed Nigerians at home? The tax revenue from such private sector investment accruing to the federal and state governments where the industries may be sited would help sustain the minimum wage of even a $90.00/N8,3700.00 minimum wage. Unemployment is a means to poverty. Elimination of mass poverty in the next millennium is a task that must be accomplished. Otherwise, peace and security will hang on a delicate balance at all times and ethnic and tribal tension will always push the country to the brink.

Very important factors for investment are a safe and secure environment, adequate supply of basic infrastructure, of literate manpower and favorable economic policies. To do business, investors want good returns on their investment or capital. Secure environment includes stability of the Government and the population that provides the local workforce. A disillusioned population can be disruptive. Hoping that the incoming civilian government must reckon with these factors, it is my vision for the next millennium that investment is a key area in which Nigerian leadership has to focus on seriously.

If Nigeria's civilian leaders fail to grasp the opportunity, the country will be left in the dustbin of history if one might recall the Chinese Red Guard's slogan during their parade in 1967 in Peking against the Chinese workforce. My fear though for the new millennium is that foreign multinationals are right now repositioning themselves by concluding international and intercontinental mergers. The mergers are going to produce giant global corporation capable of intimidating and buying off the whole productive assets and resources of small developing countries. In the competition in the new millennium, unfocused, unprepared African Governments and leadership will succumb to this intimidation by the multinationals whose operating budgets may match or surpass those of black African countries with weak economic bases.

My vision for the new millennium includes a nation where an able-bodied citizen can find productive work or gainful employment. If one doesn't get employed in the factory, one can find other suitable options in running one's own private business. We need a nation where farmers will get a decent price from the produce of their farms! It will be marvelous to fulfill an old urge of a past generation to "Let everybody be employed, and employed in the right occupation or best capacity of which his nature is capable, and die with the consciousness that he has done his best" (Simmons?). I am inclined to think that in the incoming millennium, if a majority of the population is gainfully employed, people will be happy with their leaders and the government. Crimes induced by revenge and neglect, such as bursting the oil pipelines in the Delta States by angry youths, embezzlement of government allotments by staff or civil servants, looting the treasury by some of those in authority, will be so few that the culprits will be transparently vulnerable to detection. With fewer crimes, the new Police and the Judiciary will be more capable of coping with cases of criminality and the punishment of perpetrators.

EDUCATIONAL INSTITUTIONS

It is characteristic of Nigerians, especially the educated class, not to take kindly to criticism, even if constructive. They seem to know it all. But they surprise me that upon all that they know, they lag far behind their White counterparts in Europe and the USA in terms of achieving the desired results. Nigerians will, doubtless, perform very well when they work in Europe or USA for the Whites but hardly achieve the desired results for their own country when left to manage their own affairs. There are so many educated Nigerians, yet our schools lack proper textbooks and writing materials at home. If it is so expensive to import them from abroad that parents cannot afford it, why can we not produce ourselves reading and writing materials of high quality for our schools, colleges and universities? (I chuckle at the quality of the brown envelopes I receive as mail from Nigeria. The gum or glue at the flap of the envelopes is obviously not supposed to keep the flap sealed for its journey by post, many arrive half open.) Universities are established in almost every State. Scarce funding appears to have stifled any meaningful research and development efforts. Research institutes left for us to manager after the British left such as the rubber and oil palm research institutes have been consigned to past history. Medical and pharmaceutical research is critically needed for the next millennium in this country.

The country also needs an effective quality control body to help monitor and prevent the low quality drugs now imported into the country. Traders and pharmaceutical companies should not to be left to decide on the quality of drugs they can import into the country purely from their commercial point of view or profitability. Nigerians are not used to accountability and are proud to fight any attempt to make them render an account of their stewardship. Our institutions such as the colleges, universities, including the Lagos Law School, Government Departments and Ministries never respond to inquiries or suggestions to enable them to improve. Instead they hate the inquirer or the person making suggestions to them for improvement. For them, the customer is not always right.

If you write from abroad to any of the Nigerian institutions, you cannot receive a reply. Typical examples are the JAMB headquarters or Lagos Law School at Victoria Island prior to their move to Abuja. So if you are requesting application forms or inquiring if they would accept a bank draft or money transfer as payment, you are wasting your time. Perhaps, the institution cannot spend N30-50 for postage and bill, together with the cost of the form. Why? If you have dealt with them, you will obviously find out the reason. This attitude has to change as we enter into the next millennium. There is but one exception worth mentioning here. It is a pleasant distinction from my other experiences. The only reply I ever received from a Nigerian Government Office or high official was from the former Minister of Foreign Affairs, Major-General Ike Nwachukwu (Rtd.). I had to write to him in his capacity as the Federal Minister of Foreign Affairs. I offered my suggestions as to how the Government should deal with the Italian ships which dumped drums of deadly toxic waste material in a village near Warri, former Bendel State, sometime in 1987 through a deal with a Nigerian businessman. The Honorable Minister of Foreign Affairs, though a very busy man, acknowledged receipt of my letter, appreciated my concern as a Nigerian patriot and assured me that the ideas I suggested would be part of the Government's strategy if normal diplomatic means fail in resolving the matter. Compare the attitude of those Nigerian institutions and those in charge of them to UK and US institutions. In 9 cases out of 10, a UK/US institution will respond to your inquiry for information or your suggestions on how to solve a problem of public concern. In the UK/USA, the leaders and the elite see their mission as serving their community in particular and society at large. In Nigeria, they are not in business to serve the community or society at large; rather, they are there as masters of everybody who crosses their jurisdiction. How can this kind of attitude help our next generation who are fast learning from us, our leaders and the elite inclusive?

BASIC INFRASTRUCTURE, UTILITIES AND RESOURCES

Looking at the present pitiable condition of basic infrastructures or utilities in the southern halves of that country, Nigerians visiting from abroad get either of two impressions: Nobody seems to be in effective control of affairs or the State Governments concerned do not care and have taken leave of their statutory responsibility. Take for example, the federal and State roads, many of which have seen no serious maintenance since the First Republic was overthrown. Another example is the Nigerian Electricity Power Authority (NEPA). This is the most unreliable, mismanaged, dysfunctional statutory bodies in the country comparable, perhaps, to the Nigeria Airways. In some Local Government Areas (LGAs), entire communities have had electricity supply cut for as long as 3-4 months. The management and modus operandi of NEPA belongs to a long, forgotten, bygone era. At this dawn of the next millennium, NEPA is an anachronism and its services a slander to Nigeria's sense of responsibility, independence and self-image. NEPA's complaints are unending. Either there is no oil or fuel, no available replacement equipment, or the overhead cable is cut or stolen by people. Yet knowledgeable Nigerians know that if one asks NEPA to connect one's house to the main power line, it is the customer who pays for the electric poles or pylon that will be required, no matter the quantity involved. In addition, it is the customer who pays for the cables and gadgets at grossly inflated prices, no matter the quantity required.

The customer also pays for the labour provided by NEPA staff and technicians. One then wonders what NEPA does with its allocation of funds by the Government!

When eventually your home is connected to the main power line, you may have light or power supply at the rate of 2-4 hours per day. You may not have power for another 4 weeks after which you will be given a quarter or half current and then your power supply will still go off the next hour for weeks or months. When you inquire from the NEPA, their field boys will tell the same story every time, such as the oil is finished so they need to buy a drum of oil or the cable is cut somewhere so they need to buy cables, or the main fuse is burnt. Then they will add: It may take months and months to get the parts and materials required if they rely on their Head Office, however, if any consumer can give them the amount required, they will be able to buy these materials. NITEL is another critical area that is a disappointment to Nigerians. It has had a face lift lately but the state of telephone system within Nigeria and between Nigeria and other countries, especially the Orient, is deplorable to say the least. If one arrives at the Airport, it is virtually impossible to make a phone call to a hotel for reservation. One cannot get through from Ikeja airport to downtown, Victoria Island or Ikoyi. One of my most frustrating experiences is calling Nigeria outside Lagos from the Orient, Middle East or Far East, such as Cambodia, Malaysia, Thailand, Israel, Damascus. Using public telephones, one faces embarrassment as other people waiting to use the truck line service would be wondering which primitive part of the world you have been trying to reach for so long without success.

Why should our country always lag behind in such vital technology as Satellite telecommunications? We can have access by subscription only. The primitive state of the telephone lines rules out the use of facsimile (fax) in that country as an effective business tool. I know of a community which has been cut off from the telephone network for more than 4 years. A Government contractor was carrying out some construction work at Arochukwu at the far eastern flank of Abia State, at the border with Akwa Ibom State when the contractor's ignorant laborers willfully or ignorantly cut the underground telephone cables. Since then half of the entire town of roughly 1,000 subscribers with a potential of another 1,000 subscribers are cut off till date and no attempt by NITEL to replace the telephone cables.

The Water Boards are apparently created to give a semblance of providing potable water supply within the rural development program. This body is a joke. It neither provides advice on water treatment procedures nor equipment. It does not drill bore-holes to supply communities within its jurisdiction with potable water. It is obviously there to charge fees for doing nothing. However, when a community or individuals spend about a quarter of a million Naira to half a million Naira to drill a borehole, the agents of this body will appear at the site to collect fees and mandatory tips. They threaten court action if their demands are not met. The purpose of water boards, as I know it abroad, is to provide from its own resources potable water supply, using its equipment, and thereafter charging fees monthly or quarterly for the services provided. In South-East Nigerian, they have no equipment to provide anybody with water supply; they do not drill borehole; they do not even supply chlorine or sodium chloride or any other water treatment chemical or equipment.

It has become evident that with each layer of regulatory body created in good faith in the country, another layer of exploitation of the people or of bribery and corruption is created with it. To stop this as we enter the next millennium is a task for all Nigerians of goodwill and nationalistic zeal. Roads have deteriorated in the country to the point of being a death trap to motorists and travelers. The state of the roads in Nigeria can only be likened to the state of roads in Cambodia after 21 years of war in this country during which Pol Pot's regime sent millions of Cambodians away to farmlands in the hinterland to till the soil, leaving the cities empty. At times, I wonder whether those leaders at State and Federal levels actually travel along those roads. Many of the dilapidated roads are Federal responsibility while many are State or Local Government responsibility.

Inquiries reveal that in many cases contracts were awarded for reconstruction or rehabilitation of the roads but the contractors abandoned the project after having shared the money for the project with officials responsible for awarding the contract. Is it not strange to reasonable people that the authorities concerned are not keen to hold the contractor responsible for nonperformance? It has been the practice for the incoming Local Government Chairperson not to complete any project that remained uncompleted by his predecessor.

The logic is understandable, the new Chairperson of the Local Government Area (LGA) has to initiate new projects to enable him to make his own money from fresh contracts. It is always assumed, perhaps rightly too, that the outgoing Chairperson has made his own money while in office from the abandoned, uncompleted projects.

REFORMING AND RESTRUCTURING STRATEGIC INSTITUTIONS

Reforming and restructuring our strategic institutions must start with the Constitution. The Constitution should not be a secret document that will be imposed on the people. It shall be open and subject to a referendum by the States or the adult taxable population before it takes effect. The Police have to be restructured at all levels with immediate effect. Then the newly restructured Police will be tested and put in place by the dawn of the next millennium. For the Police to be effective it has to command the respect and trust of the population which it has unduly brutalized over the decades of military dictatorship. The same applies to the Armed Forces. The appointment of the Inspector General (IG) of Police and the Deputy IG shall be subject to confirmation by the National Assembly and subsequent approval by the Senate. The same condition shall apply to the appointment of the Head of the Armed Forces and his Deputy. These positions shall also be subject to geographical rotation at the commencement of each presidential term of four years. These provisions shall be reflected in the Constitution accordingly. The next restructuring shall include the public corporations, particularly the Customs and the Passport Services, and so forth.

The most important focus of this reform and restructuring for the next millennium shall be to achieve maximum performance and accountability in public service. Performance is measurable against mission target. Any performance or accomplishment must have a time frame to be able to measure its success or otherwise. The Federal and State Governments will have to show transparency in what they do. It is not enough for the Head of State or Ministers to read over the airwaves the budget speech at the beginning of each fiscal year or on each October 1st.

The Nigerian public is entitled to know how the budget or appropriations were actually utilized so the Federal and State Governments should be required to publish an audited, certified Balance Sheet and budget performance report in one form or the other in a Government White Paper or Gazette at the end of its fiscal year as was the case during the Colonial Administration. If leaders and managers of the Nigerian economy actually intend to serve the country and not to cater for their own personal interests, why did they let our four refineries get to their current advanced state of disrepair? Importing petroleum fuel, petrol and diesel, from abroad would normally be a stop gap measure until repairs or refurbishment of the existing 4 refineries were completed to optimize their operating capacity. Importation as a way of awarding contracts to cronies and contractors with the expectation of a reward, kickbacks or disguised birthday gifts will certainly defeat the purpose of our vision. Repairs are hardly carried out in time due to our lack of a maintenance culture. The costs would have been low and the current low production and slanderous scarcity nationwide avoided.

A BILLION DOLLAR QUESTION

Where will Nigeria be in the geopolitics of the next millennium? As an onlooker? or a full player? India and Pakistan, both third world countries, both developing economies, both former British Colonies just as Nigeria also was, have far outstripped us. Both countries have their nuclear capability; they have developed and tested nuclear long-range ballistic missiles. That of India is claimed to travel up to 2,200 km. This has placed them in the exclusive nuclear club. It is only the blackman's continent which has not one member in that club. The question now is: Can Nigeria and Nigerians handle the technology to develop and exploit nuclear power for peaceful purposes in the next century? Are our people capable of developing nuclear power and anti-ballistic missiles in the next century? If so, do they possess the moral discipline to handle the safety aspects of maintaining such a hazardous facility? If our people are neither capable of maintaining four harmless, low-tech refineries for maximum production of our fuel requirement nor of providing adequate petroleum fuel for our electricity power needs, how can we dutifully safely man the much more complex high-tech reactors for nuclear power and the high-tech missiles? If we do not do it, we will continue to pay heavy price for relying on the technologies developed by other countries. Nigeria will also be paying those countries' research and development (R&D) costs! Moreover, they will not allow us to share in their technology in order to maintain their superior edge over Black African nations. The keyword for this project must be for peaceful purposes such as the generation of electricity for the next millennium.

If Nigeria believes that the benignity of foreign nations will continue indefinitely, it is mistaken. Look at the political and economic battles now going on between Europe and America over banana exports to Europe by their third-world client nations. When a deal is reached, one way or another, one side will lose; whichever side loses, it is going to be third world nations either in Africa, the Caribbean or South America. Nigeria has to decide by the dawn of the next millennium on how to assemble its R&D expertise and create an effective nuclear R&D project to take us to where India and Pakistan are now within the first quarter of the 21st century.

If Nigeria proves unreliable to accept the challenge, Black Africa will need to look elsewhere -- to the Republic of South Africa to put an African nation in the nuclear power and missile technology club. As long as we are working towards peaceful uses of nuclear energy, we will be able to maintain the goodwill of the existing nuclear club members upon whom we may depend for reactors and nuclear material. The limit of our influence in the geopolitics of the next millennium will more or less depend on our demonstrated capabilities in this area.

RECOMMENDATIONS

Any credible attempt to bring about solutions to Nigeria's multifarious problems in the next millennium must start from the top, from the leadership, to assure the population that they are serious not only by words but by their actions. It is this class that the rest of society looks up to for direction. The quality of leadership therefore is crucial to success and progress in the next millennium.

It is strongly recommended to include in our laws a charge of perjury without limitation of time against any leader who makes false declaration of his assets and tax returns prior to taking up a Federal or State Government appointment and upon leaving office. To ensure that projects and contracts are properly and fully implemented prior to releasing the final payment, there shall be established a monitoring machinery on project implementation and certification. To this end, there should be a Joint Inspection Group (JIG) whose membership shall comprise representatives of interested parties to the project, including consumer groups and members of the public directly affected by the project. Members of the JIG may hold office for two years only and then are replaced accordingly by citizens known for their integrity and national interest. Accountability shall be one of the core conditions of all public office holders. It should be included in their terms of contract or appointment. Officials, officers and contractors shall not be relieved of their accountability responsibility for five (5) calendar years, during which time their service or project will be tested in practical terms by users or the public.

All public institutions to publish an audited and certified balance sheet at the end of each fiscal year in either each State's Official Gazette or its Government White Paper and in at least one national newspaper for public interest. The Federal Government and its corporate bodies, boards and commissions, shall be required to do likewise.

This is to place public information in the public domain for transparency in governance and for public policy researchers. The wages and salaries of civil servants of federal, state and local governments, including the Police, and other government institutions shall be revised to give them a decent living wage or salary above the subsistence level in the first century of the next millennium. For public servants to maintain a basic wage or salary not easily wiped out within a year or two by inflation, it is necessary to peg or index 50% of their salary/wage structure to the US Dollar. Of course, these will be payable at the local currency rate of exchange prevailing on the last day of the month when the wages and salaries are due. The Federal and State Governments are to set the criteria which traditional rulers (i.e. the Eze, Oba, Emir, Obong, Alafin, Amayanagbo or others chiefs) will satisfy to warrant their official recognition.

The king makers or chief-makers will ensure compliance with the criteria before they crown their tribal ruler. The established criteria will be the basis for granting official recognition to persons who claim any chieftaincy title within the nation. The title of Chief may be conferred for distinguished, selfless service to the nation or to humanity by an appropriate, recognized traditional authority. Evidence shall include an uninterrupted traditional use and record of the same title in the family back to at least (4) paternal generations. In other words, the Federal in collaboration with the State Government shall establish the criteria to qualify anybody to hold the title of Chief or any of its other connotations and be recognized as such. The criteria should include the total number of taxable adults under the jurisdiction of each traditional ruler or chief, together with the number of villages and village heads answerable to such a chief, the amount of tax each ruler or chief collects and pays to the treasury as well as the tax due from the chief himself. The Chief has to file an affidavit to this effect with each State Governor's office with a copy each to the State Tax Assessment Authority and to the Office of the House of Chiefs annually.

The conferring authority shall be verifiable from the conferment certificate, duly signed. There is a public need to curb the claim by almost every other person in the street to a titled Chief. There should be respect for our titled traditional Chiefs and this recommendation is made to separate them from the mercenary or bogus chiefs who parade themselves and lord it over the people. Implementation of an effective tax assessment and collection strategy for the next millennium using responsible Government officials instead of using contractors and thugs so that the Government can receive the full returns of the taxes due to it. To restructure and re-equip a new NEPA. In other to ensure healthy competition amongst the providers in the energy sector, a new NEPA will need to be restructured into about six separate zonal entities, each covering some specific zonal areas. This will make the new NEPA small and easy to manage, oversee and control. A new Nigeria Airways to effectively serve the nation in the next millennium has to be created from the scratch, from the assets that are left of the old Nigeria Airways. Suffice it to say that the Nigeria Airways is (or should be) the image of this country abroad and our national symbol in foreign airspace, flying our national colors. It must not be allowed to disappear permanently from the airspace at an age that air travel is making many countries proud. The old Nigeria Airways was handicapped by political interference. When its operational management was contracted to a foreign agency, political interference seemed to have made the contractor's job untenable. In any case, any contract to lease the Nigeria Airways out to private or foreign operators has to include a clause that the aircraft shall fly with Nigerian national colors and remain our national asset which we may redeem whenever it is deemed necessary to do so. Nigerians need a national carrier. It will be a shame if we cannot manage it profitably at a time that foreign airlines are making millions of Dollars on our route. To restructure the Nigeria Police Force and the Armed Forces and re-train and re-orientate their members(starting from the top to bottom), to a fresh commitment of rededication to their proper constitutional role for the country and its peoples in the next millennium. As discussed above under Restructuring of Strategic Institutions, the appointment of the IG, Deputy IG, the Head of the Armed Forces and his Deputy shall be subject to confirmation by the National Assembly and subsequent approval by the Senate, each sitting in formal session.

The approving votes of Representatives shall be from at least two-thirds of the 36 States (or more) of the Federation. This is to enable the incumbents to see themselves as responsible to the President, the Legislatures and the federation as a whole.

To revive and revitalize the economy by rehabilitating our basic infrastructures and institutions, namely federal trunk roads, state roads, railways, bridges and the main Nigerian seaports which are now being avoided by Nigerian and foreign importers due to port congestion, leading to high demurrage charges, and all sorts of impediments and encumbrances placed on the clearance of goods from the ports. The effect is that a significant amount of imports meant for Nigeria has been discharged at neighboring ports. In this scenario, it is Nigeria which loses the large amount of duty that would normally accrue. The bureaucracy at the Nigerian seaports has to be drastically reduced to induce importers to use these ports instead of the ports of our neighbors.

In this connection, there should be a national task to restructure and reform the Nigerian Ports Authority (NPA) and the Port Customs Service to achieve the desired results. A port friendly environment must be created for importers. To establish a proper machinery for Quality Control in our country of Medicines and Drugs whether locally produced or imported from abroad. To establish a proper machinery for environmental control, particularly for disposing of city and community refuse or garbage generated by city dwellers as well as toxic waste from industrial/chemical plants which pollute our rivers and lakes. To clean up by dredging and to revive our natural waterways passing through our cities or towns which have been polluted, thus giving stinking smell across the neighborhoods through which they flow. At the same time, to prohibit man's activities which dry up the rivers and water ways in order to make way for all sorts of building construction activities.

Finally, I deem it a national necessity to institute a maintenance culture in our society by the dawn of the next millennium. Nigerians are great in erecting imposing edifices. They are, however, not good or great in maintaining regularly as matter of routine these imposing edifices, be it Government office buildings, roads, streets or express ways, hotels, airports, seaports, or street pavements. Just one example: As a world traveler, used to staying in fine hotels, I have been dismayed at the speed of deterioration of a number of hotels I have visited in Nigeria. During the first year of their completion, the hotels are attractive and neat. By the second visit a year or two later, one hardly recognizes the same hotels due to their advanced stage of deterioration from their outward look to window blinds, from their paint-work to furniture, from their roofing to floors. We indeed need a maintenance culture in our country; if we cannot achieve it by preaching and advocacy, perhaps it is high time to do so by legislation by the turn of the next millennium.

CURRICULUM AND ADMINISTRATIVE INNOVATIONS FOR THE NIGERIAN EDUCATIONAL SYSTEM IN THE TWENTY-FIRST CENTURY

Zephyrinus C. Okonkwo

This chapter deals essentially with two ideas: Curriculum Innovations for the Nigerian Educational System, and Administrative Innovations for the Nigerian Educational System with emphasis on the tertiary level. Although these two ideas seen to be independent, they have a region of intersection which will be discussed in the sequel. In this chapter, we will discuss in some details the needed curriculum innovations at all levels of the educational system. We will also deal with administrative innovations required at the colleges and universities in order to lay a strong foundation for a stable environment where students, professors, non-academic staff, and administrators can thrive as a community whose objective encompass teaching, research, and service. Like every educational system, the Nigerian Educational System must provide:

(i) An adequate, safe and secure environment for teaching and learning where the educated must imbibe adequate skills and knowledge to seek gainful employment within the society;

(ii) College level education, which must not only provide the student with enough basic skills but must also prepare the student for graduate education within and outside the country;

(ii) Responsive dynamic curriculum at all levels of education. Such curriculum must respond to societal needs, and must include innovative methods of teaching and learning, innovative method of seeking knowledge, computer skills and information technology, strong emphasis on communication both in written and oral forms, reading and public speaking.

The curriculum at all levels must be reviewed from time to time expunging irrelevant topics and courses and including new ones.

Administrative innovations at the tertiary level must include:

(i) Tenure system at all tertiary institutions;

(ii) A method of checking the excesses of some professors and administrators through legislation and enforcement of the laws;

(iii) Provision of adequate funding for salaries and research for colleges and universities by the establishment of a stable method of funding including land-grant, Educational Tax, Luxury Tax, and Property Tax;

(iv) Streamlining teaching and research resources and reducing waste by eliminating redundancy and duplications in neighboring colleges and universities.

1. INTRODUCTION

The next millennium presents an extraordinary challenge to the people and government of the federal republic of Nigeria on all facets of life. The development of a strong educational system is very essential for the development of a strong economy, educated and skilled workforce, peace, and stability. Considering the nose dive Nigeria has suffered in the last sixteen years (from 1984- 1999) encompassing very weak economy, high unemployment, dilapidated and neglected educational system, high poverty rate, extraordinary level of corruption and fraudulent practices in both the public and private sectors, armed and pen robbery, international condemnation and sanctions, as a result of bad management of national resources, it has become a matter of urgency that our educational system must be revamped and innovated.

Nigeria is a great country and all Nigerians must have the confidence that the new leadership at both the national level and state levels has the capacity to improved the welfare and living conditions of all Nigerians by fighting the above mentioned vices. This they can do by standing on higher ground than their predecessors. Nigeria has abundance of natural and human resources. The mere population size of Nigeria is an asset as a big market for agricultural goods, manufactured goods, and other services. Nigerians need a strong collective will for the common good. It is essential to mention here that there is a strong relationship between the quality of the educational system of a nation and its technological development. It is clear that if one considers the state of education at the present time, one finds that Nigerian educational system must undergo very radical changes in terms of administration and curriculum. This is the crux of this chapter. Even though this chapter will emphasize innovations in tertiary level education, the importance of primary and secondary education cannot be overlooked. This work will also deal with primary and secondary education adequately.

Section 2 of this chapter outlines the present situation of education in Nigeria. Section 3 deals with anticipated innovations in administration and curriculum at the primary and secondary levels of education while in Section 4, we deal with administrative innovations at the tertiary level. Section 5 deals with curriculum innovations at the tertiary level. Funding of education in Nigeria is discussed in Section 6. The chapter is concluded in section 7.

2. THE PRESENT STATE OF EDUCATION IN NIGERIA

It is difficult to separate the present condition of the Nigerian Education System from the present status of the economy and Nigeria's political stability. An executive summary report on the review of undergraduate education in the United States 1996 (by the National Science Foundation) has this to say "in an increasing technical and competitive world with information as its common currency, a society without a properly educated citizenry will be at great risk and its people denied the opportunity for a fulfilling life". The Nigerian educational system has suffered unprecedented neglect since the unwelcome military intervention of December 1983. For the past fifteen years, education has become one of the main casualties of military dictatorship and misrule despite all the leap service paid to education by subsequent governments.

However, some superficial changes have been introduced since 1984 especially during the regime of Ibrahim Babaginda. One of the main changes was the creation of two tier High-School program, the Junior Secondary School (JSS)- 3 years, and the Senior Secondary School-3 years. The junior secondary school education was to give the student a general education from an adopted national curriculum while at the senior secondary level, students would be placed on career tracts after the junior secondary school education. The senior secondary school education, for example, would create suitable conditions in high schools where students interested in the sciences, technology, engineering, medicine, and the arts can enhance their knowledge in the high school subjects leading them to their chosen careers. Senior secondary schools were to be equipped with science instruments, libraries, and expert teachers employed to teach the respective subjects.

This was not to be. The senior secondary school education was also supposed to eliminate Higher School Education. The primary school education has not undergone any significant changes since the time of the British in the fifties. Neither administrative nor curricular changes or innovations have taken place. In fact, despite the fact that primary school teachers are more qualified now than their counterparts of the sixties, very few students with the First School Leaving Certificate can communicate effectively in English both in oral or written forms. The reasons are obvious. The funding for education is inadequate according to Hope Eghagha, (1999),During the period of the second republic, primary school teachers went on protracted strike, which the government ignored, apparently to underscore the perceived insignificance of teachers in the scheme of things. When the military returned in December 1983, education did not receive better attention. In many local governments of the federation, teachers do not get paid regularly. In fact, in some states, teachers sometimes go without pay for five months. This has adversely affected the morale and discipline in the teaching profession. There are tales of teachers abandoning their jobs and becoming petty traders, shopkeepers, and bricklayers. In many parts of the federation, most primary school buildings look like animal barns.

3. ADMINISTRATIVE AND CURRICULUM INNOVATIONS FOR PRIMARY AND SECONDARY EDUCATION

Since state take over of primary and secondary education from the missionaries in the late sixties and early seventies, community input and local participation in education at the primary and secondary levels have diminished if not entirely evaporated. The consequence of this is the fact that local government supervisors control the hiring of primary school teachers while the secondary school teachers are hired at the state level without community input. National, state, and the local government's education policy markers have ignored the role of communities, which are served by these schools. In order for the schools to return to their Old Glory, the importance of community involvement must be addressed. The community can play a vital role not only in the building of the schools, but also in the hiring and firing of teachers and principals. Every community should elect a governing board for each school. The governing board should participate in fund raising (may be in the form of a small education levy on all tax payers), enhancing enrollment, school security, seeking and hiring of excellent teachers, conducting workshops for the teachers on community expectation. The board should also oversee the principal to make sure that the curriculum is taught. The board should play a vital role in the hiring of school principals. The board should have regular meetings to evaluate school performance. It will make sure that all school age children are in schools. Sometimes, the board should conduct town hall meetings in order to solicit community input. Every school should also have a Parents-Teachers Association whose role should be exclusively advisory. The state should continue to play a leading role in primary and secondary education. The role of the state governments should include provision of funding from line-item budget to cover salaries, administrative, instructional, and maintenance cost for schools. The state will be responsible for in-service and retraining of teachers, as well as keeping records of evaluation of teachers for tenure at the primary and secondary levels. Curriculum innovation is not existent at the primary and secondary levels. This is not surprising since the colleges and universities, which train the teachers do not have the facilities and amenities to embark on innovation of their curriculum.

One significant change that has taken place at the tertiary level education is the discussion of the importance of computers and information technology. However, the number of computers in these institutions is insignificant to impact on a tangible number of students. Most colleges and universities do not have Internet connections and hence the importance of the World Wide Web cannot be explored. Even most instructors do not know how to use the computer.

There is an urgent need to initiate a national debate on the end product of our secondary education. There is no doubt that with the downward trend in the economy, the average Nigerian secondary school graduate is not well prepared for the workforce as well as for higher education. Every high school graduate should be able to communicate strongly (in English) both in oral and written forms. There is also a need to teach basic computer science and information technology at the secondary level. This will enable high school graduates to acquire extra skills to become employable. The federal and state governments must delineate the specific objectives of high school education based on outcomes. It is essential to mention here that select high schools such as Federal Government Colleges and private high schools, which charge exorbitant tuition and fees, which are not within reach of the average Nigerian family, are meeting such capabilities.

Most Nigeria students of high school age attend state high schools, which are located in big cities and local communities. Some of these local schools do not have teachers who hold college degrees in the subjects they teach. There are hundreds of rural high schools, which do not have qualified chemistry, physics, biology and mathematics teachers. A nation, which cannot take care of the young ones, cannot be a great nation. In order for Nigeria to transform to a strong nation with a growing technological base, it must make huge investment in education, science, and technology. There must be a national goal to train and adequately compensate all teachers. Extra compensation should be made to science, mathematics, and technology teachers. In fact, in order to initiate the growth in capacity at the primary and secondary levels of our educational system, the following issues must be considered for implementation.

(i) Federal and state curriculum standards and regulations.

(ii) Outcome based National Standards in science, mathematics, technology, communications, and social studies.

These regulations must be brought about by legislation or an act of national and state assemblies and must include:

(iii) Teacher standards,

(iv) Certification and continuing education,

(v) Technology in schools,

(vi) An outcome driven curriculum,

(vii) Implementation of national standards for tenure and promotion,

(viii) Ethical standards for all individuals working in the education sector,

(ix) A method of compensation based on merit and experience,

(x) Exit examinations at the state and national levels based on standardized tests.

If Nigerian children have to be competitive at the international level, they should be able to take standardized culturally unbiased examinations.

Administrative needs include:

(i) A national standard for hiring teachers and administrators.

(ii) Professional standards and ethics. There must be a well spelt out relationship between the teacher and the student.

(iii) Zero tolerance for discrimination based on ethnicity and state of origin.

(iv) A complete and unambiguous delineation of what constitutes sexual harassment and exploitation. There should be no tolerance for sexual harassment at the workplace or school.

There should be the law to compensate hard working teachers, and remove the lazy and unproductive teachers and administrators. Decadent teachers and administrators who embark on sexual exploitation of students or those who knowingly steal public money or property should be prosecuted and if found guilty sent to jail.

4. ADMINISTRATIVE INNOVATIONS AT THE TERTIARY LEVEL

Essential administrative changes must be made if the tertiary education level in Nigerian is to give optimal educational service to the Nation.

The roles of the Presidency, Federal Ministry of Education, the Ministry of Science and Technology, the Federal Ministry of Industries, the National Universities Commission, the Universities and Colleges, and other stakeholders are very important. The goal of this section is to delineate these anticipated administrative innovations and discuss ways in which they should be implemented.

Classification of Tertiary Institutions: As mentioned earlier on this chapter, it is important that while the present Nigerian Universities continue their role as comprehensive universities, all the nation's universities do not have equal capabilities to be designated as research universities.

It is important therefore that the Federal Ministry of Education and the National Universities Commission backed by an act of the legislature should classify our tertiary institutions as follows:

(a) Research 1 Universities,
(b) Research 2 Universities,
(c) Regional Universities,
(d) 4-year Colleges, and
(e) Two-year Colleges.

This classification has even become more important at this period of scarce financial and human resources.

Research 1 Universities. Our oldest flag-ship universities namely the University of Ibadan, University of Nigeria Nsukka, Ahmadu-Bello University Zaria, The University of Ife (Now Obafemi Awolowo University, and the University of Lagos should be designated Research 1 Universities. Each of these universities has a long history of strong curriculum. They have produced a majority of older generation of Nigerian professionals in the public and private sectors of the country as well as in the academia. These universities have comprehensive curriculum ranging from the liberal arts to medicine. The faculties at these universities have the reputation of producing research results and have published such works in international journals. They have also presented their work at national and international conferences. These universities have world class reputation. They offer a wide range of undergraduate and graduate programs. They should be permitted to continue to do so. These universities should be the host centers for

National Laboratories where advanced research and study should be taking place. Since Nigeria does not have the resources to support doctoral programs in all disciplines, only these universities should be allowed to run doctoral programs in disciplines like mathematics and physics.

The teaching load at these institutions should be 2-three hour courses a semester. Full Professors must be encouraged to make contact with young undergraduates. Assigning first and second year level courses to experienced professors to teach every year can achieve this goal. Research I Universities should be the center for excellence in teaching, research, and service. Other universities should serve as feeders to these universities.

The graduates of other universities should be encouraged to proceed to these universities for their graduate degrees especially the Doctoral programs. The Federal Government and other funding agencies should invest research money at these institutions.

Research 2 Universities: Nigeria's research 2 universities should include:

The Universities of Benin, Port Harcourt, Calabar, Jos, Ilorin, and Bayero University Kano. These universities should continue to offer comprehensive programs in most disciplines as well as Masters Programs. They should be permitted to run Ph.D. programs in select disciplines. They can however offer Ph.D. programs in Mathematics, Physics, Chemistry, Biology, and Engineering provided they can demonstrate that such programs are viable.

Viability should be measured in terms of the number of graduate students in that particular discipline. Any graduate program, which does not graduate 15 Ph.D.s in five years, should be canceled. The resources to run such programs, which include the number of qualified faculty and financial resources should be examined.

The faculty teaching load at these universities should be 9 hours (3-3 hour courses) a semester, two of which must be undergraduate courses. Senior faculty must not be allowed to delegate their teaching to Masters degree holders or graduate assistants in order to run Ph.D. programs. It is therefore the responsibility of the administration to make sure that every faculty member heeds to his or her responsibilities.

Comprehensive Regional Universities: The following universities should be designated as comprehensive regional universities: The Universities of Sokoto, Maidugiri, Abuja, and Uyo. Others are the Federal Universities of Technology at Owerri, Akure, Yola, Minna, Bauchi, and the Federal Universities of Agriculture Markudi, Abeokuta, and Umuahia. These universities should concentrate on the provision of quality undergraduate education and a few select graduate programs. Teaching load should be 9-12 semester hours. They should only be allowed to run Ph.D. programs in select disciplines if those programs are viable and only if they are in collaboration with Research 1 or Research 2 universities. They should have larger class sizes and must accommodate as many students as possible. Masters Granting Institutions: All state universities should have as their primary mission the provision of quality undergraduate education. They should expand their capacities to accommodate more students. They should hire more instructors with masters' degrees to meet such responsibilities. These masters' degree holders should concentrate on teaching lower level undergraduate courses- the freshman and sophomore level courses. The more experienced Ph.D. holders in each department should teach junior and senior level classes. Less research should be expected from the professors at these colleges especially for the sake of compensation, tenure, and promotion. These colleges can run masters programs in select and limited disciplines provided undergraduate teaching is not neglected.

Four-Year Colleges: All Federal and State Colleges of Education should be converted to degree awarding four-year colleges. They should run honors degree programs in education as well as in the liberal arts, basic sciences, and social sciences.

The mission of these institutions should be teaching and service.The Polytechnics and Institutes of Technology: The Polytechnics and Institutes of Technology should run four-year degree programs. The ND (National Diploma) curriculum should be the same as that of the first two years of 4-year degree program. This will enable a ND holder to transfer to any university for the sake of completion of his or her degree program in two or three years.

Two-Year Colleges: Because of the great demand for higher education in Nigeria, states with high population of high school graduates should consider the establishment of two year colleges. The curriculum of these two-year colleges should be the same as the first two years of the curriculum of four-year colleges. They should be feeders for four-year colleges. These two-year colleges should also be the center for the training of middle skilled technical manpower.

5. CURRICULUM INNOVATIONS AT THE TERTIARY LEVEL

The present curriculum (in all subjects and disciplines) at the tertiary level does not prepare the student for the work place or advanced education outside Nigeria. Let us illustrate this statement with an example the subject of chemistry. In the US universities, students are able to perform experiments, generate and analyze data using computers. They are exposed to different types of sophisticated equipment some of which they will use in the workplace. In fact, part of the requirement for graduation of chemistry students is to acquire some practical training in chemical manufacturing companies. This enables them to acquire hand-on skills in their discipline. On the other hand, the Nigerian chemistry graduate at the present time has minimum knowledge in both skills and the core. Very little time is spent in the classroom and the laboratories as professors are on strike most of the time. This results in the production of ill-prepared and academically weak graduate. Most of the university graduates have found an inconvenient way to deal with skill problems. Some of them enroll in computer training schools and acquire basic skills in word and data processing. This enhances their chances of securing jobs outside their areas of discipline. Others resort to accepting low paying jobs with the hope to gain skills and apply for better paying jobs.

Graduate education in the United States, Canada, Europe, and South American countries gives strong support to higher-level manpower training, as well as to academic and non-academic research. On the other hand, the present graduate education is viewed in Nigeria as advancing knowledge only in the individual subject areas and discipline, and emphasis placed more on theory rather than applications. In order to catch up with the developed world in the twenty-first century, there must be an overhaul of both curriculum and pedagogy at tertiary institutions. The future demands greater need for interdisciplinary-learning. This can be enhanced with the availability of information technology. The National Science Foundation Report Review of Undergraduate Education puts it more clearly " Many curricular and pedagogical improvements are mutually reinforcing. Also, very important is the observation made by many, particularly employers, that a well-designed, active learning environment assists in the development of other skills and traits they seek in the employees: cognitive skills (problem-solving, decision-making, learning how to learn) social skills (communications and teamwork), and positive personal traits (adaptability and flexibility, openness to new ideas, empathy for ideas of others, innovative and entrepreneurial outlook, and a strong work ethic)".

For the past fifteen years, most universities in Nigeria have lost the capacity to do pure and applied research. The low number of research reports and publications of scholarly papers in national and international journals manifest this. This setback is even worse in the disciplines of medicine, engineering, agriculture, science, and technology. Presently, our medical schools are ill equipped and the teaching hospitals lack basic facilities for theoretical and practical instructions. Professors do not have the privilege to attend international conferences which (In the past) afforded them the opportunities to interact with their counterparts in developed countries. This without a doubt reduces their capabilities to be familiar with the state of the art equipment, techniques, and resources in their respective fields. This can virtually be said about all disciplines.

There is no doubt that the quality of doctoral programs run by even the best Nigerian universities is in doubt as these universities lack the minimum facility support to run such programs effectively. Most universities lack professors who should supervise such programs. This chapter will address the panacea to these problems in the sequel.

One essential curriculum issue which has neither been tackled nor even reviewed by the Federal Ministry of Education, the National Universities Commission, or the colleges and universities themselves is the non uniformity of the undergraduate curriculum. At the present time, it is difficult if not impossible for a Sociology undergraduate from the University of Ibadan to transfer to the University of Lagos in the same discipline. This is essentially because the undergraduate courses of study in Sociology at these two universities are different. Although the courses of study in Sociology in these two universities may have similar content, there is no uniform delineation of course sequencing, making it extremely difficult for faculty advisors to match course by course the course of study for Sociology. The lack of uniformity in the undergraduate curriculum makes it difficult for students to transfer from one university to another. A student, who for whatever reason, cannot continue his education at one university will either start from the beginning at another university or loose his chance for college education. Faculties also have the same problem of mobility. Unless a special arrangement is made within the department, a faculty member cannot secure a job at another college or university without losing his benefits at the previous university. Several Nigerian Colleges and Universities adopted the credit-course system, which are common in American Universities. What they have not implemented adequately is the flexibility that comes with such credit-course system. If the credit-course system is adopted and adequately implemented, then, the flexibility that comes with it will be beneficial to the Nigerian undergraduate in many and varied ways.

Since College and university curriculum has to respond to societal demand, the need to create new degree programs and discontinuation of low demand and redundant disciplines need not be overemphasized. For the past fifteen years, our country has witnessed an upsurge in criminal behavior and different forms of deviant behavior. There is a need therefore to establish degree programs in criminology. This way, these negative issues that confront our nation at this present time will be carefully researched. A department of criminology should not only train the civilian workers for the prison system, security agencies, and employees dealing with law enforcement, it should also partake in the professional training of our police force. Indeed, it is feasible to establish a strong link between the Police Colleges and Criminology Departments of the universities. This will undoubtedly enhance the capacities of our policemen and other law enforcement officers.

Another discipline that needs to be established in Nigerian Universities is Special Education. As the nation continues to develop in the twenty-first century, there is a greater societal responsibility to Individuals with Disabilities and other special needs. The present practice whereby the caring of such individuals is left for the their families or religious organizations, is no longer desirable. Individuals with Mental Retardation have same rights as other individuals in the society and must be accorded the right to education.

In order to achieve this in the next century, special education programs should be established to train teachers who will teach these individuals at the Elementary School and High School levels. There is doubt that cases like the ones made above can be made for other emerging disciplines. Social life for university and college students should not only be tolerated but also supported by the university administrators to the extent that it does not constitute a hindrance to the goals and mission of the university. Moreover, as young adults, they have the right to social life. Unfortunately, while the majority of college students are law-abiding citizens, there is a small percentage of them who should not be found at the college campuses. Deviant and decadent behavior, intimidation, murders, and occultism has no place on campuses. In the last fifteen years, occultism has taken over the social life of college students. Murder has become rampant as a result of occultism and this is not well investigated or prosecuted by the courts. The majority of college students live in fear as a result of this. Occultism has no place in the university and college environment.

Streamlining: If the federal and state governments are to realize the optimum benefits of investment in higher education, streamlining college and university curriculum as well as degree offerings must be addressed. While the supporters of higher education decry the poor funding of higher education, the nation must face the real fact that in this period of meager resources, duplication of degree offerings and the running of parallel programs in neighboring universities do not help the case. It is important therefore that the following important questions must be addressed:

(a) Do Nigerian Universities need to produce one thousand graduates with degrees in philosophy? If Nigerian universities produce them, is there any job market for them?

(b) The University of Lagos has undergraduate and graduate programs in Urban and City Planning (in the Geography Department). Does Lagos State University, The Federal University of Agriculture Abeokuta need to run the same program? Is this not a waste of National resources?

(c) Where should a degree program in Material Science be best run- The University of Illorin (which is close to Ajeokuta Steel Complex) or University of Maiduguri or University of Sokoto?

(d) Is it feasible that the University of Calabar run an independent Ph.D. program in Mathematics while the University of Port Harcourt, The Federal University of Technology Owerri run similar programs? Is there anyway these universities can share resources?

(e) Should every university in Nigeria be in the business of running Ph.D. programs? What quality of Ph.D. are these?

(f) Are Nigerian Colleges and Universities adequately responding to societal demands and the job market need or are they there to produce "half-backed " graduates with little or no skills?

(g) Is the teaching load of professors adequate or are they under utilized?

Some of the answers to these questions are obvious. Let us address the issue of sharing resources with a concrete example. The City of Owerri, the capital of Imo State, has four-degree granting institutions.

At the present time, none of these Universities has minimum resource to support the academic programs being offered at these institutions. In fact, the classrooms are inadequate and sometimes too small to accommodate enough students. The libraries are substandard with few books and most of which are old. Is it feasible for the government to build a well equipped library at one of these institutions and students, faculty, and staff at these colleges can share such a library resource? A good library costs millions of Dollars to build and millions more to maintain. The University of Port Harcourt has a Ph.D. program in Mathematics. The Federal University of technology Owerri (FUTO) does the same thing. These universities are seventy miles apart. There is a World Renowned expert in Partial Differential Equations at FUTO and an expert in Fluid Mechanics at the University of Port Harcourt. Is it not feasible for graduate students from Port Harcourt to take 3 courses in Owerri one semester and the graduate students of FUTO to take course in Port Harcourt the next Semester, and vice versa? It is my view that the National Universities Commission should stop the new federal and state universities from running doctoral programs.

They do not have the resources to do so. These resources should better be directed towards the improvement of undergraduate programs.

Barriers to curriculum changes at the college level (in the United States) have well documented in Toombs W, and Tierney W (1991). According to these authors, in order to implement these changes the following must be taken into account:

Create a climate, even a demand for change.
Diminish the threat associated with innovations and avoid hard-line approaches.
Avoid being timid.
Appreciate timing.
Gear the innovation to the organization.
Disseminate and evaluate information.
Communicate effectively.
Get organizational leaders behind the innovation.
Build a base of active support.
Establish rewards.
Plan for the period after adoption.

It is therefore clear that in order to effect any worthwhile changes in the tertiary education curriculum, government leaders, university and college professors, and the university teachers' union (ASU) must be brought on board. By doing this, the threat to innovation will be greatly diminished and tangible and effective changes can be implemented.

6. FUNDING OF EDUCATION IN NIGERIA

Events in the last twenty years suggest that it is impossible for the federal and state governments to adequately fund all levels of education in Nigeria.

It is essential therefore that funding of education has to be reexamined. In this section, we shall advocate for different sources for funding education. This will create financial stability for the Nigerian educational system.

FEDERAL AND STATE FUNDING FOR EDUCATION: The Federal and State governments should continue to lead in the funding of education in Nigeria.

Land grant Designation: Nigeria is endowed with abundant natural resources. However, funding for education has not benefited from the country's wealth for the last fifteen years. If the Federal Government is serious about educating Nigerians, there must be a percentage of the Federal budget allocated to education every year. This percentage cannot continue to fluctuate. Machinery must be put in place in order to make sure such monies reach the levels of Education and for the purpose for which it is allocated. In other words, there must be an efficient mechanism to direct the monies to accomplish specific goals. Apart from direct funding through the Federal Ministry of Education, the Federal Government must mandate all ministries to support education with parts of their budgets. Such funding may be in the form of research grants to professors, consultation with professors and provision of work experience for undergraduate and graduate students. The ministries and other independent federal parastatals should be encouraged to rent and utilize university facilities for training and retraining of their workers.

Nigerian Science Foundation: The Federal Government should establish the Nigerian Science Foundation- a Foundation similar to the National Science Foundation (NSF) of the United States.

This foundation should have as its primary mission the promotion of science research, teaching, and learning at all levels.

Education and Luxury-Tax: All taxpayers and companies should pay some percentage of their yearly net income as education tax. Individuals who have benefited from the society and who buy expensive vehicles, live in expensive houses, have private planes, yachts, and vacation homes should be made to pay taxes on their luxurious life-style. Vehicle license tags should be renewed every year and taxes should be paid on them.

Private Foundations: Nigeria has very affluent people. The private foundations in the United State support not only education and educational institutions in the United States, but all over the world. Grants awarded by the Ford Foundation helped several Nigerians earn Ph.D. in the sixties and seventies. The Nigeria government should encourage private individuals, communities, and companies to establish charitable foundations not only to support education, but also to support community development. Government can enhance this by giving tax incentives to such individuals and companies, as well as awarding nation honors for such benevolence.

7. CONCLUSION

The path to greatness requires very careful and sometimes radical changes in the national polity. If Nigeria is to become the great Nation it aspires to be the Nigerian education system must undergo radical changes. Several changes in both administration and curriculum have been suggested in this chapter. However, these suggestions are not exhaustive. It is my view that the Nigerian leadership must confront these problems in our educational system at all levels.

In order to achieve meaningful changes at all levels, those changes must begin in our tertiary institutions. Change requires financial support. Nigeria as a nation has the financial resources to improve its education system. It also has the human resources to do so. Financial support for education is inevitable if Nigeria is to have a competitive workforce in the twenty-first century.

Chapter VII

THE NIGERIAN ELITE AND THE GENERATION THAT WAS LOST

Adeolu Esho

"Arise O compatriot, Nigeria's call obey
To serve our fatherland with love and strength and faith ...."

Thus go the opening lines of our beautiful National Anthem. The original anthem, "Nigeria We Hail Thee" was equally a masterpiece. Behold, how nice would it have been if all Nigerians hold the lines in these anthems dear to their hearts and live and die to serve their country with honor and faith. One wonders if people actually stop to reflect on the meanings of these lofty words or just mumble along with a gaping yawn of indifference.

Our goal in this chapter is not to provide an academic discussion on the state of the elite group and its societal influence on our country, but rather a personal discourse into the ills of our country and how the elite group that were supposed to put the country on the right track and let her hold her head amongst other countries of the world has engaged in a systematic bastardization of a people and scuttled the aspirations of a generation.

THE BEGINNING

Nigeria under colonization definitely was a more stable and more presentable country. Although the British had their own agenda to get as much resources out of the country as they could, they had systematically used the existing institutions to perpetrate and perpetuate the inhumane practices. Without the traditional political groups' help the British agenda would have been unsustainable. One should however give credit to the many leaders that stood their grounds and only had to give in after being arm strung with "Arm Boat Diplomacy". The British used "Divide and Rule" tactic and eventually got her hands on almost all our institutions in all over our land. Well, we all know how the history went. The elite group during this period consisted of the traditional rulers. However, in spite of all the shortcomings of colonization, whatever infrastructure the British put in place worked. The telephone system worked if you were fortunate to get one. The Electricity Company was efficient in its own little way. Radio Transmission was very well up and running into the few homes that had access to it. Goods and services could be moved without too much hassles. Things just worked.

What was missing was the principle of self-determination -- being our own People. A People not under any domination and subjugation to external powers. A People that could be allowed to define its own future the way it deems fit. A People that could be left alone to plan for itself, make mistakes and learn from those mistakes in the painstaking effort to build a nation that everyone is proud of.

THE NEW ELITE

The opportunity to rescue the country from the clutches of foreign powers came knocking after it was discovered that the white man was not that superior to his black folks after, having seen them afraid to die in war and seen them actually die just like their black counterparts in the world wars. This was a real turning point in the general perception of this strange looking person to whom some super natural and extra terrestrial powers had been mistakenly arrogated. The emerging elite group, now different from the original elite who were the traditional rulers and the aristocrats, were full of energies and had accumulated all the academic degrees under the sun from the white man's country and even out performed them in every department in the course of achieving these academic laurels. One could then begin to imagine how fired up these new group would be with these eye-opening events of the World Wars.

The struggle for independence grew with leaps and bounds and we eventually won our independence with little or no resistance from the British. The new elite, with all intent and purpose, had the fire and the determination to see their country develop just the way they had seen the European countries develop. They believed down inside them that they were up to the task of building a country of their dream. The problem however was that the country itself was flawed in the way it was setup. It had been setup as a political and economic convenience of the British. The scramble for the continent and the eventual outcome of the Berlin Conference of the late 1800s, which began the process of Nation States in Africa leaves much to be desired. In fact that deserves a thorough examination and is beyond the scope of my present contribution. As a result of this random demarcation of the land, not long after independence the cracks in the wall of our nation began to surface and they grew and grew and we have been trying to make amends ever since. The fact is that Nigeria is a country of many peoples with distinct political and national identities.

Apart from the imperfection of our the Nigerian entity, the new political elite group seemed to have forgotten their initial goals as they started enjoying the trappings of power and felt that they needed to first sort themselves out and provide for the survival, dominance and perpetuation of their lineage. Of course this goal could not be achieved if they remained honest. So a new equation came to fore. They had to dip their hands into pockets beyond those of their "Agbada, Sokoto, Babariga, and Kente" and this took them to the bottomless pit of the National Treasury. Having made a success of pulling from the treasury at will, a new precedent was set and the new implicit goal of future members of the elite group was how to dip deeper with perfection. The rat race had just begun. The initial goal of serving the fatherland was pushed to the back burner and replaced with "what can I gain from it financially? In all fairness to them, they did manage to keep some of the infrastructure that had been put in place by the colonialist working and in some places actually had actually improved on them. They still managed to keep the momentum of pride in fatherland going during the honeymoon period. When the honeymoon was over and it came time for re-election they were not yet ready to leave the stage having tasted from the sacred cow.

They bribed, cajoled, beguiled, lied and rigged their way back into office. Of course they needed more funds to achieve this and as such the looting got worse.The army saw how rosy the cheeks of the political elite was and decided they wanted a piece of the action and of course as the gun was mightier than the pen, they have been able to do it longer than any other group. In their own situation the treasury actually became their private accounts from which they can withdraw and draw cheques at will. This newly defined illimitable spoils of power that had just been discovered by the ruling groups became the single most important reason for the scramble for power by the groups in the country, be it the civilian, the military. This is not to say however that there were not office seekers who were very honest and only sought office in other to serve. The reality is that when such people get into office, they either join the bandwagon or the dishonest ones make it impossible for them to function with integrity. They might even loose their lives in the process as the evil doers see them as being in the way.

Responsibility without Accountability

It is said, "To whom much is given, much is expected". Responsibility means having "control" or "authority" and the other piece of the equation is being "accountable" for one's actions during the exercise of the authority. While the elite group readily accepted the first piece - Responsibility, they have expunged the second piece – Accountability, from the national polity. The military successfully established and perpetuated this practice of responsibility without accountability in almost every facet of their activities as they have the monopoly of the instrument of coercion.

Of course the political elite did not like the fact that they had been kept out of the treasury looting game for too long and having discovered that they can not out run the military with the stroke of the pen compared to the latter's instrument of oppression, they became wise and started forming alliances with the military, begging for a piece of the action even if they were just crumbs. Especially now that responsibility does not come with its twin brother, accountability. They started lobbying to be appointed to ministerial and parastatal positions promising to be loyal and sing the tune of the military irrespective of how diametrically different the military involvement in politics is to their political philosophy. Even seasoned politicians that had built a great political career full of accomplishments fell prey to these. What eventually happened was that they lost all their political clouts in their home base and are now condemned to a life of irrelevance and perpetual regret. What people will do for a sack of gold!

This dangerous trend has been the centerpiece of Nigeria's problems. A new culture emerged in the country. We now see governance and being associated with someone in government as being a sign that we "have arrived" – a status symbol. People now do not question where people get their wealth. As long as you get it and use it to know them, who cares? I happen to have a friend who once told me that there was an elderly poor man whom he had a lot of respect for.

One day the old guy called him and prayed for him that God will elevate him (my friend) to the position of those who could readily get their hands in government money and that when he finally does, he would have plenty of it to pull. This shows how much we have sunk as a "nation". Of course, my friend educated the old man on why he should see those people with such greed as criminals and not heroes. But before long this new endemic problem found itself into the fabric of our cultural psyche. If you are bold to question someone's source of wealth you are seen as being jealous. So everyone just went with the flow. If you steal government money and you are not caught then you are a true smart hero. This condoning of fraud also includes those of contractors who get awarded contracts to supply goods or build structures and they supply inferior goods or build inferior structures or don't even build at all even though the money for the contracts had already been disbursed. What a way to build a viable nation!

Tactics for Self- Preservation

As stated above, the Nigeria nation was flawed from inception. The emerging political elite groups know about this and have used and continue to use this imperfection to sustain its hold on power. The political and military elite having tasted the joy of wealth that being in power had afforded them now had to devise a method to keep membership of the coveted groups as small as possible. The second thing they needed to do was to ensure that the torch could be passed on to their off springs without any problem. One must admit though that this happens in all societies of the world. Who would not like his off springs to have easy access to such spoils of power? But at least in majority of the other societies the patriarch had had to build his reputation or dynasty on his selflessness in the service to his community and to his country and not selflessness in the looting of the National Treasury.

To perpetuate themselves the tactic employed was to capitalize on the loyalty of their political followership by emphasizing those areas of differences amongst our people instead of concentration on those things that are similar and unite us. Thus the various groups in the society were pitched against each other in a zero-sum game fashion while the elite gloat at the top looking down with utmost satisfaction that at least they can continue to enjoy their wealth for a long time to come. Behind the scene the elite have common bond amongst them no matter how stern they are in criticizing their colleagues wherever and whichever side of the Niger they are. One needs to look at the structure of most organizations and companies in the country to appreciate what I am trying to say here. They therefore have fueled tensions amongst and within the groups so they could continue to be seen as being relevant to their aspirations. This was the same tactic employed by the colonialist.

This situation continued and eventually the country became the big looser for it. People saddled with authority either : willingly given in an election; stolen in an election; or forcefully acquired with the use of guns, have greedily and maliciously decimated the hopes of a people for an affluent and prosperous society in which they are proud to live in or return to after a sojourn in foreign lands.

What eventually happened was that a sizeable number of members of the newer generation of Nigerians, having been let down by the so called elite groups, had to seek greener pastures abroad, thereby contributing to the Gross National Income of the host countries.

THE GENERATION THAT WAS LOST

Wole Soyinka, the world renowned writer and a Nobel laureate once said that his generation was a wasted generation because of his belief that the generation was not given the opportunity to contribute to the best of its ability to the upliftment of the country. If this was the case, one should be able to safely say without any fear of contradiction that the generation that came after him was a completely lost generation. People in this generation have had to endure a lot of adversities and you can see them struggling everyday just to be relevant somehow to their society. They have had little or no opportunity to make significant contribution to the prosperity of the country.

When growing up, members of this generation, just like other generations before them, were told to be studious in their academic pursuit, strive for excellence in anything they are involved in, be good citizens and they would have the passport to better living automatically given to them. They actually have witnessed that the members of the generations that came before them did just that and the door to prosperous living was opened to them. But while they kept their side of the bargain the country reneged on its own side. Majority of the members of the lost generation studied and acquired so many degrees both at home an abroad, shattering numerous academic records along the way, just as is typical of Nigerians of all generations. Those amongst the generation that were not that academically inclined have had high hopes that whatever business they might want to get involved in, the country will be with them every step of the way and help them to succeed. What happened was that the country left them in limbo. The policies of successive administrations in the country and the free looting of the national treasury, massively carried out by people in power, stifled the economy and politics of the country, thereby leading to economic malnutrition and political kwashiorkor. There were simply no jobs for them to go into and for those that were business-inclined, no conducive climate existed for any honest business to thrive.

The result of the foregoing was that people that had the opportunity to leave the country left en-masse. The big loser in this new trend was of course the country. Thus a whole generation of a people became marginalized, and rendered almost irrelevant to their country and thereby lost. It is possible to argue that citizens in diaspora are actually contributing by other means to the country and as such not marginalized or completely lost. Well, my response would be- how many of them are actually happy where they are? Would they have remained in those countries if conditions at home were better? How many enjoy the type of work they are doing and the number of hours they have to put in everyday to make a living? How many really feel they are being appreciated or even welcomed where they are?

Finally, how many of them see themselves as being relevant to the society they now call home? Frankly, it is my believe that given the opportunity to live in an economically advanced and politically stable Nigeria, many of our countrymen will gladly stay at home and just be satisfied with the opportunity to travel abroad on vacations. I cannot count the number of Phd and other single and multiple degree holders that have had to become security guards, dish washers or cab drivers in these countries just for the sake of survival. Many Nigerians abroad have had to retrain in professions that are totally different from what they started with, not because they liked the new professions, but because they needed to keep body and soul together. Moreover most of the new professions are not ones they would be proud to admit to friends and families in Nigeria that they had trained in, talk less of practising them when they return home.

Majority of our people in diaspora was so much elated with the political trend in the country that cumulated in the presidential election of 1993. In some cases some of them had actually purchased one-way tickets home for them and their offspring as they perceived that political tradition had started taking firm roots in the country and they wanted to be part of it. It was therefore very disappointing that the whole process was reversed by the Babangida regime with the prodding of some elements within the country who felt they would be irrelevant under the incoming dispensation.

MILITARY DISENGAGEMENT AND THE ELECTION OF 1999

The elections of '99 have come and gone and the eyes of the world are now on us. It had been possible for another round of elections to be held due to divine intervention. The events that paved way for fresh electioneering were not entirely palatable, especially since the country lost the person mostly believed to be a dully-elected President in the process. We of course also lost the head of a junta that reversed the course of progress and scuttled the political traditions that were beginning to take firm root and therefore becoming institutionalized in the country. Whether we realized it or not, Nigeria was able to conduct and actually peacefully removed people from office through the political process a number of times during this period. Though these elections were not perfect, at least it was the beginning of a process, the beginning of a tradition, the beginning of a culture of believing that we have that ultimate power to vote leaders out of office if they do not perform to the people's expectation. The entire process would have been complete and a milestone reached if the result of the election that would have finally brought in a nationally democratically elected President had been allowed to stand. As the results that were released showed, Abiola had won in places that ordinarily would not have voted for someone not of their own. That was the kind of things that needed to be happening if we were to sustain Nigeria as we know it. Ethnic barriers needed to be broken willingly by the people rather than being forced. But what happened after is well known to all of us – The course of progress was reversed and we sank deeper into darkness.

As stated above, the untimely death of two of the key players in our polity paved way for another round of elections. While I am not entirely satisfied with the exercise due to all the electoral malpractice that have been reported by international observers, which was a far cry from the clean bill of health they gave to the last election held in 93, I want to add my voice to those of the well meaning Nigerians that have surmised that we accept the result, notwithstanding its imperfection. It was also a good thing to see the opposition go to court to seek redress on the outcome of the election. This is so much welcomed. This is the kind of tradition that needs to take a firm root in our society if we are to move ahead and join a comity of enlightened nations. The opposition went to court and the case was brought to a logical conclusion through a due process. It eventually conceded the election, not because it thought the acclaimed winner actually won, but because it felt we needed to move the country ahead and keep the power out of the grasp of the military boys.

We should realize that the bane of our country apart from the bastardization by the now unpopular military is the general attitude of the average Nigerian politician. Their credo had always been that -- "If I can't have it nobody else can have it". This is a jungle mentality and it was what destroyed the previous presidential election. If the opposition party had insisted to the military that it accepted the results, Babangida and his folks would have found it difficult to sustain the annulment and we would have been singing another song now. Look where the attitude eventually led us ----.

I particularly did not and still do not like the idea of having an ex-military running for the Presidency, especially not in the first election, if the military really wanted to show us that they mean well for the country. Obasanjo should have gracefully rejected the nomination and if the PDP still wanted someone from the south as its flag bearer, I believe there are more credible Southerners in the party that they could bestow the job on. If this had happened, we would have truly established a 3 Party System with membership cutting across diverse groups. But what happened? One party is now being seen as the party of the military and the others are in an alliance to stop them. This is not good for the health of our national polity. Well, as I mentioned earlier, it is time to move on. We should congratulate whichever 'civilian' is 'elected' and get the uniform guys out of the way. The next goal is to get the political machinery institutionalized. This is the beginning of something we can build on. Eventually there will be realignment of the political forces within the country and every group will find its level and the military might eventually be confined to the place they belong for good – the barracks. We should remember that it is a lot easier to get a civilian president out of office than to get rid of a military dictator. Our experience over the years has shown this to be true.

THE WAY FORWARD

It is imperative as we approach the next millennium that Nigeria wakes up from its slumber and position itself in a vantage position within the comity of nations. If our current political elite fail to take advantage of the new lease of life that has been so graciously handed to us by the invincible hands of the creator, they would have committed a high crime and misdemeanor and posterity will never forgive them. Not many people get to have a second chance.

Accountability with Responsibility

We as a nation should insist that whoever is given responsibility of leading us is also accountable to us for all actions taken on our behalf. Once this tradition is firmly established at the top it will undoubtedly trickle down to other people and other aspects of our society. We know all along that our people are very good followers and that all that has been lacking in our land is good governance.

Transparency

Our leaders should endeavor to be very transparent in everything they do in the day to day running of our societies. We should borrow a leaf from the great countries of the world where the leadership place all policies on the table and explain to people the why, what, how and when of all their policies. Nothing should be shrouded in secrecy.

Responsiveness

Rulers should show responsiveness to the problems of the people. They must identify with the day to day struggle of the people and comprehend the battles they fight to provide a living for their families. They should continuously strive to formulate policies that make these daily struggles a lot easier to bear.

Principled leadership

We need leaders that are principled. Leaders must have the courage to leave the stage whenever they feel things happening are against their principles. Our history has shown us that our leaders are not ones to leave the stage when things being done are against their personal convictions and principle. They always manage to stay around because of the fear of becoming irrelevant. We have witnessed formidable leaders that have spent a lot of years building their political identity shoving all what they have spent a lifetime building to the side just for a sack of gold. No need to name names, I am sure we all know who they are. This is a very selfish disposition and the trend needs to stop if we are to build a country we could all be proud of.

Absolute power corrupts absolutely

It was Lord Acton who once said that "Power corrupts and absolute power corrupts absolutely". We must ensure that the principle of separation of powers as provided in the constitution is implemented to the letter so we do not see the other arms of government as being an extension of the executive.

In our past political experiences we have witnessed situations where the executive had been too overbearing that it kept the judiciary and the legislature in tow. The result in that kind of environment is like having a military government with its unitary command structure imposed on the country.

Aggressively pursue the revitalization of the economy

Our economy as it is now is malnourished. Overwhelming majority of economic activities still revolve around the government. The government needs to consciously formulate policies that will make it conducive for businesses to thrive. It is only when there is opportunity for businesses to operate and grow that it would be possible for economic activities to revolve around the business community rather that the government. This is the trend that will help creative an expansive economy with the capacity to absorb the human resources that had hitherto been involuntarily rendered idle.

Adequate means of collection of taxes

There is need for an adequate method of tax collection in Nigeria. It is a known fact that a very small proportion of taxes meant for the government actually get into the government coffers. Some of them are plainly just not collected while others get collected but miraculously find their ways into the pockets of some unscrupulous tax collectors who are getting rich at the expense of the government.

Building of Infrastructure

Whether we believe it or not, a country that does not have the necessary infrastructure solidly in place will have a stunted growth. Excellent infrastructure is a precondition for economic growth. This includes facilities like Roads, Telecommunications, Electricity, and Water/ Sewage Systems to mention a few. If these were not in place, businesses would not be able to thrive properly and put them in a position to compete with other businesses in the world. As an example, there are instances when you have someone hit the road from one company to the other just to inform the other company that the answer to the question asked was "no". If there had been good telephone system he could have phoned faxed or e-mailed the other party. In this example, there was one more car on the road that should not have been if the phone system worked.

Change our societal values

Our people should learn to question things that do not look right. For example, history has shown that our people do not question individual's source of riches. There are people in all works of life in our society who had amassed ill-gotten wealth. Instead of questioning the source of such wealth we would rather love to be associated with the "success" of these monstrous individuals and criminals. We see it as a sign of being associated with people in high places. This has to stop. We need to cease pandering to such people and emphasize probity in our society. There is nothing wrong in having people who are wealthy, but such wealth should come from the labor of one's sweat and not from stealing from the public coffers. We should also desist from measuring success from the point of view of material accumulation and how fat the account balances are.

You do not have to be rich to be successful.

Emphasize things that unite us rather than dwell on mundane and divisive issues

As stated earlier, the Nigerian entity was flawed in its composition by the colonial masters. We however have to find a way to make the best of the situation in which we involuntarily found ourselves. We should try to emphasize more things that unite us rather dwell on the petty and mundane things that divide us.

Restructure the Federation

Our federation is in dire need of restructuring. The center should be made less attractive by concentration of more powers in the hands of the state. Revenue allocation should be revised to ensure that we do not strangle the goose that lays the golden egg. Some of our existing States are not viable and efforts should be made to reduce the number of the states. A State that relies on the Federal Government for more than 70% of its funding definitely is not viable and should be scrapped. Our local leaders should stop being selfish trying to make ward in their area become States. A state that can not support itself is as good as dead.

'If I can't have it, nobody else can have it'

The mentality of - no one can have what I can't have - must stop. It is a jungle mentality. We should learn to be magnanimous in victory just as we are gracious in defeat. We should accept that if we don't get something that we want this time around there is always a next time. This is the best legacy to pass on to the children. Our leaders have been so guilty of this that it has reached an epidemic level. No one should arrogate monopoly of wisdom to himself.

The military must be restructured and made more professional

It should be a crime to bear arms against people that had been politically elected by the people. We should criminalize army takeover. An American friend of mine, Leanne Moore, who is an avid student of African politics, impressed upon me that this military act is a "Cowardly Act". Her argument goes:

The only reason such criminals in military uniform could do that and get away with it was due to the monopoly of the instrument of coercion. If one is interested in leading a people, one should submit himself to the people for endorsement instead of putting a gun to their head. After all, these instruments of coercion were purchased with the people's money in the first place and with the sole purpose of protecting them.

There you have it. I couldn't have put it any better.

Emphasis on technological development

It is a known fact that as at the present time, technology drives all the economies of the world. Any country that could not take advantage of the advancement in technology to revolutionize its economy does not deserve to exist. In Nigeria we are so blessed with citizens who have trained extensively in all aspects of the industry and we should find a way to harness all these knowledge to the betterment of the country. Our educational institutions should be well equipped with state of the art technology/computer systems so they could be in the forefront of the revolution.

It is a real shame that much needed computer systems are not available in our institutions of higher learning. We produce Computer Engineers that hardly ever worked on computers. This has to change. If we fail to introduce far reaching programs that will propel our country forward during the current dispensation then we would have squandered the new lease of life that had been magnanimously extended to us and we should forever cover our heads in shame. Our country can be as beautiful as we want it to be. It is a place that we all would love to come back to with pride. We should not have to fear to go back to our fatherland. We shouldn't have to be ashamed to defend our country at every opportunity that we have to do so. These could only be possible if there is purposeful leadership in the country. The time to act is now. Nigeria should awake from its slumber

PART III: FOREIGN POLICY ISSUES

Nigeria foreign policy has suffered tremendously under the past two military leadership and particularly under the Abacha administration because of his record level human rights violation which led to the suspension of Nigeria from the commonwealth and reduction of what remains of the Nigeria's influence on the continent. At the same time, Nigeria continue to play an important role in the west Africa sub-region and attempts to restore stability and democratic governance in Sierra Leone, why resisting calls for democracy at home. The task that faces the new Nigeria leadership is the daunting task of restoring Nigeria credibility abroad while re building confidence in its foreign policy constituency at home.

Chapter VIII

A SURVEY OF NIGERIAN FOREIGN POLICY: 1960 TO 1998

Olayiwola Abegunrin

The foreign policy of a nation is the part of its national policy that relates to other countries and is based upon a-priori conceptions of national interest. In short, a nation's foreign policy is the totality of its dealings with the external environment. Foreign policy is more than just a collection of official documents, formal records of actions and public statements. Foreign policy is the key element in the process by which a state translates its broadly conceived goals, and interests into concrete and specific courses of action in order to attain these objectives and preserve its interests(Abegunrin, 1992, 69).

Therefore, no country, big or small, rich or poor, can exist in isolation from the other states within the international system. Leadership capability has always been one of the factors that exerted decisive influence in foreign policy of a nation. The leadership impact, and the role of Nigerian leaders since independence had influenced Nigeria's foreign policy. Therefore, to do justice to Nigeria's foreign policy during the periods covered in this study, (1960-1998), the foreign policy of each administration will be treated separately. We shall do this, because the personality of each leader that have ruled Nigeria has affected, and influenced the country's policy either negatively or positively, no matter how stable or unstable the political situations of the country have been under each regime.

FOREIGN POLICY IN THE FIRST REPUBLIC 1960-1966

Nigerian foreign policy in the First Republic has often been described as conservative and timid. The colonial legacy which restricted the policy options of the immediate post-independence leaders, the relative poverty of the country at the time, the lack of experience in international affairs, the conservative outlook of the first prime minister-

Abubakar Tafawa Balewa, and other members of his cabinet, and the domestic divisions which led each region within the federation to open its own consulates abroad are some of the reasons that have been advanced for the low-profile foreign policy(See Idang, 1973; Akinyemi; 1974; Aluko, 1982) It has been said that the collapse of Nigeria's First Republic was as a result of a crisis of leadership. When asked by a Daily Times correspondent about the serious political, and social disturbances in the former Western Region of Nigeria, Prime Minister Balewa said, "When people are excited, they can do anything. It is to be hoped that they will soon see reason, and the whole thing will pass away"(cited in Abegunrin, 1992, 79). The government of the Western Region at the time had lost the power to govern, and the federal government led by Prime Minister Balewa had no political will to exercise its responsibility to maintain law, and order in that region. The result was chaos which spread nationwide, and finally led to the collapse of the First Republic(see Abegunrin, 1992).

A major aspect Balewa 's foreign policy was its pro-Western orientation. The pro-Western posture was inspite of an avowed policy of non-alignment--that is neutrality in relations between the East and the West, which was so popular among the newly-independent third world countries. However, Nigeria pursued a policy of hostility towards the Soviet Union, and other members of the Eastern bloc, which was partly informed by Balewa's personal fear of communism. Among other anti-Soviet Union actions,was the Nigerian government refusal to open an embassy in Moscow, and only reluctantly allowed the Soviet Union to open its mission in Lagos. Nigeria also placed restrictions on travels to the Eastern bloc countries and communist literature; refused to recognize the Peoples Republic of China(PRC), and Mongolia, and rejected aid, and bilateral agreements with communist countries, including Soviet Union scholarships for Nigerian Students. Trade relations with the Eastern Bloc were insignificant and even not encouraged. For example the leader of the Northern Peoples Congress(NPC), Alhaji Ahmed Bello, the Sardauna of Sokoto, refused to accept a low-interest Russian loan by saying, "That is not our policy. We have to work with those we are accustomed to."(Daily Times, January 1960). To show the extent of Balewa's fear of communism, China was not invited to Nigeria's independence day celebrations, and the Soviet Union that was invited was told it would have to wait in line to open an embassy. The Prime Minister also publicly complained that Jacob Malik, the Russian delegate to the celebrations, had tried to bully him into speeding up the embassy opening(The Times, London, 11, 1960).

By contrast, relations with Britain, and the West were conducted in a manner that sometimes cast doubts on the country's independence, for example when Nigeria was admitted to the United Nations, on October 7, 1960, as the 99th member-nation of the Organization, addressing the General Assembly, the Prime Minister spelt out the fundamental basis of Nigerian foreign policy, and went further by promising that: "We shall not forget our friends," meaning Great Britain(Schwarz, 1965). Another example of Nigeria's dependent foreign policy on Britain was that, "throughout the Balewa administration, the Cabinet was totally excluded from formulating foreign policy which was exclusively done by the Prime Minister, and the Cabinet Secretariat headed by Balewa's British expatriate private secretary, Peter Stallard, who was originally in the

British colonial service"(cited in A.B. Akinyemi, 1974). For instance, It took protests from university students, the opposition party in the Parliament-the Action Group(AG), and progressive elements in the country for the federal government to abrogate its defense pact with Britain(Daily Times, 11, 24, 1960).

On the decolonization of Africa; Nigerian Foreign Minister, Jaja Wachukwu, tabled a formal resolution in the United Nations General Assembly in September 1961, calling for an end to colonialism in all parts of the African continent by 1970. "This resolution from Africa's largest populated country shocked other African States who wanted an end to African colonialism at least by 1965"(UN General Assembly Official Records, 1961).

Nigeria defied African opposition to British policy on the (former Rhodesia) Zimbabwe, after Ian Smith unilaterally declared the independence of Southern Rhodesia on November 11, 1965, and tried to discourage African countries from breaking diplomatic ties with Britain over the Rhodesian issue. Over the Congo crisis Nigeria government actively supported the West. Nevertheless, on a few occasions when the federal government was forced to defer to public opinion demands at home or when Nigeria's strategic interests were at stake, the federal government showed a sign of independent policies. The Nigerian government after the independence has forthrightly identified its national interest, and its ideology, which the Prime Minister called as a primary consideration in the formulation of the nation's foreign policy. Nigeria's national interests include, the preservation and survival of Nigeria as a sovereign state; the security, and protection of its citizens, and maintenance of its territorial boundaries. As a result of these principles, Nigeria treated South Africa's policy of racial discrimination as a threat, and the killings in Sharpeville on March 21, 1960, of 69 Africans who were carrying out a peaceful demonstration. Nigeria again in 1961, defied Britain to champion the expulsion of South Africa from the Commonwealth. Also in 1963, Nigeria broke diplomatic ties with France over that country's nuclear testing in the Sahara Desert, despite reassurance from Britain that the tests would have no effects on Nigeria.The federal government under Balewa administration tried to reduce its dependence on Britain by diversifying its trade relations, and strengthening relations in other areas with the U.S., and other Western Powers. However, Nigeria's foreign policy in the First Republic remained pro-Western, and was greatly influenced by its close relations with Britain.

In its relations with the outside world, the conservatism of the Balewa regime led it to emphasize the legal principles of international relations. This was evident in the country's participation in the international organizations to which it was a member-the United Nations, the Commonwealth of Nations, the Non-aligned Movement, the Group of 77, and the Organization of African Unity(OAU), where it insisted on the principles of non-interference in the internal affairs of other countries, peaceful resolution of conflicts, inviolability of national boundaries, peaceful co-existence and good neighborliness and others. The use of these international organizations as the main channels of foreign policy was also a sign of the administration's legalistic approach to foreign relations. However, the Balewa government also supported the formation of powerful Third World commodity organizations as a way of improving the terms of trade with the Industrialized nations. To this end it sponsored the meeting of the Africa Primary Agricultural

Producers in 1962, and was a founding member of both the Cocoa Producers Alliance, and the African Groundnut Council. From the time of independence, Balewa has articulated the afrocentricity of the Nigeria's foreign policy which gave a clear signal of a readiness to assume the "manifest destiny" of African and black leadership, when he said that;

> ....the creation of the necessary economic and political conditions to secure the government, territorial integrity and national independence of other African countries and their total liberation from imperialism and all forms of foreign domination;... creation of the necessary conditions for the economic, political, social, and cultural development of Africa;... promotion of the rights of all black and oppressed peoples throughout the world;...and promotion of African unity;(Otubanjo, 1989).

Nevertheless, Balewa administration lacked political will, and radical orientation required to play the foreign policy roles set out for itself. For instance, on apartheid policy in South Africa, Nigeria was one of the few countries in Africa that favored dialogue with white minority regime in Pretoria. To the surprise of many African States, Nigeria, invited apartheid South Africa to its independence celebrations. Balewa even announced that, "he would if asked, exchanged ambassadors with South Africa, and if invited would visit South Africa to help make the country change its apartheid policy." In a similar statement at the Commonwealth Prime Ministers' Conference, Balewa said that, "he would not oppose the Rhodesia's' Prime Minister Roy Welensky coming to Nigeria because he was not a racist, and Africans in the then Rhodesia, contrary to South Africa, could hold political meetings"(Daily Times, 1962). There was incoherence and inconsistency in Nigeria's foreign policy, because at the same time Balewa was advocating for dialogue with the white minority regimes in Southern Africa, he was championing the expulsion of South Africa from the Commonwealth, and the International Labour Organization. Also following the Sharpeville massacre of 1960, Balewa's political party, NPC established a trust fund for the victims, and banned further employment of white South Africans in the northern regional public service.

Nigeria was a foundation member of the Organization of African Unity(OAU), but favored the functional approach to continental unity as opposed to the more radical political approach championed by President Kwame Nkrumah of Ghana, who advocated a United States of Africa. This and several other disagreements, like supporting anti-Lumumba forces in (former Congo), Democratic Republic of Congo in opposition to Ghana, were some of the manifestations of a rivalry between Nigeria and Ghana for the leadership of Africa. Nkrumah's radical, pro-communist inclination, and support for radical opposition groups in Nigeria also underlay the rivalry between the two countries as pointed out, "anti-Nkrumahism was a major theme of Nigeria's foreign policy in the First Republic"(Nnoli,1989). But this rivalry only made Nigeria more determined to assert its leadership in other areas. Thus technical assistance in the form of manpower was given to several African countries, "Nigeria sent a battalion of her troop to Tanzania to put down the army mutiny in that country in 1964, and Nigerian soldiers and police first acquired a higher reputation during the participation of African military contingents in the United Nations Peacekeeping Operations in the Congo in 1960 to 1964"(Abegunrin, 1992).

Nigeria under the First Republic initiated the establishment of the Chad Basin Commission, and the Niger Basin Authority in 1964, though these were directed purposely at sustaining a policy of good relations with immediate neighbors.

However, on balance the criticisms of Prime Minister Balewa's conservative policies and his failure to assert Nigeria's rightful role as an independent country, and leader of Africa, which are oblivious of the inexperience of the regime, and the divided domestic terrain between the Southern and Northern regions of Nigeria. Nevertheless, most of the guiding principles of foreign policy in the post-independence period were established under the First Republic. These were mostly, the commitment to the total liberation and development of Africa, a pro-Western orientation despite non-alignment, and the defense of Nigeria's national interests.

FOREIGN POLICY UNDER THE FIRST MILITARY RULE 1966-1979

Nigerian foreign policy underwent major dramatic transformations during the thirteen years of the first phase of military rule. The transformations were particularly part of efforts by the military to redeem the country from the failings of the First Republic. However, the changes were not always the result of deliberate policies. A good example was the oil boom of the 1970s, which enabled the country to pursue more assertive policies, and actualize its manifest destiny, was a matter of circumstance. The same can be said of the civil war, which marked a turning point in Nigeria's relations with Eastern European countries, particularly, Nigerian-Soviet relations. In fact, successive military regimes in that period consciously set about asserting Nigeria's position in the West African sub-region, Africa continent, and the rest of the world.

In this first phase of military rule, the main thrusts of the nation's foreign policy under the three military regimes were more militant, and radical approach to the liberation of Southern Africa, and other countries under colonial domination; the assertion of Nigeria's role as a black, and African leader, positive neutrality, involving the diversification of relations to the Eastern bloc countries, and vigorous challenge of western global hegemony, and the promotion of regional integration. Compared to the conservative Balewa regime, the military administrations were more adventurous, pragmatic, and populist in their approach, and this meant less reliance on the legal instruments of international relations. The emergence of oil as a major weapon of foreign policy strengthened this orientation. Another major reason for more adventurous policies, especially after the civil war, was the relative peace, and unity in the country which modified the effects of the regional cleavages on foreign policy-making. Another important factor in this was the size of the post-civil war army. Nigeria by 1978 spent about 8% of its GNP on defense($2.7 billion annually). Nigeria's role as a military power in Africa was emphasized in the annual reviews of The Military Balance, published by the International Institute for Strategic Studies of London. For two years in a roll (1978-1979) Nigeria came third after Egypt leading all Africa with a total of 895,000 men in its armed forces, South Africa was second with 345,000 while Nigeria had 232,000 men in its own armed forces(IISS, 1979, and West Africa, 1978).

The Obasanjo regime made strenuous efforts to step up and improve the training of the defense forces at all levels (Abegunrin, 1992, 78). Efforts were also made to strengthen the structures of foreign policy formulation, and management, and improve the quality of policies. Thus, in addition, to the restructuring at the Ministry of external affairs, the Nigerian Institute of International Affairs (NIIA) became the think-tank of foreign policy, the National Institute for Policy and Strategic Studies at Kuru, Jos also emerged as a major actor in policy formulation. From time to time, foreign policy consultative forums were also set up to review policies. Although these led to a marked improvement in the logic of policies, the policies still suffered from incoherence and discontinuity.

There were marked differences between each of the three military regimes from 1966 to 1979, in the tempo of their foreign policy. This had to do partly with the prevailing circumstances, and partly with the orientation of each military leaders. However, domestic problems did not allow the Ironsi regime to articulate, and pursue any serious foreign policy other than to maintain policies inherited from Balewa. "The brief six-month period of the first military administration illustrated clearly that no state which is extremely disturbed, and is unstable domestically can be effective in international relations"(Ofoegbu, 1979). Nevertheless, Ironsi stopped the practice of sending regional economic missions overseas, and closed down regional consulates abroad. However, the short-lived regime of General Aguyi-Ironsi (January 15-July 29, 1966), and the succeeding one of General Gowon continued the policy of non-violence opposition to apartheid and racism in Southern Africa, but certain important acts differentiated them from Balewa government. The major opposition to racism and colonialism was taken by Ironsi regime early in July 1966, when it decided to henceforth deny the use of Nigeria's air space, sea ports facilities to South Africa apartheid regime, and Portuguese aircraft and ships, and to all other aircraft and ships traveling to and from South Africa. The Ironsi regime also terminated the Portuguese diplomatic mission in Nigeria (Polhemus, 1977(11)). The political crisis of 1966-1970, especially the civil war, made the Gowon administration only a little better than Ironsi at the initial stage, since most external relations hinged on the crisis.

However, one of the major gains from the civil war was closer ties with the Soviet Union, China, and Eastern European countries which came to Nigeria's rescue when Britain, and other West European countries refused to sell heavy weapons to the Federal government to prosecute the civil war, this was partly due to the powerful and successful propaganda launched by the secessionists(Biafrans), which presented the war as genocide against the Christian Igbo by the Muslim North. Though, Britain refused to sell heavy guns, bombs, and aircraft to the Federal government, but continued to supply light weapons. The Federal government then turned to Soviet Union which supplied military hardware from August 1968, and provided technical support to the federal forces, and Egyptian Airforce contributed in training the Nigerian airforce fighter pilots. Britain's refusal to play a more supportive role also led the federal government to downplay the relevance of the Commonwealth in its foreign relations.

However, the oil boom of the 1970, helped Gowon pursued, a vigorous regional and African policy after the war. The international situation after the second military coup of July 29, 1966, forced the Gowon government to maintain very close friendly relations with African countries in order to explain the Federal Military Government's position, and to offset the propaganda that was being disseminated by the secessionists against Nigeria. The Gowon regime restated the Balewa government's policy to uphold, and maintain all international obligations, treaties and agreements with foreign governments or companies, and that there would be no interference in Nigeria's internal affairs. "Foreign policy then became a tool to help secure the integrity of the nation by denying recognition to its secessionist elements"(Abegunrin, 1975).

Let us now examine the nature of foreign policy under the military regimes at three levels; regional, continental and global. We shall begin with the continental level because almost every policy was anchored on African interests which Nigerian leaders saw the country as leading, of course this was secondary to Nigeria's own national interest where the two clashed. The African-centredness of the military administrations was clearly articulated by Ironsi regime after he came to power thus:

In the whole sphere of Nigeria's external relations, the government attaches the greatest importance to our African policy. We are aware that because of our population and potentials, the majority of opinion in the civilized world looks up to us to provide responsible leadership in Africa; and we realize that we shall be judged, to a very large extent by the degree of success or failure with which we face up to this challenge which this expectation throws on us. We are convinced that whether in the political, economic or cultural sphere, our destiny lies in our role in the continent of Africa(cited in A.T. Gana, 1989: 123).

The liberation of Africa from the last vestiges of colonialism and racial domination, and the development of the African countries, and the continent as a whole were the major pillars of the African policy. Nigeria's foreign policy was preoccupied with the liberation of apartheid South Africa, and other Southern African white-ruled territories Zimbabwe(former Rhodesia) and Namibia, as well as of Portuguese-ruled Angola, Mozambique, Guinea-Bissau, Sao Tome and Principe, and Cape Verde which were the last colonies on the continent. The international organizations, like the U.N., the Commonwealth, the O.A.U., the Non-Aligned Movement, and other international forums remained a major channel for the initiatives on liberation, but bilateral material assistance to African liberation movements, and other diplomatic channels also grew in importance. Of all the anti-colonial offensives, the liberation of South Africa and the independence of Rhodesia, and Angola provoked some of the most radical, militant, and pan-African foreign policy postures in Nigeria's history(Abegunrin, 1992). On South Africa, Nigeria rapidly moved under Gowon away from dialogue to full support for armed liberation.

Most importantly, was the support of the South African white minority regime for Biafra, and the active roles of white South African mercenaries in secessionist army during the civil war led to this shift(Abegunrin, 1975).

THE NEW NIGERIA FOREIGN POLICY: MUHAMMED/OBASANJO REGIME 1975-1979

The Mohammed/Obasanjo regime took Nigeria's assertiveness to the populist height. It pursued the most radical, progressive, and Pan-Africanist policies of the three military regimes in the first phase under consideration in this section. This administration made the greatest use of the oil weapon in the pursuit of foreign policy objectives. Many Nigerian observers have described the 'new' Nigerian foreign policy under Muhammed/Obasanjo regime as more nationalistic and radical.

Many referred to it as the beginning of a "new revolutionary foreign policy"(Daily Times, 12, 17, 1976). General(now President)Obasanjo himself described it as not only a "new dynamic foreign policy" but a new orientation" in the country's foreign policy. His Foreign Minister Major-General Garba, referred to it as "dynamic and nationalist." Nigerian intellectuals referred to it as "dynamic and progressive foreign policy (Abegunrin, 1992). After the tragic death of General Murtala Muhammed, on February 13, 1976, the nation's foreign policy did not weaken as some sections of the foreign press had expressed very pessimistic views of what might have followed this tragic incident. The tempo received added impetus. As a result of the Adedeji Foreign Policy Review Panel, in a policy statement on June 29, 1976, the new head of state, General Olusegun Obasanjo, identified Nigeria's foreign policy objectives as follows.

1. The defense of our sovereignty, independence and territorial integrity.
2. The creation of the necessary political and economic conditions in Africa and in the rest of the world which would foster Nigerian national self-reliance and rapid economic development. This would facilitate the defense of the independence of all African countries.
3. The promotion of equality and self-reliance in Africa and the rest of the developing world.
4. The promotion and defense of social justice and respect for human dignity especially the dignity of black men.
5. The promotion and defense of world peace.

Spelling out foreign policy position and objectives is one thing, its effective execution and reality is another. In reality, some of these objectives spelled out are beyond the capacity of Nigeria, especially numbers 2, 3, and 5. In most of his speeches during his military administration, General Obasanjo tended to emphasize three major objectives as being central to Nigeria's national interests, namely (1) territorial integrity, national unity and stability; (2) the defense and maintenance of Nigeria's independence; and (3) rapid economic development through application of modern technology.[1]*

The country's overall commitment as well as financial, and material support to the liberation movements in Southern Africa led to Nigeria being given the status of an honorary Frontline State, and the chairmanship of the UN's anti-apartheid committee being reserved for Nigeria's permanent representative in the world body.

Nigeria intensified its anti-apartheid campaigns for the imposition of more sanctions on the regime in Pretoria, and its further isolation. The country spearheaded the boycott of international sports meetings, notably Commonwealth, and Olympic games, to back these protests. On Rhodesia, the Obasanjo administration nationalized the assets of British Petroleum, and Barclays Bank in Nigeria in 1978, as a reprisal for the sale of oil to the Ian Smith regime in Rhodesia; this was one of the factors that forced the British government to defer to the demands for an all-party conference which ultimately led to the independence of Zimbabwe in 1980(Abegunrin, 1992, 176). The Africa-centered featured was demonstrated most vigorously by the Muhammed/Obasanjo regime, which recognized that the continent of Africa is the most vital environment for the realization of Nigeria's foreign policy goals.

The character of the interactions among African states could have a decisive impact on Nigeria's ability to defend its national interests in global affairs. "Consequently, the African centerpiece makes African crises a central concern of Nigeria's foreign policy"(King, 1998). This regime was distinguished by its assertive foreign policy leadership. The most notable foreign policy action was the administration's diplomatic recognition, and total support of the government led by the Popular Movement for the Liberation of Angola(MPLA). Nigeria acted over strong opposition from the West, especially over the objection of the United States. General Murtala Muhammed, in a remarkable speech before the OAU extraordinary summit in January 1976, insisted that Nigeria and Africa were capable of defining their own interests. He rejected U.S. President Gerald Ford's attempt to pressure African countries into supporting Western cold war policies in Africa, with regard to Angola. In replying to President Ford's pressure on African, General Murtala Muhammed pointed out that: "gone are the days when Africa will ever bow to the threat of any so-called superpower. Not content with its clandestine support and outpouring of arms into Angola to create confusion and bloodshed, the United States President took it upon himself to instruct African Heads of State and Government, by a circular letter, to insist on the withdrawal of Soviet and Cuban Advisers from Angola as a precondition for the withdrawal of South Africa(white minority regime's troops) and other military adventurers. This constitutes a most intolerable presumption and a flagrant insult on the intelligence of African rulers"(A.B. Akinyemi, 1979).

The Nigerian government's decision of November 1975, rejecting U. S. government advise not to recognize the MPLA government marked a turning point in African independence, and especially in Nigerian foreign policy. In a run-up to Angolan independence Nigeria opposed the U. S., which supported UNITA and FNLA, by strongly backing the MPLA and mobilizing the rest of Africa behind that position. The anti-American efforts, including military and material support to the MPLA, and diplomatic shuttles, was estimated to have cost Nigeria over $20 million. Many Nigerians believed that the assassination of General Murtala Muhammed in the abortive coup of February 13, 1976, led by Colonel Dimka was linked to U. S. determination to eliminate the threat posed by Nigeria. The U. S. later friendly overtures from the Carter administration, including a state visit in 1978, were in acknowledgement of Nigeria's new "African superpower" status, which arose not only from the Angolan connection but also from Nigeria's emergence as an oil power (Abegunrin, 1992, 72).

Nigeria allowed the Zimbabwe African National Union-Patriotic Front(ZANU-PF), as well as the South West African Peoples Organization(SWAPO), the African National Congress(ANC), and the Pan-African Congress(PAC) to open offices in Lagos.

Nigeria in effect became a member of the Frontline States, and insisted on the right to be consulted as such. Nigeria use its influence to bring pressure on Western powers, especially Britain and the U. S., to support decolonization of Southern Africa. Nigeria's Africa policy facilitated the process that brought Robert Mugabe's ZANU Patriotic Front to power in Zimbabwe in 1980.(Abegunrin, 1992). Nigeria's new-found status as an African leader and champion of anti-imperialism on the continent, particularly under Muhammed/Obasanjo regime, resonated in many other areas of its African policy.

This took the form of financial and material support to many African countries for a variety of purposes: to assist drought-affected countries like Ethiopia, Chad, Mali and Senegal; to assist newly independence countries like, Cape Verde, Sao Tome and Principe, Mozambique, Angola and Zimbabwe; and to Cameroon, Sudan, Gambia, and Zambia and other countries for miscellaneous reasons.

In addition, technical assistance was offered to Algeria, Botswana, the Gambia, Swaziland, and other countries, while scholarships were made available to students from all over the continent, most especially students from Southern Africa. Nigeria was particularly generous to its neighbors, partly to compensate them for their support for the federal government in the civil war and to elicit their support for the country's initiatives on regional integration. Nigeria sold oil at consessionary rates to West African countries, although this was also used to punish regimes to which Lagos was opposed, for example, Jerry Rawlings in Ghana in his first military government of 1979. Other acts of generosity included funding the building of a presidential palace, and a petroleum refinery in Lome, Togo; provision of electricity from the Kainji dam to Niger; and the granting of a N2 million interest-free loan to Republic of Benin. This was in addition to, among other projects, investing N7.2 million in joint cement and sugar projects and building the N1.8 million Idiroko-Port Novo stretch of the TransAfrican highway. Most of these donations were initiated by the Gowon regime, but one of the consequences of the petro-naira mentality was that financial assistance to African and black countries became an integral part of Nigeria's Africa policy. This was entrenched institutionally by the establishment of the US$80 million Nigeria Trust Fund at the African Development Bank(ADB) from which needy African countries could draw loans on easy terms. Such donations as these, even those which involved investment, were criticized at home as irrational display, squandering of wealth, and economic waste. At the West African sub-continental level, Nigeria maintained a policy of good neighborliness, and peaceful co-existence. The generous contributions to several African countries mentioned above was a major aim of this policy, as was involvement in the peaceful settlement of disputes between countries, and the search for solutions to protracted Chadian civil war (Gambari, 1989, 73-85).

By far the most important landmark of Nigeria's West African policy was the formation of the Economic Community of West African States(ECOWAS) in 1975, under Gowon administration. Regional integration was aimed amongst others, at consolidating the gains of good neighborliness and the above-mentioned peaceful co-existence, enhancing the bargaining and competitive capacities of the countries in the sub-region in their dealings with European Economic Community(EEC), now European Union(EU), and other economic powers, and underlining Nigeria's leadership roles (Edozien and Osagie, 1982). Given the suspicions, and envy with which many countries in the sub-region, especially the Francophones which already had formed their own economic communities, purposely to counter ECOWAS (the most notable of these was the Communaute Economique de l'Afrique de l'Ouest), the emergence of ECOWAS was scored as a major foreign policy achievement by the Gowon regime. The Muhammed/Obasanjo administration gave more attention to African continental wide issues, but they also worked to consolidate the gains of ECOWAS.

At the global level, there was a more positive approach to non-alignment, following the opening of diplomatic relations with the Soviet Union and other East European countries. There was also an attempt to extend Nigeria's delinkage from Britain, which had become a competitor in oil production (Britain's oil from the North sea),, by further diversification of trading partnerships. Thus, although it remained the major source of imports and destination of non-oil exports, Britain's share of Nigerian trade declined considerably, instead U. S. became Nigeria's most important trading partner, because she bought nearly half of the country's oil export. "By the same period, the U. S. consumed 58% of Nigeria's oil production, while Britain buys only 12%"(Abegunrin, 1992, 72). However, Nigerian-British relations, which had flourished under Gowon regime despite the civil war became turbulent under Muhammed/Obasanjo, whose populist and anti-imperialist policy and militant offensives against the Ian Smith white minority regime in Rhodesia, and the apartheid South Africa put Nigeria on a collision course with Britain. As was mentioned earlier, the British Petroleum(BP) and Barclays Bank assets in Nigeria were nationalized in 1978, over British violation of sanctions against Rhodesia. Relations deteriorated to its lowest point in 1976, when Britain was accused of complicity in the assassination of General Muhammed, and refused to extradite General Gowon to face charges over the coup.

The increased delinkage with Britain was part of Nigeria's emergent radicalism and assertiveness in its foreign policy, whose hallmarks were the efforts to establish its political and economic autonomy, positive non-alignment, and a challenge of U. S. and European hegemony. The attempts to indigenise the domestic economy, stepped up under the Muhammed/Obasanjo regime, were an integral part of the new orientation. Nigeria joined other developing countries to demand restructuring of the International Monetary Fund(IMF), the World Bank and General Agreement on Tariffs and Trade(GATT) which perpetuated Western hegemony, and a new world economic order. For these purposes it sought greater collective action by the developing world at forums, including the Non-Aligned Movement, and the Group of 77.

Nigeria was also instrumental in the formation of the Africa-Caribbean-Pacific(ACP) group which strengthened the bargaining power of those countries in economic agreements with the EEC/European Union. But the major factor of the country's autonomy-seeking foreign policy initiatives was the oil weapon which was reinforced by membership of Organization of Petroleum Exporting Countries (OPEC) where forces were joined with the powerful Arab states to establish a third force of power play in the international arena. But oil was also the major cause of the decline in the adventurous foreign policy in the early 1980s. The slump in oil prices, which was attributed to Western conspiracy, and the start of a period of recession forced Nigeria to relink with the capitalist industrial powers on terms dictated by them. This was to be the country's lot in the 1980s and 1990s.

FOREIGN POLICY IN THE SECOND REPUBLIC 1979-1983

The Obasanjo regime kept its promise and became the first military government to hand over power to an elected civilian regime. The 1979 presidential elections brought to power the government of Alhaji Shehu Shagari. The Shagari administration continued to support the African-centered policy of Muhammed/Obasanjo regime.

This was evident when President Shagari declared that, "Nigeria will no longer tolerate provocations by South Africa or the dilatory tactics of her allies in the Western bloc with regard to self-determination and majority rule in Namibia"(Tijani and Williams, 1981).

He further pledged Nigeria's support for armed struggle in South Africa, and pointed out that, "sanctions alone will not destroy apartheid and racism in South Africa. They can however, be used to support the armed struggle.... We shall continue to assist, encourage and support that struggle with all our might and resources"(Tijani and Williams, 1981). However, Otubanjo gave an insight into the Shagari administration's foreign policy as:

> The... regime of Shehu Shagari inherited a foreign policy which was very popular with the people as well as being the object of respect in the international system. But while adapting its principles, goals and rhetoric, the regime quickly showed that it neither had the zeal nor the competence to keep up the pace it inherited.... The result was that Nigeria's foreign policy remained at the level of routine observance of existing relations and obligations.... The four years of the regime were, therefore, a period of recess for Nigeria's foreign policy (Otubanjo, 1989, 6).

Assessment like this above under play the differences in the foreign policy setting between a military regime, which has its right of way, and is not accountable to the people, even when its policies are populist, and a democratic regime whose autonomy of action is seriously constrained by a complex network of legislative controls, intra, and inter-party differences, accountability to the electorates and so forth. In the case of Shagari administration, the crisis of legitimacy that attended his attainment of power in 1979, and the economic recession, mismanagement, and corruption of the regime, which imperiled the Second Republic, and caused Nigeria to risk losing the little amount of autonomy it had managed to execise in its foreign policy towards the Western Powers, under the Muhammed/Obasanjo administration.

Also this had consequences for foreign policy of the country under Shagari, and even after. However, foreign policy in the Second Republic was, like that of the First Republic, conservative, cautious, pro-Western and unpopular, which Okolo (1989) attributed to the fact that President Shagari was a political student of the Balewa government. President Shagari nevertheless, showed some flashes of non-conservatism, as in the strong opposition to the bloody coup d'etat that brought Master-Sergeant Doe to power in Liberia in 1980, and subsequent attempts to isolate the regime, and the opposition to the Reagan's policy of engagement in Southern Africa. But as was pointed out by Otubanjo, it was mainly just routine, meaning that Africa remained the centerpiece of the country's foreign policy.

At the African continental level, decolonization and eradication of racism remained the main focus, and the OAU, the UN, the Commonwealth, and other international forums were the major channels for articulating demands for sanctions and isolation of the white minority regime in South Africa, and mobilizing the support of other countries. Support for the liberation movements in Southern Africa was maintained, although in 1980, the decline in the economy led the federal government to stop the yearly allocation of $4 million to aid the liberation movements. However, immediately after the Zimbabwean independence, the Federal government gave a grant of $10 million to Zimbabwe.

The grant was to help Zimbabwe establish an institution for manpower training, and to enable Mugabe government to acquire the assets of the white-controlled Zimbabwe Herald newspapers from its white South African owners(Abegunrin, 1992, 177).

The Shagari administration pursued the anti-apartheid struggle in other spheres, although, more consciously than many Nigerians would have expected, especially in its dealings with the U. S. and other Western Powers. Following the pressures from home, and from the liberation movements, Shagari administration was forced to take a hard-line positions against the U. S. on Southern Africa. Thus, Nigeria opposed Reagan's so called "constructive engagement" policy in South Africa, and its linkage of the Namibian independence to the withdrawal of the Cuban troops from Angola. In other spheres of African relations, there were no major departures from the past, but there was considerable interest in the affairs of the OAU. Nigeria was strongly criticized for failing to rally support for the OAU summit in Tripoli, Libya in 1982. This was manifested in Nigeria's frontline role in hosting the OAU Economic Summit, which adopted the Lagos Plan of Action of 1980. The plan advocated African economic self-reliance, and the emergence of an African Common Market by the year 2000. Nigeria also provided troops for the OAU peace-keeping force in Chad(Gambari, 1989).

At the sub-regional level, commitments to ECOWAS were maintained, although the federal government was forced, as part of the desperate measures to arrest the precipitous decline in the economy and check the rising spate of religious riots in which several west African nationalities were claimed to have been involved, to adopt more realistic approaches to its policy of good neighborliness, and its role as a regional benefactor.

For this reason the Shagari administration embarked on a massive deportation of illegal aliens, originally from Ghana and other neighboring countries who had flooded Nigeria in the wake of the economic decline in their own countries. There was also a drastic reduction in aid to countries in the sub-region, although concessions continued to be made on oil sales. One area where Shagari administration drew serious criticisms, especially from the military leaders, was in its response to border disputes with Chad and Cameroon, and the incursions into Nigerian territory by soldiers from these countries, especially soldiers from Cameroon. Shagari's preference for "peaceful resolution," which top military officers saw as detrimental to Nigeria's status, was one of the factors that led to the overthrow by the military in 1983. The Shagari administration's Africa policy extended to the question of reparations. President Shagari brought the issue of reparations for Africa before the U.N. General Assembly. President Shagari declared that "Africa bears the scars of a long history of spoliation and deprivation, of the ravages of the slave trade and foreign aggression, of both political and economic injustices.... I believe the time has come for the international community to address itself to the serious issue of reparations and restitution for Africa"(Tijani and Williams, 1989, 90-91).

At the global level, Nigeria was preoccupied with negotiations with the IMF, and other Western creditors. The negotiations were stalled over the refusal of the Shagari regime to accept the hard conditionality of devaluation of naira and removal of oil subsidies, Nigeria also remained committed to OPEC despite strong pressures to pull out because of the limitations it placed on production quotas.

The final major notable global relations worth mentioning was the increased U. S. presence in the country, marked by the visit of Vice-President George Bush to Nigeria in 1982. This was in connection with Nigeria being a major supplier of oil to the U. S., and its assistance to Shagari's Green Revolution Program, and Nigeria's operation of U. S.-type of presidential System. Nevertheless, Britain remained a traditional ally, albeit its influence in Nigeria had waned considerably. During the Shagari administration oil production fluctuated and oil prices declined. Since about 90 percent of Nigeria's export earnings came from petroleum resource, it became more difficult to use economic power as an instrument of foreign policy. The diminished economic resources meant that Nigeria was less able to support its foreign policy declarations with actions. The "oil shock" affected Nigeria's declining economic fortunes, increased corruption, economic mismanagement, and intense divisions among political elite, especially after the elections of 1983, and rapidly declining living standards among the masses all provided a rational for the military coup of December 31, 1983.

FOREIGN POLICY UNDER MILITARY RULE 1984-1998: BUHARI ADMINISTRATION 1984-1985

When Major-General Muhammadu Buhari became the new head of state in 1984, the linkage between foreign and domestic policy was evident from the inception of the regime. A basic rationale for the coup was to arrest Nigeria's rapidly deteriorating economic situation and improve the well-being of the generality of Nigerians. Despite its pre-occupation with economic recovery, the Buhari regime managed to articulate an aggressive foreign policy posture in line with its claim to be an offshoot of the Muhammed/Obasanjo administration. However, the realities of the economic situation made its posture less adventurous than that of the previous military regime. The other major difference between the two regimes with implications for foreign policy was that in contrast to Muhammed/Obasanjo regime, the Buhari regime was unpopular with the vast majority of the people. Thus, even though some of its policies were well received at home, it could not match the wide acclaim that had added to the vibrancy of foreign policy of the Muhammed/Obasanjo administration. Support for Buhari regime's policies was muted.Given the regime's short life, which was not sufficient to make any lasting changes in Nigeria's foreign policy, we need only highlighted its most important initiatives. It kept Africa as the center-piece of foreign policy, and attempted to redress the weakness of the Shagari administration. As usual, South Africa and Namibia were at the top of the agenda, and the Reagan administration's policy of constructive engagement towards Southern Africa was opposed, even more vigorously than before. Monetary and other contributions to the liberation movements through the OAU liberation committee, which were suspended by the Shagari administration were restored, and foreign minister, Ibrahim Gambari, undertook a tour of the Frontline States to reassert Nigeria's commitment to the liberation struggles. Policy on South Africa received a great boost with the appointment of Joseph Garba, the exuberant former foreign affairs minister under Muhammed/Obasanjo regime, as the country's permanent representative to the U.N. ; and thus to the chairmanship of the anti-apartheid committee.

In addition, the federal government recognized Polisario as the legitimate government of the Saharawi Arab Democratic Republic(SADR), this facilitated the latter's admission to OAU membership. Within the West African sub-region, the realistic policies initiated by Shagari regime were maintained. This led to the second wave of expulsion of more illegal aliens, and the closing of borders to check smuggling and sabotage the change of the Nigerian currency-the naira. The regime also dealt decisively with the threats from Chad and Cameroon by stationing military contingents along the borders with those countries. At the global level, the Buhari regime, found itself unable to pursue the assertive policy of Muhammed/Obasanjo, mainly on account of the debt trap. Albeit, bold statements were made about the need for a new international economic order, these lacked substance. The continued decline of oil prices and the inability of OPEC to do much to change the situation, and the counter-trade and other alternative economic arrangements into which Nigeria was forced could not bring about the much desired autonomy of action.

The Buhari administration, for instance did not agree to the IMF conditionality, for devaluation of the naira, and abolition of petroleum subsidies, for borrowing loans or rescheduling debts. As a result, the Western creditors, led by Britain's Export Credits Guarantee Department(ECGD), rejected Nigeria's proposal to reschedule debt payments.(Forrest, 1989). The Buhari government was overthrown in August 1985, in a coup led by Major-General Ibrahim Babangida.

FOREIGN POLICY UNDER THE BABANGIDA REGIME 1985-1993

Like all other issues, foreign policy under Ibrahim Babangida was quite eventful. Although its cardinal goals, national interest, Pan-Africanism, good neighborliness and greater integration of the West African sub-region, remained basically unchanged. The period witnessed certain experiments, and bold initiatives which reinforced the country's claim to being a power in Africa. The most notable among these were the attempt to organize a "concert of medium powers," and introduction of the Technical Aid Corps program under the foreign ministership of Bolaji Akinyemi, the "economic diplomacy" initiative, the active response to the perceived threat from apartheid South Africa, the opening of diplomatic ties with Israel, and the deployment of a peace-keeping mission to the war-torn Liberia(Vogt, 1992). Nigeria enjoyed some good moments under Babandiga. In 1990 General Joseph Garba became president of the 44th session of the U.N. General Assembly, while Emeka Anyaoku became secretary-general of the Commonwealth. The government sponsored General Obasanjo's bid for the office of U.N. secretary-general, but did not succeed.

Despite being unsuccessful, it was a high point of the country's rising international profile. Nevertheless, as with previous regimes, there was little or no coherence, and continuity in the foreign policy initiatives. This was even more serious in the Babangida periods as the foreign policy arena greatly reflected the confusion, and political turbulence in the domestic scene. This situation proves that foreign policy of a nation is an extension of its domestic policy. This also shows Babangida's sad legacies in Nigerian political history.

For example, the minister of foreign affairs was changed five times under Babangida, Akinyemi, General Ike Nwachukwu, Rilwanu Lukman, again Nwachukwu and Mathew Mbu. As usual we shall analyze Babangida's foreign policy under three levels: the West African sub-region, Africa continent, and international environment. At the West African sub-regional setting, good neighborliness and ECOWAS remained the center of foreign policy. In pursuit of the former, borders closed for long periods under Buhari were reopened. Nigeria mediated, with varying degrees of success, and setbacks, in the seemingly intractable Chadian crisis, the border clashes between Mali and Burkina Faso, and the disputes between the leaders of Togo and Ghana. However, the decision to initiate the peacekeeping mission in Liberia under the aegis of ECOWAS stood out as the most remarkable and historic sub-continental peace initiative.

This was influenced by a number of factors, including, but most important was the close personal relations between Babangida, and the former president of Liberia- Samuel Doe which led Nigeria to support Liberia in many ways before the civil war started in that country; the evolution of a regional approach to solving regional problems which was welcomed by the United Nations, whose peacekeeping capacity was overstretched, and financially weak; the reluctance of the U. S. and other major powers to intervene; and the potential threat of the Liberian civil war to collective security of the sub-continent, and also its implications to the African continent as a whole(Vogt, 1992). The final factor, which made Ghana, Guinea, Sierra Leone, Gambia, Senegal, and other countries in West Africa sub-region readily to support Nigeria's initiative, had to do with what was perceived as a grand design by Mummar Gadafi's Libya to destabilize the sub-region, and install reactionary regimes in some of these countries. Using Burkina Faso as a springboard, Gadaffi sponsored Charles Taylor's declaration of war in Liberia. This action was to be only the first stage of a well planned process which quickly spread to Sierra Leone. The intricate involvements of Ivory Coast, Sierra Leone and Guinea, Liberia's neighbors in the war easily made it a sub-continental affairs, and Nigeria's deployment of troops to help the Sierra Leonian government ward off the rebels associated with Taylor's National Patriotic Front of Liberia(NPFL) in Liberia was part of its strategy to "contain" the crisis before it spread to the neighboring countries in the sub-region(Nwolise, 1992). This is a brief background of the formation of the ECOWAS Monitoring Group (ECOMOG) after the failure of several attempts by ECOWAS leaders to reconcile Doe and Taylor. The complexity of the issues in this war, opposition to ECOMOG by Ivory Coast, and Burkina Faso, tended to divide ECOWAS; the involvement of the U. S., Russia, France, and other foreign powers; Charles Taylor's NPFL's long drawn-out opposition to Nigeria's intervention on account of Babangida's closeness to Samuel Doe; and lack of clarity of ECOMOG's mission and mandate, was it for peacekeeping, peacemaking or peace enforcement, strongly militated against ECOMOG's efforts(Vogt, 1992).

Many Nigerians were very hostile towards the ECOMOG initiative, which they saw as extension of Babangida's personalization of the country's foreign policy.

Most important concern was the wastage of Nigeria's dwindling resources, and the several losses of lives (Nigerian soldiers), and weapons in the protracted civil war in Liberia. Nigeria was chief financier of ECOMOG, although the U. S. supported Nigeria's initiative and at various points made financial, and logistics contributions, including $2.8 million in 1990. The exact size of Nigeria's total expenditure was not known, because the Babangida regime refused to disclose it to the Nigerian people; but was believed to have been a major, and an expensive economic waste for the country's revenue from 1990, till the end of that war in 1997.

The windfall from oil sales during the Gulf war in 1991 was believed to have been wasted on Liberian war. According to one source an estimates of N470 million, following the original overall ECOMOG budget of N500 million (Babawale, 1995); but according to African Guardian, September 28, 1992, Nigeria's total expenditure was over N2.8 billion. "Domestic hostility, the mismanagement of the country's resources in the name of ECOMOG and the apparent complication of the intractable civil war in Liberia due to

ECOMOG's intervention cast a shadow over what was without doubt a pioneering, and commendable foreign policy initiative"(Vogt, 1992).

During the Babangida administration, however, Nigeria did a lot to reactivate ECOWAS which went into a rapid decline in the early 1980s, especially during the Shagari's administration. The country continued to carry the largest budget of the organization, its average annual contribution was 33.3 per cent. Nigeria built, furnished, and maintain its secretariat, host its summits in 1986, 1987, and 1991; chair the organization when no other country was willing to do so, and provide various forms of support to member states including, most important, oil concessions, and financial aid. Nigeria also championed the restructuring of ECOWAS in other important areas. In 1990, a comprehensive trade liberalization scheme involving relaxation of the restriction on the free movement of unprocessed goods, handicrafts and industrial goods was adopted. This complemented the minimum agenda for action, which entailed signing the second phase of the protocol on the free movement of persons, goods and services, as well as implementing the ECOWAS insurance program. As part of the moves towards monetary cooperation, Ecobank, and the West African Clearing House were established. Despite this progress, the growth of ECOWAS continued to be retarded by the separatism of the Francophone countries and suspicions of Nigeria's "big brother" gestures. At the continental level, OAU remained the major channel of the "traditional " commitments to eradication of apartheid system in South Africa, liberation of the entire continent from colonial rule, and the advancement of unity. Babangida became the OAU chairman in 1991, when Nigeria hosted the organization's summit. In 1986, Nigeria led thirty-two other countries in boycotting the Commonwealth games in Edinburgh, Scotland, in protest of Britain's reluctance to apply comprehensive sanctions against the apartheid regime in South Africa, and continued to function as an honorary Frontline State. Nigeria also maintained its financial contributions to the liberation movements from both private, and official contributions to the Southern African Relief Fund(created by the Muhammed/Obasanjo regime, in 1976), and Namibia Solidarity Fund.

For instance, in 1989, Nigeria gave SWAPO $1.5 million, the ANC $1 million, and the PAC $600,000. Nigeria continued to chair the U.N. anti-apartheid committee, and General Obasanjo was appointed to the Commonwealth's Eminent Persons Group in 1986, as a recognition of the country's role in the liberation struggle. The release of Nelson Mandela in February 1990, after twenty-seven years imprisonment, and the subsequent negotiations to end apartheid were celebrated in Nigeria as a major victory. Nigeria continued to play a leading role in the search for a peaceful settlement.

This was evident by F. W. De Klerk's visit to Nigeria during his diplomatic shuttle across Africa at the times of the South African negotiations for democratic majority rule. Besides, Southern African liberation, Nigeria pursued the goal of African unity, and development in decisive ways. It played the role of a mediator in several internal disputes, including those in Uganda, and unending civil war in Angola, although most of these efforts were channeled through the OAU. It played very crucial roles in the formation of, and signing of the treaty for, the African Economic Community in 1991, as well as the establishment of a Department for Conflict Prevention, Management and Resolution in the OAU. Under Babangida regime, Nigeria made donations both in cash and kind to several countries, purposely to make good its image, an example was the monetary assistance given to Zimbabwe when that country hosted the Non Aligned Movement summit in 1990.

Nigeria's most notable African policy innovation by far was the introduction of the Technical Aid Corps Program(TAC) in 1987. This program was conceived in lines of the peace corps in the U. S.; the program involved the sending of Nigerian graduates and professionals - medical doctors, nurses, engineers, lawyers, teachers, and others, to various African countries, Caribbean, and Pacific countries, completely at Nigeria's expense. This program was used to boost the country's image and status as a major contributor to the Third World, and particularly African development (Osaghae, 1998). At the global level, Nigeria maintained its pro-Western posture in trade, and other socio-economic and political relations, and the legacy of colonialism was evident as the regime attempted to address the persistent economic hardship by restructuring the domestic economy. Babangida encountered the same difficulties as Buhari administration, as he attempted to get Nigeria's debt rescheduled. The IMF, a Western dominated institution, continued to insist on conditionalities that resulted, in increased economic hardship among Nigerians. Nevertheless, "when the regime introduced the so-called Structural Adjustment Program(SAP) in 1986, this was expected to increase its ability to borrow and enable it to reschedule its debt. However, problems relating to debt rescheduling persisted despite SAP"(King, 1998). As usual, debt rescheduling, procurement of more credit lines and promotion of foreign investment were the main themes of the so-called "economic diplomacy" which was vigorously pursued under General Nwachukwu as the foreign minister. Nigeria remained a committed member of OPEC, which continued to peg member countries' production quotas in its bid to shore up oil prices in the international market.

However, in 1987, purposely to strengthen the use of the oil weapon by African countries, following the example of the Organization of Arab Petroleum Exporting Countries(OAPEC), and as part of "economic diplomacy", Nigeria joined Algeria, Angola, Republic of Benin, Libya, Cameroon, Gabon, and Congo to establish the African Petroleum Producers Association (APPA). Ivory Coast, Egypt, Democratic Republic of Congo (formely Zaire), and Equatorial Guinea, joined the association in 1988.

The main objective of APPA was to promote cooperation among member states in hydrocarbon exploration, production, refining, petrochemicals, manpower development, and acquisition, and adoption of technology. "APPA never became any serious strategic benefit to Nigeria, since member states found it difficult to reconcile their divergent interests. OPEC therefore, remained the country's main collective platform for employing the oil weapon."(Osaghae, 1998).Nigeria remained committed to the U. N., the Commonwealth, and the Non-Aligned Movement through which position on major global issues were articulated. During the Babangida regime, Nigeria became a full member of the Organization of Islamic Countries (OIC), although, this had no significant impact on foreign policy, except for the emergence of Islamic financial institutions in the country. Also Babangida regime restored normal relations with Britain, which was strained under the Buhari regime, strengthened existing relations with Germany, and France, and established diplomatic relations with Israel. The tie with Israel was a major achievement considering the historical opposition of the conservative Northern Muslims leaders to relations with that country. It should be noted that Babangida's virtual dependence on Israeli security was very crucial to the restoration of ties. It was Israeli security protection that saved (him) Babangida in the April 1990 bloody coup, that led him to move from Lagos to Abuja the new capital, shortly after that coup.

The international community was not very supportive of Nigeria in the Babangida years because of the criminal activities of the regime, especially the leadership committed several unspeakable atrocious that led to its loss of its credibility, both domestically and internationally. For example, the country's emergent image as a major channel in the international drug trade (Klein, 1994), led to the decertification of Nigeria by the U. S., resulting in blocking of aid, and the placing of an embargo on direct airflights between the U. S. and Nigeria. This was a major and serious foreign policy problem, but a more serious problem with the international community, especially, the United States and other Western powers, arose over the scuttling, and unending of the democratic transition process. Seen the authoritarian, oppressive rule, criminal activities, and the human rights abuse of the Babangida regime, the Western powers lent material, and other necessary forms of support to the Non-governmental Organizations, and pro-democracy movements which spearheaded the stirring up of civil society, and forced Babangida out of office. The anti-militarism (led by National Democratic Coalition-NADECO), of the Babangida years and after was encouraged by the favorable and supportive international opinion, and the direct criticisms and opposition to military regimes by the Western Powers.

THE "SURVIVALIST" FOREIGN POLICY OF THE ABACHA REGIME 1993-1998

The anti-militarism, and the serious pressures both from the domestic civil society, human rights groups, and the international community, after the annulment of the June 12, 1993 elections, apparently won by M. K. O. Abiola, forced Babangida out of office on August 26, 1993. This paved the way for an Interim National Government (ING) that he created by decree, and assumed power on August 27, 1993.

The ING was headed by Ernest Shonekan. The ING continued the foreign policy of the Babangida administration, but the regime was short lived. The Shonekan led ING, was very unpopular nation-wide, and pressured by the military, eventually resigned after three months in office. General Sani Abacha immediately took over, and set up his own government in November 1993. The Abacha regime claimed its intention to honor Nigeria's international obligations, and solicited for international support. At the same time, Abacha was dismantling all of the democratically elected institutions at the local, state, and national levels. The international community very strongly protested this action, and the continued refusal of the military to restore democracy in Nigeria. Indeed, any remaining credibility of the military dissipated with this latest betrayal of the Nigerian electorates by the military dictator. Meanwhile the Abacha regime became ever more dictatorial, very brutal, ruthless, and oppressive. Abacha represented the most tragic era in Nigeria history up to this point.

Nigeria's effectiveness in international affairs deteriorated to its lowest point ever, under the Abacha regime. The hostility towards the Abacha regime, and its condemnation both domestically, and internationally was intensified, and his foreign policy was mostly reactive and incoherent. However, Abacha concentrated his energies mainly on consolidating his hold on the country, and working on getting the international recognition and acceptance, therefore, foreign policy was made to serve the need of this struggle for survival, recognition, and consolidation. Thus the activities of the foreign-based "opposition" and ways to combat them became a major determinant of foreign policy for the Abacha regime. Therefore, foreign policy was turned to a survivalist imperative, and a strategy to divert attention away from the internal crises and tensions. Another Abacha strategy to cause distractions was what he called the "war" declared on foreign based oppositions, and Western imperialists who were accused of a conspiracy to destroy Nigeria, the clash with South Africa, and the border disputes with Cameroon over Bakassi peninsula (Osaghae, 1998). As was previously done under each regime, we shall examine the Abacha administration's foreign policy at the regional, continental and global levels. At the West African sub-regional level, ECOWAS remained the major focus, but Abacha regime was less active than it had been in the Babangida regime. one of the reasons responsible for this, was due to the francophone countries being more involved in the affairs of a parallel economic union, the West African Economic and Monetary Union (UMEOA), formed in January 1994, following the devaluation of the CFA franc. From that time the Francophone heads of states rarely attended the annual summits, and ECOWAS became increasingly an Anglophone affairs. The second reason was that most countries in West Africa were seriously troubled by political instability, and economic decline, and were each preoccupied with solving these problems.

Nigeria itself was in the same situation, and between 1994 and 1995, Abacha did not attend ECOWAS summits, and other crucial meetings, due to domestic economics, and political crises confronting him. However, in 1996, Abacha became chairman of ECOWAS, and Nigeria seemed set once again to salvage the organization.

This was part of Abacha's isolationist, and survivalist policy, as well as part of his strategy of the preparation for transformation to a civilian president, planned for August 1998, but Abacha's self-succession plan died with him. ECOMOG remained the most important collective undertaking in which Nigeria was involved, but the intractability of the Liberian civil war led to threats by Ghana, the other major participant in the peace-keeping mission, to pull out. Nigeria also considered pulling out, but its involvement in this war was very unpopular at home, but the international acclaim from its involvement was seen as a good counter-balance to its isolation, and condemnation, dissuaded Abacha regime from pulling out. The ECOWAS summit at Abuja in July 1996 initiated a new peace offensive under which an interim government was formed in Liberia, and the warring factions agreed to disarm, and prepare for elections. Outside ECOWAS Nigeria maintained its shaky sub-continental "superpower" role despite its increasing insolvency. However, Nigerian troops remained in Sierra Leone where they assisted the government of that country in warding off rebel attacks. Abacha regime pursued other collective development projects, one of which was the gas pipeline project jointly funded by Nigeria, Togo, and Ghana, involving the laying of pipes to supply gas from Nigeria to these other countries. The agreement on this project was signed in September 1995.Nigeria's relations with other countries in the region was also affected by the regime's determination to contain opposition activities, as well as the responses of these countries to its isolation by Western powers. For example, relations with neighboring countries, such as the Republic of Benin, under President Soglo were strained by that country's support for the oppositions. Relations only improved after Matthew Kerekou, a long-time friend of Nigeria, returned to power after defeating Soglo in the 1996 elections. However, Nigeria made efforts to secure the support of other West African States in its struggles against the Western-led international oppositions, including South Africa, especially when it boycotted the 1996 African football Cup of Nations hosted by South Africa. For this purpose, it relied partly on article 83 of the revised ECOWAS treaty which provided for the formulation, and adoption of 'common policies on issues relating to international negotiations with third parties in order to promote and safeguard the interests of the region,' but its efforts on this were unsuccessful.

The policy of good neighborliness was mostly shaped by the regime's survivalist agenda. There was much more serious problems with Cameroon which grew out of the long-standing dispute over the Bakassi peninsula. There were constant skirmishes, and a few serious battles between the armies of the two countries, as well as a massive build-up of military units along the borders. Nigeria constantly accused Cameroon of being the aggressor, and of having French backing. Several unsuccessful efforts were made to resolve the dispute, including mediation by the international Court of Justice. However, this worked in Nigeria's favor in so far as this continuous crisis helped to divert attention away from the problems at home, but temporarily(King, 1998). At the continental level, the end of apartheid, and the entry of South Africa on the scene as a major power, brought changes which seriously affected Nigeria's policy towards the continent.

With apartheid gone and the entire African continent liberated from the last vestiges of colonialism, the only major issue which previously gave coherence to the country's policies had been removed. Even the OAU, which was a major channel of Nigeria's African policy, seemed to have lost its relevance, at least for the time being.

In the process of charting a new African policy in the post-apartheid era, it is inevitable that Nigeria would sooner or later have to confront South Africa, as its rival for continental leadership. It has started, with South Africa been able to conduct successfully, two democratic elections within five years, whereas, Nigeria with almost forty years of independence still unable to do so and not able to maintain democratic rule and political stability. The opportunity came through South Africa's attempt to play a leading role in the resolution of the Nigerian crisis. Initially, Abacha regime seemed ready to accept South Africa's intervention which, unlike that attempted by Western powers, was based on dialogue and mutual respect. Thus Mandela's emissaries, Archbishop Desmond Tutu and Vice-President Thabo Mbeki, achieved good result with the coup trial and detention of political activists, where others have failed. But even at that stage, strains could be observed in the relations between the two countries, because of South Africa's open-door policy towards the opponents of the Abacha regime, especially the Nigerian pro-democracy groups. Relations deteriorated to the lowest point after the killings of the nine Ogoni leaders in November 1995, which President Mandela considered a personal blow since he had received assurances that these activists would not be killed. Mandela decision to champion the African arm of the international opposition while other African states maintained a low profile and had muted reactions to the executions, led to accusations by Abacha regime that South Africa was a stooge of Western powers. Abacha went to the extent of accusing Mandela that he was not a "true African nationalist." At the height of the bad relations, Nigeria withdrew from the 1996 African football Cup of Nations which South Africa hosted. The Abacha regime gave an execuse for this action that, the country withdrew on the ground that the South African authorities had refused to guarantee the safety, and security of its contingent. However, steps were initiated to restore normal relations between the two countries, but things were not normal as they were before the November 1995, Ogoni killings, and relations were cool until after the death of Abacha on June 8, 1998.

It was at the global level that the Abacha regime faced the worst opposition and hostility from the very beginning. Abacha's adamant nationalism, and ruthless dictatorship which, led to the abrogation of liberalization policies in 1994, and his anti-Western stance on many issues, reinforced this hostility. The U. S., and other Western powers actively encouraged and supported opposition groups in the country as well as those abroad. Late in 1994, the former military head of state, and now newly elected President of Nigeria, Olusegun Obasanjo, and his deputy Shehu Musa Yar'Adua were alleged of plotting a coup d'etat to overthrow Abacha regime.

They were tried and sentenced to life imprisonment early in 1995, but later commuted to 15 years in prison. The international opposition to Abacha dictatorial rule reached its height with the Ogoni killings in November 1995. Nigeria was suspended from the Commonwealth instantly.

This was followed in December 1995, when the U. N. General Assembly's social, humanitarian, and cultural committee representing all the 185 members of that organization overwhelmingly condemned Nigeria's execution of Saro-wiwa, and eight of his members of his movement. The U. S. increased its sanctions against Nigeria, but refused to place an embargo on oil trade with the country. (King, 1998, 27). Abacha's response to the international opposition to his regime was to invoke the non interference clause of the U.N. and other international organizations to oppose interference, in the internal affairs of the country; and sought to rally the support of other third world states, especially the pariah states like Nigeria itself, Libya, Iran, Iraq, Sudan, and Syria. As during the Nigerian civil war in 1960s, the Abacha regime searched for alternative allies in the Arab countries, and the old Eastern bloc, but not much was achieved. Still the major channels of its global policies remained the U. N., and for major economic policies it remained committed to OPEC, of which a former Nigerian foreign affairs and petroleum minister, Lukman Rilwanu, was Secretary-general. In spite of all this, the country remained pro-Western, and the U. S., Britain, Germany, and France its major trading partners.

CONCLUSION: NIGERIA'S FOREIGN POLICY IN THE YEAR 2000 AND BEYOND

The persistence of military rule in Nigeria is inimical to its foreign policy. This is especially so since more and more African people are demanding a voice in their government, and democratic movements are challenging authoritarian, and dictatorial regimes throughout Africa. Still, the forces of the colonial heritage, Pan-Africanism, and Non-alignment are likely to continue to provide continuity in Nigerian foreign policy whether the regime is civilian or military. Since the independence in 1960, Nigerian governments have been leading actors in Africa, and have pursued foreign policies commensurate to the country's perceived standing. During the 1970s, a clear policy focus, matched by some economic power, gave the country an important stake in the African continent, and its policy overtures beyond the continent were consequently listened to with some respect. In this sense, the country gained status within the international community, which at times translated into real influence. Since the early 1980s, and particularly during the 1990s, a combination of forces, some of which we have spelt out in the previous pages, have brought a deterioration in both domestic and external factors that influence foreign policy options, and orientations.

It would be wrong to claim that Nigeria has lost all its capability in policy; rather, it has failed to exert influence to the extent that it did in the past. As in other African states, a troubled position in the contemporary global economy limits its options, and the country's failure to develop a diversified competitive economy and to democratize indicates a continuing weakness in pursuing foreign policy issues beyond the continent.

The ongoing inertia of ECOWAS, combined with the real potential of the new South Africa, appear also to limit, and is going to limit Nigeria's continental role in this coming twenty-first century. But Nigeria still retains some options and potentials. Transfer of power to a capable, well disciplined, uncorrupted, and democratically elected civilian government in 1999 could provide fresh impetus to the economy, to human rights, to relations with the major industrial powers, and to better policy overall.

Unfortunately, this appears unlikely. Nigeria's potential is considerable without any doubt, especially within the West African sub-region. However, without corrective actions, it will simply remain potential, and the country's aspirations of continental and regional leadership will remain unfulfilled, as well as its hopes of becoming the continent's largest democracy.

Chapter IX

THE SIERRA LEONE IMBROGLIO:
A PERSPECTIVE ON THE QUESTION OF NIGERIA'S
INVOLVEMENT

Nowamagbe A. Omoigui

In 1971 Sierra Leone became a republic with Siaka Stevens as President. Subsequently, along with Nigeria, Liberia and 12 other West African nations, Sierra Leone became a signatory to the Treaty of Lagos, which established ECOWAS on May 28, 1975 barely two months before the overthrow of General Gowon. But following elections in 1977, Stevens adopted a socialist style constitution in 1978 making the country a one-party state under the All People's Congress (APC). Stevens survived a number of assassination attempts, of which the most perilous was organized by one Brigadier Bangura in 1971. Then Corporal Foday Sankoh was arrested and jailed along with others for an attempted coup, but released seven years later in a 1978 amnesty and dismissed from the Army. Siaka Stevens' tenure was also marked by many riots as well as political scandals. Upon his retirement in 1985, propelled by his preference for a strong hand to maintain internal security, he appointed Army Chief Major-General Joseph Saidu Momoh as President. This decision was rubber stamped by the APC which made Momoh the sole candidate in the elections. However, once in power, citing continuing unrest, Momoh appointed a "national unity" civilian cabinet and publicly dissociated himself from Stevens' policies. But all was not well. The country continued to decline economically and the alienation of its peasant class continued. Inspite of its diamonds, the country was fast becoming the poorest in the world. Life expectancy for men and women was 41 and 45 years respectively. In 1989 Momoh put down a coup attempt. By 1990 peasants had begun boycotting private and public transport because of exorbitant fares and illegal taxes. Faced with public disclosures of massive corruption among government officials the Newspaper Amendment Act of April 1990 was passed to control and suppress information flow. Faced with growing calls for a multiparty system the government initially reacted by placing ministers and members of parliament who were deemed sympathetic to multipartyism under surveillance for treason. But other events in the subregion were to take on significance in Sierra Leone.

NIGERIA, ECOWAS, OAU AND THE UN WADE IN AS THINGS FALL APART

On Christmas eve of 1989, the Liberian warlord Charles Taylor (who had escaped from a Boston jail) launched an attack from Ivory Coast with the intent of removing President (former Master-Sergeant) Samuel Doe from power. This attack introduced a new element into West African politics. Encouraged by Nigeria, the Economic Community of West African States (ECOWAS) viewed the development with alarm and deployed a military monitoring group (ECOMOG) to Liberia in 1990. Nigerian troops were thus inserted into the minefield of "Mano River" politics, eventually reaching a strength of almost 6,000 (2 infantry brigades) in Liberia and 1,000 (1 infantry battalion) in Sierra Leone by 1996. In 1991, following the eruption in Liberia, two major developments took place in Sierra Leone. Ex-Corporal Foday Sankoh founded the Revolutionary United Front (RUF) to take up arms against the system.

Crossing in from Liberia, the first attacks were launched in March, exemplified by decapitations in the eastern Kailahun district. Major-General Joseph Momoh held a referendum for a multi-party system, which was endorsed by 60% of voters. Six parties came together to form the United Front of Political Movements (UNIFORM).

On April 29 1992, pre-empting the introduction of a multiparty system, President Momoh was overthrown by 26 year old Captain Valentine Strasser who styled himself initially as 'Chairman of the National Provisional Ruling Council' but later changed this to 'Chairman of the Supreme Council of State'. Barely 8 months later in December, Strasser arrested nine of his colleagues and had them executed for an alleged coup plot along with 17 other prisoners. In part because of economic sanctions imposed by Britain in 1993 and other types of international pressure, (UN, OAU, ECOWAS) Strasser eventually made a commitment to a 2-year transition to civil rule. But in January 1996 Strasser was overthrown by Brigadier Julius Maada Bio allegedly because Strasser was in the process of reneging on his promise to hand over to civilians. Brigadier Bio kept his word and supervised multiparty elections a few weeks later in February. The February 1996 elections were violent but adjudged "free and fair" by international observers and monitors. Both RUF rebels and Government troops were accused of cutting off people's hands to prevent them from voting! However, about 60% of the electorate reportedly turned out and elected Alhaji Dr. Ahmed Tejjan Kabbah of the Sierra Leone People's Party as their President.

Once in power President Kabbah was initially preoccupied with putting down the rebellion of the RUF militarily. Dissatisfied with the performance of the regular Army, he encouraged the arming of traditional hunters, the largest faction of which were the Mende "Kamajors" in a Civil Defense Militia. As might be expected, the Army was resentful - Major Johnny Paul Koroma and others were arrested in September on charges of coup-plotting. Parallel to these events, although the RUF did not recognize the elections they agreed nonetheless to meet with Kabbah. This led to the November 1996 Abidjan Accord for which the government of Cote d'Ivoire, the UN, OAU and Commonwealth were to act as "moral guarantors". A crisis of confidence soon developed, however, and Foday Sankoh was detained by Nigeria on March 2, 1997 on charges of possession of arms and ammunition. Two months later, mutinous Sierra Leonean soldiers in pick-up trucks broke into the Freetown prison and released Major Johnny Paul Koromah. They seized power after a firefight with ECOMOG (Nigerian) Guards deployed at the State House and National Assembly as part of an ECOMOG arrangement to protect the government against the RUF. The National Treasury was burnt down. Kabbah escaped to Guinea. Major Koromah assumed power on May 25, accusing Kabbah of foot dragging on the Abidjan Accord.

He then invited the RUF to help form the government alongside the "Armed Forces Revolutionary Council." (AFRC) The coup was opposed by the international community as well as the Kamajors. Within Freetown there was an initial attempt at civil disobedience as well as massive emigration by much of the country's legal elite.

But clumsy military attempts by Nigerian troops in Sierra Leone to dislodge the coupist failed. A Nigerian unit was even surrounded and held hostage. Nigeria's ruler, General Abacha, himself a coupist, was not amused. A "cat and mouse" game then began in which attempts at negotiated settlement were launched while the Koromah regime consolidated and secured support allegedly from countries like Burkina Faso, Liberia, Libya and others in Eastern Europe. Every now and then a fire-fight would break out with ECOMOG units. ECOMOG, meanwhile was gradually reinforcing its positions in the country while working out its own internal differences on the use of force. ECOWAS was by no means united on the issue. Kabbah continued to muster the international community. The Commonwealth suspended Sierra Leone from membership in July just as the Sierra Leone government-in-exile was engaging 'Sandline International', led by former British Commandos to provide technical support for a counter-coup. In neighboring Liberia, an internationally brokered peace accord enabled a presidential election in August which led to the transformation of Charles Taylor from warlord to President.

On October 8, 1997 the UN imposed an oil and arms embargo against Sierra Leone and authorized ECOMOG to enforce the embargo. On October 23, 1997 the "Conakry" accord was reached guaranteeing the coup leaders safe passage while assuring the peaceful return to power of Kabbah on April 22, 1998 preceeded by disarmament and demobilization of combatants. This plan was to be monitored by ECOMOG, assisted by UN military observers. Like the Abidjan accord, this agreement was not implemented either. By January 1998 it was apparent that Koromah had no real intention of keeping his word, particularly the item that called for demobilization of combatants. In a curious twist of fate, the opportunity afforded by Charles Taylor's insistence on the premature disengagement of thousands of Nigerian troops from Liberia provided a cover for the prepositioning of operational units in Sierra Leone to enforce the Conakry accord. Beginning on February 5, 1998, civil defense units (Kamajors) launched an attack in the Bo and Kenema areas against the junta. Reportedly responding to an attack by junta forces, ECOMOG (Nigerian) troops overran Freetown, and subsequently moved to secure the rest of the country. President Kabbah was restored on March 10. The UN lifted its Arms and Oil embargo three days later.

Furor erupted in London when it became known publicly that Sandline International had provided helicopters for logistic support and reportedly arranged air freight for 35 tons of Bulgarian automatic rifles in contravention of an existing UN Arms embargo to which Britain was a signatory. A major road in Freetown was named after late General Sani Abacha, then Nigeria's leader, while then Colonel (now Brigadier) Maxwell Khobe who led ECOMOG (Nigerian) troops into Freetown, was named Sierra Leone's Chief of Defense Staff charged with rebuilding the Sierra Leonean military establishment. Although many were captured, including a large helicopter-borne batch that was apprehended while escaping to Liberia, quite a number of former junta leaders (including Major Koromah) eluded arrest. As they retreated from the ECOMOG onslaught they implemented a scorched earth policy, inflicting mindless violence on civilians in much the same way as became standard during the Liberian civil war next door.

However, the RUF and Junta rebels added a new subregional twist - wholesale mutilations and machete amputations of limbs - on a scale far beyond what had been reported during the 1996 elections. Children and women were not spared. People were also raped, shot, and burned alive. Some had their body parts eaten raw in an ancient cannibalistic ritual designed to transfer the strength of the victim to the malefactor.

It must be mentioned that although an external appearance of pride and gratitude for ECOMOG's success in Sierra Leone was projected, internal differences among ECOWAS members soon emerged. Indeed, at a March 12 ECOWAS ministerial summit in Yamoussoukro shortly after Kabbah returned to Freetown, divisions emerged among ECOWAS member states on issues of force structure, legality, control and deployment of ECOMOG as the basis for a strategic peace-keeping mechanism in the region. While Nigeria pushed for the retention of ECOMOG as constituted to remain as a standing peace-keeping army, francophone states like Burkina Faso, Cote d'Ivoire, Senegal and Togo were more interested in pre-positioning task-oriented troops in different countries to be assembled as needed on a case to case basis. The fear was that a standing ECOMOG army as a Nigerian dominated force would evolve into hatchet-man for Nigeria's dictates in the region. Charles Taylor of Liberia, a longtime ally of Foday Sankoh, was not pleased with the ECOMOG (Nigerian) offensive. In his usual passive-aggressive style, he not only fussed about the interception of AFRC renegades in Liberian airspace but also moved to accelerate his efforts to get ECOMOG to remove its headquarters from Monrovia thus denying it a logistic hinge-point from which to launch ground operations in Sierra Leone next door. This was inspite of the Liberian peace accord which had brought him to power after a supervised election and assured a role for ECOMOG in restructuring and retraining the Armed Forces of Liberia. [Paradoxically, Taylor's push in January to get ECOMOG out of Liberia may have accelerated the demise of the Koromah regime.]

The UN on the other hand, commended ECOWAS. In June, the UN Security Council established a monitoring unit in Sierra Leone (UNOMSIL). It had both a military and a civilian element contributed by many countries and a projected one year budget of over

31 million dollars. In support of the government of Sierra Leone and ECOMOG, the disarmament, demobilization and reintegration of about 33,000 former combatants was a key objective. UNOMSIL observers were later deployed alongside ECOMOG units in Freetown, Bo, Kenema, and Makeni as well as the Lungi and Hastings airports. Given the estimated 500,000 refugees displaced within and outside the country (Guinea, Liberia, Cote d'Ivoire, Gambia and Senegal), the UN also continued to appeal to all member states to provide humanitarian assistance. As the rainy season began, activities of the AFRC/RUF rebels lulled but this eventually turned out to be a pause to regroup and rearm. The lull in guerrilla activities appeared coordinated with an apparent improvement in relations between Liberia and Sierra Leone and coincided serendipitously with a government ban on diamond mining as well as the sudden cardiac death of Nigerian strongman General Sani Abacha in early June. On July 25, the new Nigerian leadership released RUF Leader Foday Sankoh to the Sierra Leonean government.

Meanwhile Kabbah had set up treason trials in five Freetown courts against persons who were allegedly involved in the May 1997 putsch. Of the 96 initially charged, 77 were later sentenced to death. In early November, another 16 of 21 defendants were found guilty of collaborating with the former AFRC. Former President Joseph Momoh was also sentenced to jail. Beginning in late August and September during the run-up to the Sierra Leonean dry season, RUF/AFRC rebel attacks resumed in force revealing a level of determination, organization and strength in numbers and equipment which surprised ECOMOG and UNOMSIL observers even as they issued "rebel body counts" and public statements to the contrary. In mid-October, 24 military officers were shot for their part in the 1997 coup while Foday Sankoh himself was subsequently found guilty of treason on October 23. Along with other civilians so convicted, he is appealing the verdict. Competition by international Lawyers to defend Sankoh has been intense with several bids as large as almost $5,000 daily plus expenses. Not to be outdone, a Nigerian legal team offered to do the job for $2,000 daily. Eventually a British MP and former conservative government Agriculture Minister got the nod, with an international human rights organization underwriting costs. Subsequently, mutually suspicious Liberian (Taylor), Sierra Leonean (Kabbah) and Guinean (Conte) leaders met in a subregional 'Mano River Union' summit in November and issued the usual exhortations to work toward better relations. This was particularly crucial at the time because of flared tempers resulting from an alleged coup plot against Taylor which had led to shooting in Monrovia as Taylor attempted to arrest Roosevelt Johnson, a former rival warlord and now cabinet minister. Kabbah had allegedly tipped Taylor off about the putsch but Taylor later turned around to accuse Kabbah of "meddling." Taylor, on the other hand, was opposed to the executions of convicted AFRC/RUF elements and repeatedly put pressure on Kabbah to negotiate a political solution to the crisis even as Kabbah was accusing Taylor of backing the RUF. Clearly, there was no trust.

By December it was clear that UN sanctions targeted at non-governmental organizations in Sierra Leone were not being enforced. The rebels had signaled that not only were they better armed and trained than had hitherto been the case, they were well on their way in executing a major dry season offensive, advancing southwards towards Freetown from the North-west and diamond-mining eastern region in a move they said was aimed at "forcing the government to the negotiating table." But this was not all. The rebels also implemented a wave of kidnappings of priests and journalists while maiming and killing any "neutral" civilians along with agents of the state, including policemen. As if the conflict with the AFRC/RUF was not enough, the Kabbah government had to deal with a University lecturers strike and appeal against massive corruption among civil servants demanding bribes before service - for long a key grievance of the rebels.Faced with an increasing threat, Kabbah offered conditional amnesty to five important rebel commanders; ECOMOG imposed selective curfews; while Kamajor militia resorted to executions of suspected rebel sympathizers as well as illegal diamond miners. Civil Defence units also attempted to create a buffer zone along the Liberian border to prevent infiltration.

Many demobilized former soldiers of the Republic of Sierra Leone Military Forces (RSLMF) were re-inducted by the Sierra Leone government to fight alongside ECOMOG and the Kamajors against the AFRC/RUF rebels. This turned out to be mistake because many of these soldiers simply switched sides at critical junctures.On December 19, the alliance of deposed RSLMF and RUF rebels seized the diamond town of Koidu and then advanced on Makeni while probing ECOMOG defenses at Waterloo. ECOMOG renforcements, (long sought after by both Generals Khobe and Shelpidi) were rushed in by Nigeria. But by December 30 rebels had captured Lunsar, an important road junction. Panic gripped Freetown. Foreign nationals as well as international workers were evacuated, anticipating full fledged urban warfare. The pattern in each town was similar. Rebels would probe, then ECOMOG would withdraw "to save civilian lives" or "prevent our lines of communication from being cut off." Now and again ECOMOG would retake their previously held positions. It was the typical scenario of a regular army fighting against a guerrilla campaign in unfamiliar territory.

On January 6, aided by probable leaks from the Sierra Leonean ministry of defence and coordinating their attack with already pre-positioned elements, a rebel force consisting mostly of disaffected rural children and teenagers entered Freetown from the east having first slipped through the Kissy Safecon Terminal supposedly protected by the 93 mechanized battalion of the Nigerian Army. The Statehouse (located in the historic "Granville town") was seized and burned along with key parts of the city center. Within days they came very near to capturing all of Freetown humiliating ECOMOG and forcing Kabbah to call for peace and cessation of hostilities even as confused, undertrained, underarmed, poorly logistically supported, allegedly underpaid and poorly motivated ECOMOG units regrouped. With some international logistic support, thousands of Nigerian troops were rushed in. By mid-January anywhere from 15-20,000 Nigerian soldiers were reportedly in the country. After weeks of fierce fighting the rebels were cleared out of most parts of Freetown, even though further attacks have occurred in and around Freetown and Kenema. Additional troops from Ghana, Guinea and Mali were also flown in after equivocations and conditionalities typical of the ECOWAS membership. Meanwhile, Togo, leading a group of countries with no troops on the ground, quickly offered to host peace talks, citing its current chairmanship of the ECOWAS. Anywhere from 5-6000 civilians were killed but the true numbers will never be known. For Nigerian troops, the casualty rate was horrific. Although the government has kept mum about figures, foreign news agencies and some Nigerian newspapers reported an average figure of 30 deaths on a daily basis for all of January and early February. News reports (quoting former US President Jimmy Carter) of poor medical treatment for wounded ECOMOG soldiers surfaced along with reportedly secret mass burials. The Army (predictably) reacted angrily to these news reports as well as allegedly "false" and "culturally abominable" reporting about dead officers who were actually alive, ethnic selectivity in deployments to Sierra Leone and non-payment of the federal minimum wage to soldiers - all matters potentially capable of inciting soldiers to mutiny and causing disaffection among the war-weary and ethnically polarized Nigerian public. However, as of the time of this write-up, the government has still not released its own official casualty reports either for Sierra Leone or the preceding eight year adventure in Liberia.

To compound the public relations crisis, newspaper reports have surfaced that some Nigerian officers in Sierra Leone have made diamond mining and trading their preoccupation rather than conducting a counter-insurgency war.

But perhaps most provocatively, a Sierra Leonean Minister announced that the conflict was costing Nigeria 1 million US dollars daily! This has not been denied by any knowledgeable Nigerian official. Faced with declining oil prices, deteriorating conditions of living in Nigeria (with internal security implications), a transition program to civil rule and the anticipated emergence of a democratically elected President on May 29 this year, Nigeria's leader, General Abubakar, hinted that Nigerian troops may be pulled out of Sierra Leone before he hands over. This announcement by Nigeria has caused panic and increased pressure not only for more vigorous international interest and support for Sierra Leone but also for a political settlement. Kabbah has agreed to allow Sankoh meet face to face with his RUF colleagues in a confidence building measure. Unconfirmed rumors have circulated that Presidential candidates in the forthcoming democratic elections in Nigeria have been lobbied by warring factions in Sierra Leone seeking to influence Nigerian foreign policy after May.

THE DEBATE

It is debatable whether it is time to bring our combat troops home, giving the importance of the commitment for Nigeria which views itself as a regional power. Furthermore, as is obvious from the foregoing review, there are sentimental family and congregational attachments between Nigeria and Sierra Leone. Even the first "Nigerian" GOC, Nigerian Army and our first military leader, General Johnson Thomas Umunakwe Aguiyi-Ironsi, had Sierra Leonean paternal ancestry. However, my position (based on the foregoing 212 year perspective), is that it is time to do so. Whether this should be done in one fell swoop or in gradual phases depends on the tactical and political situation on the ground. But the direction should be clear. Sierra Leone's civil war has been going on since 1991. Nigeria had nothing to do with it. It started against a backdrop of decades of resentment by disenfranchised, particularly young rural folk against a corrupt older coastal urban elite. This resentment has spread to engulf foreign elements (including

Nigeria) viewed as propping up the Kabbah regime which is seen, along with the money-driven electoral process that brought it to power, (fairly or unfairly) as representing a system that has consistently exploited the country's resources for its own personal interests while looking down at the rural aborigines with contempt. Encouraged and fostered in part by conflict in neighboring Liberia (since 1990) diamonds have also been a key factor. Mercenaries have fought on both sides usually with a tacit quid pro quo for payment in diamonds. To complicate matters, the RSLMF, a descendant of the West African Frontier Force (WAFF) like its Nigerian and Ghanaian counterparts, has been rendered dysfunctional by multiple coups (since 1967), poor leadership and corruption. This frustrated the lower ranks who have been driven to exasperation in fighting a brutal counter-insurgency on behalf of a system that it owed little or nothing. The now disbanded RSLMF is an active part of the problem, rather than a partner in helping to reestablish order and legitimacy. To be sure, the RUF does not (at this time) have palpable mass support, primarily because of its (allegedly) brutal tactics.

Much of the savagery in the war has been attributed to the RUF although the Kamajors and even ECOMOG have been accused (by the UN) of human rights abuses, including summary executions. [Another common complaint against the RUF is the use of "drugged" child soldiers and the targetting of children and women for barbaric mutilation. But even Kamajors have recruited child soldiers, who were also a prominent feature of the Liberian civil war. The phenomenon was similarly noted during the Chadian conflict and the Lebanese civil war. In Vietnam, children were used to deliver booby traps. During the Iraq-Iran war, they were used to clear minefields.] It must also be a cause for pause that a movement that supposedly has no mass support has been able to wage an eight year long insurgency and create problems for the Nigerian dominated ECOMOG equipped with artillery and ground attack aircraft. The young ragtag fighters care little for their personal safety and are fanatically loyal to their commanders. The tendency to view a resistance movement as illegitimate and not worthy of attention and respect simply because it is savage in its behavior on the battlefield is shortsighted. Disgusting reports of machete mutilation by RUF rebels are not original. As far back as 51 B.C., Julius Caesar crushed a rebellion in the town of Uxellodunum and cut off the hands of all Gauls who had risen against Rome. Barbarous savagery was also a characteristic of the RENAMO rebels in Mozambique.

This did not prevent a negotiated settlement to that country's long civil war in 1992. The Islamic front in Algeria has not been particularly civil either, not to mention the Hutus and Tutsis of Rwanda and Burundi. Furthermore, the technology of amputation should not mislead us. The most effective method of mass amputation is not a machete. It is the landmine, produced cheaply by many "developed" countries many of whom have expressed horror at the RUF while doing little to curb the production of mines. To this day, Africa remains the most mined continent on earth. Angola has about 70,000 amputees - not to mention those who did not survive and the 40 individuals who get killed monthly. In the subregion, history teaches us that wholesale burning of towns and massacres are not new either. King Jimmy burnt Freetown in 1787. The British burnt entire towns and villages in the hinterland during the Temne and Mende Hut Tax wars. In Liberia, massacres were frequent during the civil war, including the notorious Marshal massacare in August 1990 during which 1000 Ghanaian immigrants and their associates were slaughtered by Charles Taylor's NPFL in retaliation for Ghana's involvement with ECOMOG. But Taylor was not alone. Samuel Doe's soldiers sealed off the Lutheran church premises and liquidated more than 600 citizens from the Gio and Mano tribes from which Taylor drew support. Roosevelt Johnson was also notorious for savagery. Most will remember the manner in which he supervised the "slicing" to death (on videotape), of late Samuel Doe, who was not a saint either, having savagely murdered William Tolbert and others with bayonets. But Taylor eventually became Liberia's President while Johnson became a cabinet minister! Their style is a feature of the "Mano river" political landscape. Nor is the tendency to renege from signed agreements new to the subregion. Temne chiefs did so in 1787 and 1801. The creole-aborigine trade wars of the late nineteenth century were a study in misunderstood expectations and broken promises. The British took possession of Sierra Leone in 1896 and began taxing it without bothering to inform any locals. The events surrounding the elections and coup of 1967 & 1968 (described above) were consistent.

So were the preemptive coup of 1992 to forestall the results of an agreed upon plebiscite, followed by Strasser's attempt to back out of the promised 1996 elections, and the failure to follow-through on the Abidjan and Conakry agreements. Over 200 years of such behavior cannot be coincidental. [Similarly, during the Liberian civil war observers will recall that Charles Taylor was notoriously unreliable with agreements.] These factors make Sierra Leone a slippery political slope for any outside nation seeking to get too deeply involved. One possible good that may come out of our adventure in both countries may be a sobering recognition of what can go wrong in Nigeria.After the RUF attack on Freetown in January, I made the observation that the RUF's dry season offensive was somewhat reminiscent of the Vietnamese TET offensive of Jan 1968 [Tet Mau Than] and the gradual escalation of Nigerian involvement bore similarities to US involvement in Vietnam. But by publicly stating that there was no intelligence failure on the part of ECOMOG (as happened during Tet), Sierra Leone's Defence Chief, Brigadier Khobe has blamed the Freetown disgrace on poor leadership, singling out the Nigerian Battalion Commander of the 93 Mechanized Infantry Battalion, who is supposedly the subject of a Board of Inquiry. He also complained bitterly about lack of timely reinforcements and disunity within ECOWAS.

Other reports have raised questions about the loyalty of Ministry of Defence officials in Freetown who leaked details of ECOMOG deployments. Even NGOs have not been spared suspicion. The Red Cross was accused of providing electronic communications support for the RUF. However, getting preoccupied with tactical specifics in Freetown risks missing the forest for the trees. The Sierra Leone involvement long ago ceased to be a peace-keeping (or monitoring) operation. It evolved into a peace enforcement / counter-insurgency operation with bursts of full scale conventional war requiring overwhelming force running side-by-side with dishonest political dialogue. The ratio of space to force in such a strategic context demands a force configuration that ECOWAS was simply not willing to commit. At one point during the peak of the RUF offensive, only one helicopter was available to ECOMOG at Lungi, rendering the force dependent on truck transport and vulnerable to ambush. ECOWAS reportedly expected every unit in the

Army to contribute 100 soldiers each of whom was issued 5-10 bullets - as if it was an internal security operation against unarmed university students!! When member countries were asked to send their complement of troops they dragged their feet, asking for guarantees against combat! In the short term, my prediction is that ECOMOG will prevail temporarily in a tactical military sense (like the US) but the horse has left the barn. The Nigerian public is appropriately questioning the whole adventure with increasing disquiet (like the American public did) and the outgoing government is now looking for an exit strategy (like the US did).

Nigeria will continue to assist in retraining the Sierra Leonean Armed Forces. Nigeria may punish Taylor for sponsoring the RUF (like the US bombed North Vietnam) in order to force a respectable peace treaty with the rebels. But eventually, my hunch is that Kabbah will fall unless he takes drastic statesmanlike action to associate with and assimilate his enemies, while 'containing' the new RSLMF. There will be many refugees (as with Vietnam). Even the 'amputee' brutality of the RUF against civilians, policemen and civil servants 'collaborating with ECOMOG and Kabbah' is classic VC style to ensure "political correctness".

A comment about the French is apropos. Back in 1968 they criticized the US policy in Vietnam. In 1999 they are not excited about the regional projection of power in West Africa by anglophone countries like Nigeria and Ghana with British and American assistance. So it is no surprise that we are witnessing certain passive aggressive resistance from francophone countries secretly backing Taylor to humiliate Nigeria. The French have always had designs on the Sierra Leonean hinterland. Even as we herald the establishment of a new garrison in Freetown (under Col. Buhari Musa), legitimacy has to come from within through political dialogue and the re-establishment of a social contract between the leaders and the led. One cannot legislate or decree a political culture by force imposed from afar unless long term colonization is the goal and one is willing to forcefully impose oneself over decades. The Sierra Leonean quarrel is very deep and years of brutality and counter-brutality have undermined a basic sense of civility. The economy is in ruins.

The US entered Vietnam to prevent the domino spread of communism which threatened its ruling class. Nigeria entered Liberia and eventually Sierra-Leone to prevent the domino spread of warlord instability in West Africa, fearful of a precedent that would someday threaten the Nigerian ruling class. In 1990, our own dictator, General Babangida, himself a coupist (like Samuel Doe), sent Nigerian troops to Liberia to prevent Taylor from coming to power. But Taylor eventually did and has (understandably) kicked out the Nigerians (ECOMOG). Nigeria needs to avoid misjudging the geopolitical intentions of the RUF/AFRC and their ally, Charles Taylor along with those francophone countries acting as surrogates for France. While they need to be assessed, overstating the danger they pose to Nigeria's stability could very easily lead us into an abyss. Much of the Gulf War oil windfall may have been sucked up by our Liberian adventure. Practically speaking, with or without Taylor, among ECOWAS states, Guinea and Liberia will always have the greatest opportunity to influence Sierra Leone because of proximity. Quite apart from the more recent effect of instability in Liberia, the impact, for example, of events in Guinea on the politics of Sierra-Leonean independence in 1961 have already been reviewed. In the present conflict, however, Burkina Faso and Libya also appear to be playing a geopolitical role that needs to be carefully studied and understood. We need only recall our own experience during the Nigerian civil war to avoid being frustrated by the lack of unanimity among countries in the region. African countries took sides then Why does it surprise us that they take sides now? The bottom-line is to determine the threat to Nigeria. But we know that the greatest dangers to Nigeria's stability are internal. What eventually becomes of Nigeria depends on how we handle our own affairs. The closest thing to an 'across border warlord affliction' in Nigeria today is represented by the activities of fanatically religious Chadian rebels in some parts of northern Nigeria. Destroying the RUF in Sierra Leone will not solve this problem. It has become fashionable in recent months for international groups to talk about a "dual-track" strategy to the Sierra Leone crisis - negotiating while fighting. Then a situation where fighting and negotiations are conducted simultaneously may emerge. In fighting while negotiating, the side that fights more strongly will compel the adversary to accept his conditions." Thus, we must not underestimate the resolve of the RUF.

Winning the hearts and minds of the generality of the Sierra Leonean people (rather than the elite) needs to underlie a more subtle and farsighted strategy in the region. Even so, in the long term, it may be unwise to view the people and leadership of Sierra Leone through a Nigerian (or ECOWAS) prism. Their short and long term collective goals may not be identical to ours. We need to understand the history, culture, politics and habits of the various leaders of that country as well as the other "players" in its conflict. Much of this essay has been dedicated to this understanding. Raw military force is not always the answer, but if needed we need to be assured of the real support of others. The US, for example, can offer satellite technology to pinpoint sanctuaries and arms trails. It can also fire stand-off missiles to destroy targets to minimize the risk to allied human life. There is no reason why every commonwealth country cannot support Sierra Leone with money and troops.

Sierra Leone is practically a failed state. With the scale of destruction done over the last eight years to its state apparatus and infrastructure, (which was marginal to begin with) it will take many years of loyal and consistent military and police support along with a ceasefire among combatants for the country to be rebuilt from scratch. Just bringing the ubiquitous and intangible RUF insurgency under control, blocking arms trails and searching for and destroying sanctuaries along and on either side of all borders may require the entire Nigerian Army. [We need to recall that the Nigerian Military grew from 10,000 to 262,000 between 1967 and 1970 in response to a civil war over an area that is roughly the size of Sierra Leone]. Brutal (and probably unacceptable) methods may need to be employed as was done by the British during the Mau-Mau rebellion in Kenya. One particularly nasty operation - "Operation Anvil" - led to the clearing of Nairobi. Modern superior technology could theoretically be made available by western countries, supported by political (and military) pressure on external sponsors. The country's borders can be electrically fenced (like General Graziano did in Libya). But even then, high technology and brutality may not prevail against popular will unless the interests of the disenfranchised are aligned with those of the leadership. Whenever I want to get a reality check about any foreign military adventure, I ask myself whether it would be worth it if my father, brother or son were to die during such an operation. If the answer is "No", then I become reluctant to send other people's parents, children and brethren into harms way. The attitude of other countries may also help place this in perspective. After Somalia, the US became very uninterested in placing the lives of its servicemen on the line in Africa.

Africa (which Europeans scrambled over in the last century), just isn't worth shedding "white blood" for today. The Belgians left town in a hurry when some of its peacekeepers were killed in Rwanda. The UN Security Council turned a blind eye to credible intelligence reports predicting the Rwandan genocide because the US did not have the political will (or interest) to take decisive action. Right now in Sierra Leone, the US and Britain (as 'step-parents' of Liberia and Sierra Leone) are playing a stand-offish role in the conflict, offering small aliquots of cash, some logistical backing and plenty of moral support but being careful not to place the lives of their citizens at risk or get involved in combat. Every time the RUF approaches Freetown there are calls for a massive evacuation of foreigners ("as a precaution").

Even UNOMSIL observers can only be deployed alongside ECOMOG units if the security situation permits - because contributing member countries are quite clear about precisely what role they expect their citizens to play and what risks they will accept, irrespective of their moral support for "democracy". It is, therefore, important for the Nigerian leadership to to develop sensitivity to "Nigerian life" in much the same way. Its got to be worth something. There are other dangers to Nigeria of prolonged involvement in foreign wars. They include the transmission of AIDS (from high risk returnee soldiers to the domestic population) as well as exposing Nigerian businessmen and travellers abroad to terrorist reprisals by aggrieved combatants. I have already shared one such example suffered by the Ghanaians in Liberia.

Given the increasingly prohibitive human and material costs of the campaign, it is vital that there be an honest national debate in Nigeria about the limits of our involvement in Sierra Leone. Fortunately, the advent of civil rule in the country enhances such a debate. It will be important to see Sierra Leone in the context of genuine regional and international consensus, unless our security is directly threatened, necessitating unilateral action. Regional indicators of genuine security need rather than want, ego or ambition should guide our decisions on military spending. Lastly it is important to recognize that there are problems that cannot be solved. No matter how desirable it may be to take certain actions, if costs are too high, one must develop the discipline to resist temptation and seek alternative approaches. Pragmatic politicians know, for example, that one should generally avoid forcing a vote on an issue unless one has the votes to win.I have heard some say that Nigeria has a "responsibility" to lead as the "Giant of Africa". In my view the concept of an economically impoverished, undemocratic, politically unstable and extremely corrupt Nigeria as the 'Giant of Africa' is frivolous. One hundred million souls perched nervously on some barrels of Oil does not qualify as a "giant nation". Nigeria is a poor country. There is just no way one can justify spending 1 million US dollars daily for the Sierra Leonean conflict. The experience of the Soviet Union teaches us that projecting super-power status abroad is NOT a game for an economically unstable multiethnic country to play. [The USSR was simply outspent by the US and then dissolved into small nations.] The predominant question was if active and retired Nigerian soldiers choose to fight in Sierra Leone "on contract" for the democratic government? This is an interesting angle which takes away some of the official emotional and economic costs of the adventure from the Nigerian state.

During the Nigerian civil war there were Nigerien and Chadian mercenaries who fought on the federal side as well as European and American mercenaries who fought on the Biafran side. In each case, the host combatant (not their countries of origin) was responsible for paying the soldiers of fortune. Even Britain, Nigeria's colonial master and assumedly the foreign entity with the greatest interest in preserving Nigerian unity only provided us weapons for a fee. Nothing was free. The Sierra Leonean government would have to decide about such an arrangement, perhaps as a form of insurance against its new Army.

CONCLUSION

As we debate a pragmatic policy in Sierra Leone, we need to review the outcome of Nigeria's sacrifices for African liberation and causes during the seventies and eighties. What have we received for it? In 1964 we assisted Britain in rescuing Nyerere from a mutiny. Three years later he refused to support the Nigerian government in its civil war. In 1975/76, we stood up to the West and supported the MPLA in Angola. Today, the MPLA government does not have good relations with us. The South Africans and Zimbabweans view us with studied aloofness. Liberia (under Charles Taylor) practically wants to see us fail. Francophone Africa is nervous about our footprints in the region. The notion of Africa as the centerpiece of Nigeria's foreign policy is romantic and admirable but needs to be vigorously reevaluated and placed in context. The center piece of Nigeria's foreign policy ought to be its citizens and their individual and collective interests outside the country insofar as it affects their quality of life inside the country. Our subregional, regional and non-regional international ties need to be predicated on this basic framework. We cannot afford to be naive enough to assume any permanent friends or enemies particularly when our presumptions are not reciprocated and our economic survival is in doubt.

How Nigeria found itself playing this activist role in Sierra Leone bears comment. General Abacha went into Sierra Leone to restore democracy at a time of self-imposed international isolation. But there has always been unproven suspicion by the public that there were additional agendas. Whether investment in diamonds and the Sierra Leonean oil refinery business was a factor may never be known. But it is clear that Nigeria is not the only country with a humanitarian or regional security interest in what is going on in Sierra Leone. Therefore, the country needs to carefully reposition itself in the right orbit within the universe of other interested parties (bilaterally and multilaterally). We need to titrate our investments and risk-taking to the realities of our domestic situation and the current international environment. We need to return to multilateral peace-keeping, rather than near unilateral peace enforcement.

I rest my case.

Chapter X

NIGERIA AND REGIONAL SECURITY IN WEST AFRICA

Aderemi Ajibewa

The Liberia crisis raises the question of sub-regional order in West Africa. Hence, the formation of ECOMOG. The Yugoslavia crisis symbolizes similar questions of regional order in Eastern Europe, and the intervention of the EC raises similar questions to those raised by the ECOMOG intervention in Liberia.

Aderemi Ajibewa

INTRODUCTION

Considering the importance of the subject and the urgency of resolving the disparity between policy and practice, perhaps, this is as good a time as any to address the issue of regional security in West Africa. Today the security issue has been recognized by many of us- the general public, the professionals and the political leaders- as an issue of central importance rather than of peripheral importance. Of all the problems that confront modern society today, the humanity's abuse of security in all its ramification is one that holds the key to all other problems facing us. Taking security as the state of making a person safe from danger, new questions were raised-more complex and more extended in scope. These are questions pertaining to the concept of security, threats to security, regionalism and regional security. All of these invoked powerful ideologies, strong emotions and deep-seated prejudices. Hence, this chapter attempts to conceptualize the term "security" in the context of the West Africa states. Defining the concept has attracted attention of scholars, especially in the third world. It is now evident that the fundamental problem of security of West African states is found in the need for an order based on dynamic security arrangement leveraged upon common needs and aspirations of the people of that part of the world. An attempt will therefore be made in this chapter to examine specific features of regions at both regional and sub-regional levels which may hinder or help the achievement of regional security. This is necessary since the relationship among states becomes crucial for any achievement of regional security, and in particular requires the broad acceptance by states of 'rules' with one another, which presupposes the absence of major grievances that can be exploited by external powers. Moreover, because the problem of political instability in developing states is, on the face of it, one of overwhelming complexities, it is useful to clarify what is relevant to our study in the realization of a political order or the prevention of conflict either within or among states. The realist view of international politics posits that the regional leader seeks to maximize its influence in the target state or enhance its status in the regional balance of power. This is a logic which finds favor with foreign policy analysts in Nigeria who see two dimensions to ECOMOG: (1) a deliberate new direction in Nigeria's African policy; and (2) a desire on its part to engender a rethinking of certain traditional variables of intra-African relations. [2] This school of thought argues that Babangida single-handedly created a scenario in which to play a new set of rules of the game. First, he drew attention to the instability, violence and cross border conflicts in the continent in general and West Africa, in particular. Then, he championed an ECOWAS committee to mediate disputes and conflicts, invoking the Mutual Defense Pact, thus lending political weight behind the organization. Indeed Nigeria is acclaimed as the giant of the West Africa sub-region. Variables that make her a "super power" are viz the most populous, over 100 million people,[3] the largest in size, 924, 630 square kilometers and the most powerful economically and militarily due to her natural resources and the sophisticated weapons in her military arsenals. In this connection, we also looking into the economic, military and socio-political clout of Nigeria in the sub-region as to determine if she could have the surplus to defend her neighbors in the West African sub-region in line with her foreign policy posture. Moreover, this chapter should be able to ginger constructive thoughts along the line of Nigeria becoming or acting as the policeman of the sub-region or would seek accommodation with others through economic, political and defense alliances to defend the sub-region.

Various national travails like the down turn in Nigeria economy, high unemployment rate, huge indebtedness and allied problems that have been undercutting her image and reputation has not in anyway significantly affected her peacekeeping effort in Liberia and role in the United Nations. [4].It is generally believed by almost all enlightened opinion in the world that, "If Nigeria's grandeur does not arrive today it will come tomorrow".

While there are a number of variables which call for analysis, emphasis will be on the more critical ones. Specifically, this paper will assess:

- A review of Nigeria's role as the giant of Africa- i.e. the Myth Reality, "Minimalists and Maximalists" views.
- The issue of power politics, rivalry, regionalism, regional security.
- hat is the 'diplomatic basis' of regional security?
- What are the conditions required for consensus to be reached on regional security?

The trend toward a regionalist as opposed to a globalist perspective in conflict resolution and management in the Third World, offers tremendous opportunities for, as well as challenges to, regional and sub-regional organizations in the management of conflicts.[5]

THE CONCEPT OF SECURITY

'Security' in its general sense, refers to the ability of human beings to live their lives without immediate fear. It is thus one of the most important aspirations of human existence.[6] In the industrialised Western states where there is a generally acceptable domestic political order and where a high standard of economic well-being has generally been achieved, the problem of security has very largely been defined in terms of protecting the state as a whole and its population against external aggression.

In much of the world, however, these conditions are not found, and writers such as Caroline Thomas and Michael Zimmermann[7] have pointed out that a much broader concept of security is required which will include basic economic security, such as food and health, as well as threats to physical security arising within the domestic political order. By 'security', therefore, we mean a political order, both domestic and international, which protects both individuals and states against the immediate threat of physical violence. Viewed from this perspective, security can be seen in two main aspects, namely internal and external. The internal aspect of security has two dimensions:

(1) The security of the people and
(2) The security of the state or the government.

As earlier stated, the security of the people is seen in terms of the satisfaction of the social, cultural, economic, political and human rights which are needs of people.

THREATS TO SECURITY IN WEST AFRICA

Major threats to West Africa security in the post-independence era have been manifested in three different but mutually reinforcing ways.

(a) Insecurity arising from extra-regional intervention or invasion, notably by United States, Soviet Union and France under various pretexts.

(b) Insecurity arising from conflicts among states within the region, normally classified as overt conflicts between national governments and military forces and covert conflicts involving support from one state for opposition movements within another state.

(c) Insecurity arising within states, from opposition to the existing regime, or from a general breakdown of political order.

In fact, on a general basis, the security of West Africa states appears to be more threatened these days than during the early years of independence. Military coups, mutinies, insurrection, political assassinations, chaotic factional conflict and other manifestations of instability are now becoming common occurrences.

A number of other reasons could be advanced for the increase in security threats, they are:

1) The decline in the accountability of regimes, which were more democratic at independence;

2) The effects of economic decline from the mid-1970's; and marginalization in global capitalist economy;

3) The rapid rise in external arms supplies from the mid-1970s. All have significantly contributed to the internal economic and political instability.

While conceding that no two conflicts can exactly be the same, a survey and study of most West Africa state conflicts shows somewhat consistent features since 1960.8 Most wars in West Africa in particular are largely traceable to the insecurity arising within states from opposition to the existing regime, as a challenge to the repressive conditions of their existence or from a general breakdown of order. Conflicts involving ethnic groups are responsible for the greatest numbers of cases of insecurity, as in Sierra-Leone, Liberia and also Nigeria and many others. It is, however, important to point out that although the events of Sierra-Leone and Liberia are not exactly parallel, certain strands still run through them in that the undemocratic and repressive nature of the regimes, failure of the governments to satisfy the basic security requirements of the people facilitates the ousting of the government and led to chaos.

Thus, the state itself may represent a threat to the security of its people: it was regimes like those of Doe in Liberia, that created the immediate security crises which external intervention had to deal with.

In an increasingly interdependent world where the concept of absolute sovereignty is largely meaningless, inter-state cooperation, whether at the sub-regional, regional, or international level, is essential. This is particularly pertinent in West Africa where the small and weak states saw the creation of the ECOWAS not only as a way of maximizing their insurance collectively on the Sub-regional scene, but also as a more realistic and appropriate approach to dealing effectively with their common problems. The question then being asked is whether the West African states in particular, have the ability to evolve clear concepts, strategies through their own regional mechanisms for the effective management of conflicts or serious security threats. Or whether groupings of regional states can do the job instead or, more precisely, what the conditions are under which they will be able (or unable) to do so. In short, the time has come to examine whether the regional organisations such as ECOWAS, and some regional powers.

REGIONALISM

Since conflict is primarily a regional phenomenon, and our overall concern is with regional security, it is necessary to examine what a region is. Given our special reference to OAU and ECOWAS initiatives, emphasis will be placed more on regional organisation in Africa. A region may be defined as 'a set of contiguous states with a level of interaction between them, such that a lack of security within or between individual states in the region affects the security of the set of states as a whole'.9

Ghana for example, has obvious common interests, and somewhat similar problems to face as, Nigeria or Senegal which she does not have as compared with Peru or Argentina. Moreover, since conflicts having foremost a bilateral and local relevance can escalate to regional level, settlement of such conflicts is foremost a question of state to state relations. Thus, regional defense agreements or pacts are concomitant to regionalism as they are aimed at protecting the expected gains of their mutual co-operation and interests from being undermined militarily or through other indirect subtle means.

Regionalism as it applies to our discussion may be defined as attempts by contiguous nation-states, reinforced by a sense of common purpose or predicament within a definite region or defined area, to foster economic or political co-operation among themselves in order to lessen their dependence on others outside the region. It can be deduced from the above definitions that regional groupings are a continuum of three stages - co-operation, co-ordination and full integration with an ulterior motive in accommodating local conflicts. Economic integration, according to the functionalist model, contains in it a certain dynamic logic that by bargaining collectively fulfils the background functions of a pluralist political structure, similarities in economic and industrial development and ideological political structure with its inherent spill over.10 Spill over implies that success in one integration sector will then lead to advances across a much broader front just as the economic achievements of the European Community have since then generated additional political co-operation.

At the regional or continental level, attempts at fostering a strong economy and security in the region have been exemplified with a series of treaties from the OAU's 1980 Lagos Plan of Action (LPA), to the 1990 African Charter for Participation in Development, and the Abuja Charter of July 1991. Within the different sub-regions in Africa, the ECOWAS in West Africa, SADC in Southern Africa, Maghreb in North Africa and the PTA for Eastern and Southern Africa and CEEAC for Central African States were to translate these socio-economic and security issues of the OAU into operational programs at the sub-regional level.

This is against the background of the social, political, economic, ideological, geographical spread and external commitments and diplomatic problems encountered at the continental or regional level (OAU).[11] Moreover, there exist certain ethnocultural and economic similarities within each region which are far more remarkable than the differences. These are enhanced by cross-border trading and free movement of people which in West Africa pre-date ECOWAS. This does not preclude the members of the organization having areas of conflicts - for example over the artificial borders inherited from the colonial powers, and the rivalry over the relative weight and influence of member states, especially Cote d'Ivoire, the most prosperous of the West African Francophone states, and Nigeria, the largest of the Anglophone states. Analysts[12] suggest that Cote d'Ivoire's relations with Nigeria are based on rivalry because the country has a leadership aspiration in the sub-region and, therefore, sees Nigeria as a stumbling block. It has often displayed divergent views from Nigeria on inter-state issues: relations with South Africa, reopening of diplomatic relations with Israel, the Western Sahara and, during the Angola war of liberation, support for the FNLA and UNITA, while Nigeria pitched camp with the MPLA.

Therefore, as noted by M.A Vogt and others:

It should have been clear from the beginning that Cote d'Ivoire would act as a stumbling block against Nigeria's influence in Liberia; more often than not, Cote d'Ivoire strives to neutralise Nigeria's influence in West Africa, not to talk of Liberia, her next door neighbour.... when a crisis occurs and ECOWAS has met and taken a decision, Cote d'Ivoire will quickly convene a smaller grouping (CEAO or Francophonie) to deal with the same issue and come up with a different position on that issue.[13]

Nigeria, in spite of her economic potentials and large market preferred a non aggressive stance on border matters and subdued approach to conflict, which has earned Nigeria good level of relations in the sub-region and Africa in general. It appears that the basic notion of insecurity in many African states stemmed from the leadership belief system that perceives other nations as the enduring source of threat to its security. However, because of the wide range of threat possibilities,[14] the perceptual problem becomes fundamental as it affects the entire formation base on which the decision making process rests, making solutions a long lasting dilemma. Having said this, in practice, it seems clear that solutions to insecurity and instability in the world and in Africa would still be woven around the three concentric circles of national, regional and global methods. It is clear that the three should comprehensively be inter linked for an effective resolution to conflict.

REGIONAL SECURITY

For a region to be secured, there are three requirements which according to Mohammed Ayoob must be made. These are:

(1) That external powers with interests in the region (and these interests can be sub-divided into those which are off-shoots or by-products of the major powers) would either willingly desist from interfering in regional issues and problems or be effectively deterred from so as a result of regional cohesion and solidarity.

(2) That inter-state tensions within specific regions are at a low level if not totally non-existent and further that institutional mechanisms are available which can be used to find acceptable solutions to inter-state problems and conflicts within the region.

(3) That the regional states would have succeeded in successfully managing, if not totally eliminating problems that create frictions and antagonisms of ethnic, communal, sub-national of socio-economic character within these states, thereby eliminating intra-state tensions as likely sources of inter-state conflict between or among regional states.[15]

Following from the above, the high level of variation as far as security is concerned among regions in the Third World may be explained by a number of factors. Differences among regions can be in terms of their internal structure, as between regions which are highly conflictual and ones which are fairly peaceful, and between regions which have potential regional leaders and ones which do not. The existence of effective regional systems will make the region less conflictual and reasonably secure, whereas those which are conflictual and thus insecure are likely to lack such structures.

The level of superpower involvement will also affect the ability of regional actors to have a security structure in place to protect themselves. Where external powers have a major stake, the great power's involvement and intervention would naturally be deep and extensive. This is exemplified by the US presence in Central America and the Gulf, the Chinese approach towards South and South east Asia, and the Soviet involvement in the Horn of Africa, Middle East and Afghanistan. It must be noted that West Africa has been relatively peaceful, except for the Nigerian and the Liberian crises. However, the increasing fluidity in West African affairs has raised the potential of strong regional rivalry, such as that between Nigeria and Cote d'Ivoire. Security issues in West Africa are becoming more complex in their own right and more consequential for the regional balance of power. Security was uppermost in the minds of the founding governments of ECOWAS. The 1977 ECOWAS Head of States communiqué made a remarkable statement to this effect, that:

there is hardly need for us to demonstrate that development cannot be secured under a climate of insecurity...We must among ourselves establish a genuine solidarity pact to guard against external aggression.[16] It was initially contemplated in practical terms as a by-product of institutionalised regional reconciliation.

However, Robin Luckham and Arthur Koestler, illustrate the most problematic aspect of collective security from a totally different perspective. The former believes that "it may well be doubted whether state or ruling class security actually has anything at all to do with the safety and welfare of ordinary citizens".[17] In line with Luckham's preoccupation with the interest of what he calls 'ordinary citizens', Arthur Koestler points out that the motives of decision-makers are often selfish, personal, or a reflection of individual aggressiveness.[18] In contrast to the above views, Barry Buzan pointed out in his conceptual work on security and listed different sets of priorities principal to states' reasons for collective security action. He states that it is the economic, political and strategic realities confronting sovereign states that impose on them the need for collective defence on a regional or continental level.[19] However, any collective institution often becomes a major source of threat to those smaller actors it was supposed to protect. The bottom line is that a regional system can handle its functions only when problem-solving and autonomy are the subject of consensus, and have a higher value than political advantage; when burdens exceed capabilities, the system requires outside help.[20]

In this uncertainty, the future of West Africa security will depend on the recognition among West African states that they are the key to the security of the continent. The various sub-regional arrangements hold promise for states upon which their security could be based. As shown in the author's work on "regional security in West Africa", the rationale for participation and non-participation of ECOWAS member states in the Liberian action, personal/regime survival issues competed on the same value levels as national/collective security in the decisions made by respective states.[21] Growing inter-state inequalities may also be significant for making progress to fulfilling the two greatest challenges of the regions - strengthening democracy and sustaining economic reforms. In a structured regional security system of interaction among juridically sovereign states, the "influential" state has a significant degree of political dominance over the security policies of the region. As Northedge noted:

> It is a well known fact that power is not equally divided throughout the international system, and it is natural that the greatest powers should make an exceptional impact upon other states in the immediate geographical vicinity and should wish to organize them within a regional forum in which, as far as possible, a local or regional consensus on common problems can be shaped.[22]

Among the principal powers, the US has maintained an interest in the Caribbean, South America, and parts of the Middle East and Asia, France in West Africa, and until 1989, the USSR in former Eastern Europe. However, as a result of the delinking of regional security issues from Great Power competition, there are today arguably similar roles to be played by the emerging regional powers, - India having a sense of guardian in South Asia, Egypt dominance in the Arab world, South Africa in Southern Africa or even all Africa, and Nigeria regulating affairs in West Africa. The influence to be exercised by the Middle powers over other actors is concerned primarily with the economic and security relations of the region.

Although it does not totally involve the day-to-day affairs of subordinate states but the regional power's role may involve monitoring the democratic process in the region and agreement over basic features of government. Though no nation is ready to compromise those interests that constitute the bed-rock of its survival. Nonetheless, a nation may give away some of its secondary interests to another nation (regional body) in order to protect its primary, strategic and core interests. That is the only point of compromise.[23]

WHAT ARE THE PRINCIPLES GOVERNING SECURITY?

Within this strategic context, any viable basis for regional security will need to rest on 'rules', whether tacit or explicit, on which regional actors broadly agree; which relate their domestic political structures to their relations with one another. These are essential in order to provide a generally acceptable solution. For the internal political structure of each state, viable internal government should rest on principles such as democratic elections, human rights, good governance, respect for different groups within each territory, and their incorporation into the government. Based on these requirements, and the earlier explanations offered, dispute resolution is seen to be an integral to the democratic process. One fundamental democratic norm is the willingness to accept compromise solutions to contentious public issues. If we extend this norm to the regional level, then it becomes reasonable to expect democratic states to adopt compromise solutions to regional problems as well. One implication of this logic is that democracies are likely to be more amenable than others to efforts of third parties to resolve or ameliorate interstate disputes. Theoretical justification for expecting democratic political structures to inhibit conflict/war involvement at both regional and international relations are generally well known.

DIPLOMATIC BASIS OF REGIONAL SECURITY

Any mobilization of a multinational coalition to deal with a regional security issue will have to operate within a diplomatic structure which enables it to carry out its task effectively. A group is synergistic, providing a whole that is greater than the sum of its parts. A decision or a solution generated by consensus is usually of a higher quality than what the brightest and most talented number of group could produce individually. Groups come together, coalesce, and make decisions on ways of solving problems. It must, however, be pointed out that the diplomacy of coalition building is always delicate, but such coalition building may well operate most effectively when there is a coalition leader who as earlier noted, defines the task, and seeks to gain support of other coalition members. It is especially important for the regional leader to observe the 'rules' on domestic political structure - democracy, respect for human rights: one case in point is Nigeria. In addition, the coalition leader acts as both the facilitator and the coordinator when rivalry, conflict, and misunderstandings arise and threaten to disrupt the effectiveness of their mission. As a facilitator/coordinator, the leader gets things done through other coalition members. Consequently, this brings trust, respect and coalition members are perceived to tie their fortunes to the leaders, thus assisting the full execution of the mission. However, in a real sense, to share the coalition leadership might be fraught with some dangers because others as well may care about their own success (national interest) and put the leader at risk.

REGIONAL LEADERSHIP AND MANAGEMENT OF THE COALITION

In several trouble spots, from Congo to Liberia, Nigeria played admirably the 'giant' of Africa role. However, it has been wary of using its military card in international diplomacy, especially in African affairs. Nigeria's experience in Chad underscores the limit of power beyond the confines of traditional diplomacy. Despite its military and economic leverage in Africa, Nigeria could not impose its will on Chad. However, the appointment of a Nigerian to command and co-ordinate both operations was no doubt the recognition of Nigeria's leadership role in the sub-region and Africa in general. Nigeria's commitment to the peace effort was amply demonstrated by the way Nigeria used her constructive diplomatic action, political restraints in rescuing ECOWAS from internal rivalries that created rifts and factions within the community. In addition, like the Chadian peacekeeping force, ECOWAS could not convince a large number of states to contribute troops to ECOMOG because of the expense of financing the participation of their troops. Nigeria, being the coalition leader, came to the rescue of both operations by dispatching many contingents to Chad and Liberia respectively. Furthermore, she had to offset the balance of the peacekeeping cost and as of June 1991, the Financial Times correspondent reported that a substantial component of Nigeria's Gulf War windfall - between 250-500 million dollars - had been used to finance ECOMOG in Liberia.[24] Nigeria was given a free hand by the United States, and was able to define the task and role of the force and able to convince some of the regional leaders of the basis of intervention.

The question then is can Nigeria fulfill this responsibility of maintaining security in the sub-region? For any Africa country, nay Nigeria to be truly secured and aspire to defend other nations in the West African sub-region, Eyo Ate suggested the advancement of a self-sustained economic and technological growth, one leading to a marked reduction in international dependency.[25] In comparing Nigeria's natural and human resources with those of other countries in the sub-region or Africa, coupled with the killing of Nigerians at the Cameroon border and dumping of poisonous nuclear waste by Republic of Benin at Koko, one school of thought[26] feels Nigeria should adopt a policy approach that really makes countries in the sub-region her political "backyard" as America is doing in Latin America countries of Panama, Guatemala and Honduras. Problems confronting Nigeria in her bid to be the real giant of Africa, or even that of the West African sub-region, could be categorized as economic and technological dependence; domestic problems of political, economic and social nature; and problems with her closest neighbors, especially the Cote d'Ivoire, one of ECOWAS' big four.

However, the present economic situation in Nigeria with all intent and purposes makes the minimalists position holding sway; the maximalist concept would have held sway in the 1970s during the era of oil boom. The impression is that to properly secure a place one must, as they say in the military, be "on the ground" or in time of war "take physical possession". This is one of the main problems of Nigeria (though it has a defense corporation) and other Africa defense systems because they depend on foreign powers for the scientific and military technologies that would enable them to maintain a mobile force. As a military expert put it, to be able to deploy a contingent of troops either for war or peacekeeping operations, the troops must be properly backed logistically.

The inability of African states to convey an OAU force to Chad without some Western countries support gives credence to Africa's dependency syndrome, which came into sharp focus during the ECOMOG operation in Liberia. Implicitly, if Nigeria, the supposed regional leader, wants to deploy its troops outside, it would have to depend on foreign suppliers who would decide, after considering their national interest, whether to sell or not.

NIGERIA AND REGIONAL LEADERSHIP

As stated earlier, in Africa, Nigeria is one of the most powerful putting her in the group of Egypt, Libya, (courtesy of thin population and petrodollar) and South Africa, courtesy of Western capitalist countries of Europe and America. In West Africa, Nigeria is a super-power and no other country in West Africa can unilaterally challenge her in the game of power calculus. The proportional and structure of middle power model of state behavior includes mediation in conflicts between other countries, influence in world politics through multilateral and regional organization, economic and diplomatic influence, territorial and strategic status, freedom manoeuvring. [27] It was, however, difficult for any state to exercise leadership within the Chadian setting. The behavioral pattern of the superpowers during the cold war was such that if any supposedly emerging regional power in the third world challenged their interests, they will block its regional ambitions. The USA was suspected of encouraging and financing Habre's forces against Waddeye, an ally of Gadaffi; and officially supporting the OAU effort in Chad.

In the Liberian case, on the other hand, the major initiator was internal: Nigeria, the major industrial power and influential member of the ECOWAS. By reason of being a pioneering member of the organization, coupled with the fact that it funds a third of its annual budget, Nigeria felt concerned about the survival of ECOWAS.[28] To this end, ECOWAS constitutes a strong plank in Nigeria's foreign policy and one of its three concentric circles. In addition, the generosity of the Nigerian government since the inception of ECOWAS especially under the military was legendary in the sub-region. Nigeria provided both official and unofficial economic assistance to its less endowed neighbors, as and when requested, a situation that brought substantial goodwill and could be converted into diplomatic support.[29] Furthermore, there has since independence been unconcealed awareness of the historical and geographical fact that Nigeria is the 'giant' of Africa. Nigeria's responsibility to Africa and to the world is to find the destination of the drifting continent. Thus Africa has been declared the center-piece of Nigeria's foreign policy by successive regimes since independence.[30] These objectives and principles have remained constant despite Nigeria's momentous and dramatic experience on both the domestic and international scenes. The Nigerian government leadership role in this respect was of particular importance because it had to bear a substantial part of the burden of any military initiative, in terms of men, money and materials. Moreover, the country had considerable diplomatic clout because of its size, status, potential and close relationship with most members of ECOWAS.

It is pertinent to point out here that apart from its regular annual fund to ECOWAS, Nigeria pursued the same vigor even in other areas of development such as West African Rice Development Association (WARDA), established in 1971 with 17 member countries, including Cameroon which joined in 1991; only two of the 17 have contributed any funds in the last two years - Nigeria $160,000 and Cote d'Ivoire $63,000,31 while a few others such as Burkina Faso, Mali, Sierra-Leone and Togo are two years in arrears. Nigeria is better off than other countries respectively in the sub-region especially its closest neighbors. Militarily, the country has the largest standing armed forces, better trained and with more sophisticated weapons than all of the countries in the sub-region.(See Table 7 in the Appendix) There are more local training facilities like the Nigerian Defense Academy (NDA) now a degree awarding Institution. Beside Ghana, only Nigeria has a Command and Staff College and National Institute of Policy and Strategic Studies (NIPSS), in the West African region which trains the middle and high level military manpower respectively, for the three armed forces-the Army, Navy and the Airforce. Within the sub-region, Nigeria is the only country with a Defense production industry, the Defense Industries Corporation (DIC), which presently produces self-loading Rifles (SLF).[32]

Annual armed forces seminars and training conferences were held especially on non-military topics to update the knowledge of top serving officers. In addition, Department of International Relations, Obafemi Awolowo University had a joint agreement with the Defense Ministry which specified that annually, 5-10 armed services middle/senior officers would be trained for a one year postgraduate diploma program in Ife. Despite Cote d'Ivoire's relative wealth vis-a vis other Francophone neighbors, it did not have the same leverage or enjoy the same leadership status as Nigeria, which enjoyed American support. For instance, Anglophone West Africa and Guinea objected to Houphouet's chairmanship of the Committee of Five on Liberia that ushered in the series of Yamoussoukro meeting; they acquiesced only after considerable diplomatic effort by Nigeria's General Ibrahim Babangida.[33] How does Nigeria in spite of all this marked superiority, see her neighbors? Are they to be protected, bullied, or lived with in a congenial atmosphere? Through the formation of ECOWAS and other bilateral agreements with her neighbors, Nigeria, has shown a desire to live in peace with the small states of the region, and has always been its brother's keeper.

Some of Nigeria's neighbour, especially Cameroon has been a pain in her neck with frequent border clashes and taking over some portion of Nigeria's territories. Indeed, to all intents and purposes, the consciousness of Nigeria's leadership role and concern for the security of the sub-region informed the active role in Chad and its proposal to establish an ECOWAS Standing Mediation Committee "to look into inter-state disputes and conflicts which have disruptive effect on normal life within the member states and on the smooth functioning of the community".[34]

Moreover, President Babangida, while defending Nigeria's participation in the ECOMOG said:

Nigeria has evolved to the point of acceptance of the fact and reality that the conduct of Nigeria's international relations and foreign policy may at times involve certain contractual military and other obligations beyond its boundary.[35]

This security from a Nigeria perspective, can only be secured by policies of political co-operation, economic integration and adoption of a consensus. To this end, Nigeria's President despite opposition from the francophone states, successfully led ECOWAS at its Banjul Summit to organize and deploy ECOMOG in Liberia in order to prevent superpower intervention in Africa. Nigerian leadership aspirations became an obstacle to French nationalism not only because they stood to frustrate it, but also because Nigerian behavior struck at the core of French inferiority.[36]

Thus, in the Liberian setting, Nigeria provided leadership and management; and the 'rules of engagement', drawn up at the various meetings of ECOWAS Head of States and diplomats, regulate and monitor the mission of ECOMOG in Liberia as against the uncoordinated Chadian episode. It may be desirable for the role of policing the security of the region (an interventionist role, either in the observance of cease-fire or related peace accords or inter positionary capacity) to be undertaken by the regional organization, albeit with the assistance of either the United Nations or international actors. This is against the background that the regional actors are likely to be more familiar with the complexity of the issues which the region presents. To prevent conflict from reaching the point of demanding outside intervention, the regional organization requires to explore concepts of preventive diplomacy as a conflict management and resolution mechanism. This may necessitate an expansion of the Charter to remove contradictions that may exist and possibly expanding its mandate into regular peacekeeping operations and conflict mediation services. Be that as it may, such new concepts may necessarily challenge universal norms which up till 1991 had formed the basis of international relations in the continent, notably the provisions of inviolability of national sovereignty and principle of non-interference in the internal affairs of states. It may also be useful to note that the regional leader may not be able to rely on consensual mechanisms, but may also have to impose some pressure or inducement on recalcitrant regional states which are not prepared to accept the verdict of the majority: one case in point was Nigeria's pressure on Cote d'Ivoire and Burkina Faso. Other mechanisms such as a steady flow of accurate information from those smaller groups should be encouraged; in meetings, participants should be encouraged to share leadership and make consensus decisions; criticism from non-supportive group should be seen by the leader as an effort to correct performance and to increase effectiveness; management style should be made open and participatory; solving problems should be seen to be characterized by searching for a desirable alternative and when rules and policies inhibit effective performance, they should be altered or scrapped. As demonstrated in the Liberian case, when Nigeria realized that as the leader of the coalition group it was not getting the result it wanted; and when the work was not being performed up to expectation Nigeria had to take full control and change the command structure and mandate of the force.

CONCLUSIONS AND RECOMMENDATION

In a concluding observation, eight dominant themes emerged in our analysis.

1. The most basic conclusion is that an effective system of regional security in Africa, and notably in West Africa, is feasible objective. Despite all the difficulties in attaining it, the experiences of regional peacekeeping in Chad and Liberia provide a basis from which, when the appropriate lessons have been learned, this objective can be achieved.

2. One major source of regional insecurity has been the relationships between governments and political factions within the region, and external powers, whether these are superpowers or former colonial powers. The connections between individual states or factions and external powers make conflicts very difficult to resolve. With the end of the Cold War, and the decline of post - colonial ambitions, the external connections of conflicting parties in African regional conflicts are being reduced. Such a reduction is a requirement for effective regional security. One important indicator of reduced external dependence is the reduction in external arms supplies, and the creation of effective mechanisms for arms control.

3. Another major source of regional insecurity has been the conduct of governments within states. By far the greatest number of African conflicts arise from the non-existence of good government, democracy, and respect for human rights. The achievement of good government within African states is therefore a further essential condition for regional security.

4. Conflicts within African states readily affect their neighbors, through cross-frontier operations, support by states for opposition movements in neighboring states, the mass movement of refugees, cross-border arms flows, and the contagion effect of conflict in one state on its neighbors. The analysis reveals a very marked discrepancy between the actual nature of regional security and insecurity, and the established conventions of unfettered state sovereignty and non - intervention in internal affairs of other states.

5. Regional security is most effectively monitored and assured at the sub-regional level. Continent-wide organizations generally cannot be relied on to provide security, since the continent is so large and states in different regions may not share the same concerns about security. The maintenance of a continental concern is nonetheless important, because of shared identities between Africans and the need to create a common African viewpoint in order to deter external intervention. Particular difficulties arise where, as in Chad, a conflict crosses the boundaries between sub-regions.

6. Within sub-regions, an effective structure of leadership is needed for regional security. A leading actor is almost always needed to initiate and coordinate action; the role of Nigeria in ECOMOG is in this respect similar to that of the United States in the Gulf conflict of 1990/91.

Leadership cannot however be entirely divorced from issue of power and hegemony. It is therefore essential that the leading state should abide by the agreed principles of domestic government outlined under (3) above, that its leadership role should be accepted and respected by other states in the region, and that it should accordingly seek to maintain consensus among these states through appropriate consultation.

Both continental organizations (OAU) and global ones (UN) may provide legitimacy for the role of sub-regional leaders but may also provide a forum where discontented states may appeal against the authority of these leaders.

7. The analysis demonstrated that the maintenance of regional security raises extremely complex political issues, especially when it involves intervention in states where order has broken down. A fully effective regional security system would ensure that potential conflicts were resolved before they had reached the stage at which intervention was needed. Where intervention does take place, very careful political judgement is needed. Intervention forces almost inevitably become a factor in the domestic politics of the state concerned, and require clear and achievable political goals. This requirement becomes all the more essential when intervention forces move from straightforward peace-keeping to peace enforcement.

8. Likewise drawn attention to a number of very important operational requirements for effective peacekeeping forces, including notably the need for sub-regional organizations to be able to call on appropriate forces from member states, and for clear command structures, information-gathering services, logistical backing, operational procedures, and financial support.

Recommendations

The conclusions above could be regarded as leading to recommendations, such as:

1. Regional security requires African states to emphasize and strengthen, wherever possible, those interests that they have in common, while seeking to overcome those that divide them. One important aspect of this is that they need to reduce, so far as possible, their security dependence on external powers, whether these be superpowers, former colonial powers, or other states.

2. Regional security likewise requires states to develop workable conventions on the conduct of their domestic governments, including implementation of democratic political systems. There is, of course, a large literature about democracy in Africa, which this thesis cannot cover.

In order to facilitate or encourage regional solutions, some preconditions must be given. To this end, it is suggested that in the light of recent developments in the region, the necessary conditions for a stable and effective democracy in Africa should be set in motion. Some African leaders have established Centers of Democracy in their countries, notably in Nigeria, Senegal and Gambia, while the majority have set up transitional programs for multi-party elections.

3. The convention of non-interference in internal affairs of other states needs to be replaced by a recognition that all states have a legitimate concern for the means by which their neighbors are governed. This does not necessarily involve any right of intervention, but would certainly extend, for example, to discussion of internal political conditions within member states at meetings of regional bodies.

4. Coup d'etat is increasingly being understood as an international crime. The rather strong criticisms or reactions in the OAS, ECOWAS, Commonwealth condemning the coups in Haiti, Sierra Leone, Nigeria and The Gambia in 1993 and 1994 respectively show a growing international preparedness to expose the misuse of military rule.

5. It is suggested here that the regional organizations should use the current favorable opinion to declare, officially that military coups and other forms of violent usurpation of power are illegal.

There is of course, the fundamental issue of acceptable level of interference in the domestic politics by a peacekeeping and defense force. Thus it would require a joint effort to stabilize the political affairs of some countries. Though some critics may see such action as an interference in the domestic politics and sovereignty of independent states, it would appear that this interference is to be preferred to persistent instability that normally results from coups d'etat or regimes generally known to lack popular base. The ability of the sub-regional or regional organization to successfully establish a force for the continent depends to a large extent on two factors. Firstly, the ability of the regional actors to broadly agree on 'rules' whether tacit or explicit, in order to provide a generally acceptable solution, even if it involves some actors being pressurized to accept it and, secondly, the organizational ability to successfully articulate the type of pressure facing the continent in the millennium. Once this is done, it will be easier to reach a formula for meeting the principles governing all forms of security, especially if the leaders realize that democratic systems that respect human rights and seek equitable economic growth are the best guarantees of peaceful change and stability. Of course, I recognize the structural distortions and contradictions of neo-colonial development which also militate against the building of effective consensus and autonomy in the continent. Even in the case of Liberia where there was a clear case for intervention, dissenting countries like Burkina Faso and Cote d'Ivoire still stood against reason by not only refusing to contribute troops to ECOMOG but also supporting the rebels. These problems would have to be handled together, a requirement which makes the task even greater and more urgent in view of the complexity of the issues which the region presents. The emphasis here is that since peacekeeping and peacemaking have been embarked twice, therefore, there is the need for some amount of pre-planning against the next peacekeeping mission, so that we do not repeat the mistakes for the third time.

Chapter XI

NIGERIAN FOREIGN POLICY AND REGIONAL ECONOMIC DIPLOMACY

Kelechi A. Kalu

INTRODUCTION

Globally, the 1980s and 1990s will be remembered as periods of economic and political distress as well as recovery in Europe, Asia and most of Latin America. However, for Africa and especially Nigeria, the same period is largely viewed in political and economic terms as lost decades. This is a study of the political economy of Nigerian foreign policy with a focus on Economic Diplomacy within the Economic Community of West African States. This chapter asks the basic question: given the international system's constraints identified by Realist and liberal theories, how much freedom do African countries have in designing their strategies for economic development? A basic analytic assumption here is that for African countries there is very little distinction between foreign and domestic economic policies. This assumption is based on the fact that domestic policy (e.g. taxation laws) affects how foreign countries and corporations perceive their relationship with a given country. And, that the structure and operation of the international economic system forms part of the structure and operation of the international political system where the concept of power, however defined, is central.

For different reasons, both Realism and liberal theories would agree that as a developing country, Nigeria's external and/or domestic economic policies would be constrained by the international system. The international system's constraints argument presupposes the absence of freedom or options for Nigeria to design an independent foreign policy and economic strategies for development outside of the rules determined by powerful political and economic actors in the international system. A systematic exploration and analyses of the relationship between Nigeria and the member states of ECOWAS yields insights for understanding regional and internal constraints on Nigeria as well as opportunities for its foreign and domestic economic policies. This chapter (1) examines the major arguments of realism and its expected impact on a less developed state like Nigeria and a region like ECOWAS; (2) next, it explores the perspectives of the liberal school of thought on the economic development of a less developed country and (3)

applies the above arguments in analyzing the extent to which Nigeria's opportunities for regional power status is enhanced and constrained by the end of the Cold War. In light of the above, the chapter makes recommendations for advancing Nigeria's economic and political influence in the West African region.

MAJOR CLAIMS OF REALISM

Generally, political realists use an analytical framework based on the structure of the international system, whose anarchy forms the central analytical premise for explaining international behavior and outcomes. Underlying their framework are the common assumptions that the anarchic international system structure is (a) comprised of sovereign states whose foreign policies are shaped primarily by security concerns ; (b) that states are rational, and unitary actors with stable power-maximizing preferences that maintain the existing power relative to other states and/or extend them; and (c) that states will consistently prefer security over welfare in an international system whose ordering mechanism is based on balances of power. Realists of all persuasions gree that given anarchy, war retains its utility in the current international system, just as it did in the classical Greek City States. And, as Krasner points out, "...the basic explanation for the behavior of states, is the distribution of power in the international system and the place of a given state within that distribution." While behavior by states may be substantially shaped by regional balances of power, the number of major world powers will determine the structure of the international system at any given time. The key points are that states must seek to preserve and strengthen their positions in the balance of power. That position may be a regional balance (as illustrated by Iraq's bid for hegemony) or a global one (as shown by the United states' action in preventing Iraq's attempt to dominate the oil-rich Gulf region).Realist's assumption that states are unitary actors is based on the proposition that even though domestic coalitions may argue among themselves on the value and utility of a given state policy, such disagreements are not usually communicated to external actors or influence targets. As a result, in spite of bureaucratic and group "interests" and disagreements in the process of policy formation, states communicate their policies as unanimous internal decisions to the external world. Equally significant for the realist argument is the assumption of rationality. States as dominant units in the international system seek power "either as an end in itself or as a means to other ends." Thus, in part, states behave in ways that are, by and large, rational, and therefore comprehensible to outsiders in rational terms because states also tend to be responsive to constraints of structures largely determined by the state's position within the system. According to Robert Keohane, "[t]o say that governments act rationally... means that they have consistent, ordered preferences, and that they calculate the costs and benefits of all alternative policies in order to maximize their utility in light both of those preferences and of their perceptions of the nature of reality. For example, deterring attack requires warnings that are consistent, clear and unambiguously communicated, backed up by military preparations or alliance formations that provide sufficient capabilities to make the warnings credible. Realists, however, caution that a state must not rely solely on allies. It must develop its internal sources of power, for allies sometimes fail to answer the call to fight or may even become enemies, as Iraq found out during the Gulf War. Also, realists argue that for a state's policy to be rational, clear preferences must be given to the "national interest" which Morgenthau, Waltz and others, define in terms of national security preserved by military power. From this viewpoint, security policies, for example, would take precedence over economic policies, which in turn would take precedence over cooperation on human rights issues. In sum, the nature of a state's government or domestic coalitions is irrelevant from a realist perspective. Sovereign states will consistently behave in ways that preserve their national security, trusting no other state to protect them; their policies will always reflect unitary, rational calculations that privilege security over economic policies.

Although, the basic analytical premise of both classical and contemporary realists is largely similar, the goals of their foreign policy tend to differ. For example, classical realists argue that power is the most important objective of a state's foreign policy in the international political system. For neorealists, power is a means that states employ for the attainment of their most desired foreign policy objective--security.Strongly opposing the classical realists' focus on individual human nature,Waltz insists that classical realism fails to take into account the international political structure and its mechanisms that constrain states' behavior. As a result, Waltz (1979) defines political structure according to the principles by which a particular system is ordered. For him, the first principle is anarchy, a view that would lead to a definition of political structures on the basis of the specification of functions of differentiated units. However, Waltz argues that in the resulting anarchic system of international politics, there are no specifications of functions since the consequent sovereign units are all alike. Further, he asserts that since states are the central units, they are similar in their functions. For him, similarity of functions exists despite unit differences in the power of states. Indeed, states are truly equal solely in terms of the legal concept of sovereignty. According to Waltz, the distribution of capabilities across units becomes the defining factor for political structure. This means that changes in the system will only result from (a) change in capabilities or (b) change in the ordering principles within the system itself. But, given the overall fact of inequality among nations, major states will tend to exercise their powers while the small states will either bandwagon or form alliances as a strategy for economic and political survival. For Waltz therefore, foreign policy methods are heavily reliant on realpolitik and the constraints, which result from its rationales and can be explained by the diversity of both its applicants and applications.Structural constraints (which gives rise to self-help) therefore may explain why the methods are repeatedly used despite differences in the persons and the states that use them. Waltz sees a self-help system as "one in which those who do not help themselves, or who do so less effectively than others, will fail to prosper, will lay themselves open to dangers, will suffer." He insists that "Fear of such unwanted consequences stimulates states to behave in ways that tend toward the creation of balances of power." Given that states are the main actors in the international system, realists assert that those who control the affairs of each state will work to increase the power of their states relative to other states for whatever reason, but largely for the purposes of state security and power. The foregoing argument is premised on the assumption that government officials are general welfare-seeking rather than self-interested agents of the state.

A Response from Liberal Internationalism

Liberal internationalism is similar to realism in its assumptions that states are the dominant actors in the international system, that states' policies are rational and exhibit consistent preferences across outcomes and issue areas. Liberals and realists also share the view that states are sovereign entities within their territory. While states are likely to achieve absolute gains from the liberal perspective, realists see relative gains as a more important concern for realizing the security needs of states. However, liberal internationalists differ from realists in giving significant status to international institutions such as the International Monetary Fund (IMF), the World Bank, the United Nations, ECOWAS among others, emphasizing the capacity of these international institutions to mitigate the effect of anarchy, which realists argue is the main source of conflict in the international system.

Robert Keohane argues that "institutionalist theory... emphasizes the role of international institutions in changing conceptions of self-interest" to articulate areas of possible cooperation between states. To the extent that liberal internationalists emphasize the relevance of institutions as agents for states' realization of their mutual interests, the debate between realism and liberal internationalism centers around neoliberal claims that the international institutions and regimes that states establish alter their behavior in ways that realism fails to predict or account for. For Liberal internationalists, international institutions provide opportunities for citizens of different countries to meet and discuss issues other than military security in situations where the constraints of different states' objectives would otherwise make such meetings difficult. Because of individual roles in international institutions, neo-liberals argue that international regimes tend to result in more cooperation, especially between democratic states, in an otherwise anarchic state system. Thus, neo-liberals largely focus their explanation of international issues within the domestic realm, by using the type of government, the leadership, public opinion and education to argue that the international system is evolutionary and that changes are possible, especially from conflicts and war towards a more peaceful world. Therefore, Liberal internationalists regard free market economic systems, as well as free trade among states (leading to growing interdependence) as critical to global prosperity and peace. From the liberal internationalist view, international regimes are significant in strengthening international cooperation. Furthermore, internationalists take the existence of "mutual interests" as a given, and therefore argue that through regime formation, "mutual interests" can lead to cooperation under anarchy. Robert Keohane, a leading proponent of the institutionalist perspective, asserts that discord among actors does not have to result in rational egoism.

Rather:

If the egoists monitor each other's behavior and if enough of them are willing to cooperate on condition that others cooperate as well, they may be able to adjust their behavior to reduce discord. They may even create and maintain principles, norms, rules and procedures... as regimes. Properly designed institutions can help egoists to cooperate even in the absence of a hegemonic power.10 However, Keohane cautions that cooperation does not necessarily imply the absence of conflict, rather, it is the extent to which states anticipate success in resolving conflicts that results in cooperation. Realists, especially neorealists, argue that liberal internationalists do not appreciate the logic behind a state's decision whether to cooperate or not cooperate with other states. According to Waltz, states are reluctant to cooperate because of their concern over how the gains from such cooperation will be divided. Waltz would also argue that such concerns do not preclude states from desiring to cooperate in situations (e.g. military alliance) that serve the national security interest of the state. And, because states may not be certain whether they "gain more or less," they fear the probability that if other states gain more, such relative gains may enhance the other states' capacity in ways that threaten the security of the states that get less. Correspondingly, realists doubt the basic and underlying assumptions of the liberal internationalists' argument about change and cooperation among states, even if such states share a similar political structure such as a democratic system of government. According to Robert Jervis, "[b]ecause there are no institutions or authorities that can make and enforce international laws, the policies of cooperation that will bring mutual rewards if others cooperate may bring disaster if they do not. Liberal internationalists contend that international institutions and regimes created by states to mitigate the effect of anarchy,... serve state objectives not principally by enforcing rules (except when they coordinate rule-enforcement by the strong against the weak, as in the International Monetary Fund-IMF), but by facilitating the making and keeping of agreements through the provision of information and reductions in transaction costs (my italics). Thus, governments will cooperate to attain their goals only when the ends-means calculations are favorable. Also, liberal internationalists acknowledge that strong states (mainly advanced industrialized states) will cooperate in the enforcement of existing international rules that privilege the developed against the less developed states if the issue-area involves the adjustment of resources, gains or influence in the international system. In light of the foregoing, the question becomes, how well does realism and liberal internationalism explain Nigeria's (potential) influence in the Economic Community of West African States (ECOWAS)? To what extent does the end of the Cold War enhance or constrain Nigeria's opportunities for economic and political influence within ECOWAS? And, what evidence exhibits the competence of Nigerian leaders' knowledge of the potential effect of globalization and democratization on Nigeria and the region?

ECOWAS: BRIEF HISTORY AND ANALYSIS

Regionally, Nigeria has succeeded in three things. First, with Togo, it established the Economic Community of West African States in 1975. Its main objectives were for a regional free market, free movement of goods, capital and labor. The attainment of these objectives, which were supposed to lead to economic development in the region, remains elusive. While the sixteen countries in the region were amenable to signing the ECOWAS protocol, Nigeria's second success in the region is less popular—the establishment of a military peacekeeping force, ECOMOG. ECOMOG helped to end the civil war in Liberia and remains active in its efforts at resolving the civil-war-induced human misery in Sierra Leone. Third, Nigeria should be lauded for its capacity for peaceful relationships with its neighbors, which has constrained intervention opportunism for both France and Great Britain into Nigerian political independence. But, while Nigeria has largely succeeded in ensuring peaceful co-existence with its neighbors, its other two regional efforts have not succeeded as much as they should because Nigeria lacks the influence and stature that its human and economic resources should provide. Secondly, inappropriate appreciation and application of the rules in an international system dominated by major powers like Great Britain, France and the United States has constrained Nigeria's effective realization of its interests within the ECOWAS project. ECOWAS (henceforth, the Community) was established on the principle that its members shall "... promote cooperation and development in all fields of economic activity particularly in the fields of industry, transport, telecommunications, energy, agriculture, natural resources, commerce, monetary and financial [sectors]." These principles were aimed at ensuring economic stability, improved standard of living and peaceful co-existence of citizens within the regional community. Furthermore, Chapter IV, Article 27(1) of the ECOWAS Treaty provides that "citizens of Member States shall be regarded as Community citizens and accordingly Member States undertake to abolish all obstacles to their freedom of movement and residence within the Community." Consequently, governments of member states were required to "exempt Community citizens from holding visitors' visas and residence permits and allow them to work and undertake commercial and industrial activities within their territories." Consistent with the logic of the major provisions in the Treaty, Chapter XIII, Article 56 provides for an amicable and direct settlement of dispute between members.

However, should such amicable efforts fail, the Treaty gives the final decision on settlement of disputes to the Tribunal of the Community whose composition was not established a priori. Such implicit ad hoc provision for the management of potential conflicts between member states arguably creates opportunities for some members to violate the protocol of the Community.

From the Community's charter, it is clear that liberal assumptions and values informed the thinking of the founding fathers of ECOWAS. Based on the assumption that although the international system is characterized by anarchy, an individual state's desire for cooperation, economic development and peaceful co-existence with its neighbors surely overrides the state's natural tendency for selfish policies. Consistent with integration theories of the 1960s and 1970s, the founders of the Community assumed that reductions in transaction costs in trade and manufacturing, as well as an eventual expansion of the state boundaries into a larger political and economic community would override Community members' differences. Furthermore, the assumption that on-going interactions between states, largely mediated by international institutions such as ECOWAS will erase realists' predicted state selfish interests in their foreign policies. So, what happened? Why has ECOWAS failed to result in regional economic development? What, for example, explains the fact that most members of ECOWAS remain hopelessly in the low category of the UNDP 1999 Human Development Report?

While the intent of the founding fathers of ECOWAS remains honorable, both Nigeria and Togo, the sponsoring states inadequately read and understood the structure of the international system and the logic guiding the actions of major states like the United States, France and Great Britain. Especially, Nigerian policy makers inadequately understood and/or planned ahead for economic downturns, which resulted in Nigeria's violations of the ECOWAS protocol under the Buhari/Babangida regimes. In 1975, Nigeria had not yet fully recovered from the economic and political impacts of the 1967-1970 Civil War. Although, crude petroleum gave Nigeria a sense of wealth, mismanagement of this natural resource and the impacts of same on Nigeria's foreign policy initiatives may not have been anticipated. But, the policy makers ignored the fact that the sixteen members of the Economic Community of West African States were caught between a rock and a hard place in their efforts to develop strategies for economic development within the context of the international capitalist economic system. Although, the major states preach free market and liberal ideologies to the rest of the world, the history of economic development in advanced industrial countries is replete with mercantilist and economic nationalist policies.

This was especially true for the Francophone countries, whose economies and currencies were, until 1994, tied to France. As former colonies of the major powers, efforts at breaking away from the existing international division of power and labor required members of the Community to think within the same logical framework as the major states. Given the above, I argue that to the extent that the analytical and policy framework of the major states is realist in orientation, liberal policies and values will not yield the desired result of economic development for either Nigeria or members of the community. Thus, even if the prediction of institutionalist theory that international institutions will harmonize the differences between members of ECOWAS, the outcome will not have changed largely because, the Community lacks an effective underwriter that is comparable to the United States' during the formation of the European Union.Consistent with liberal internationalist argument that interdependence exposes states to differential vulnerability and sensitivity, the absence of a credible and resourceful state like the United States highlights the vulnerabilities of states more than it would otherwise.

This is evidenced by Nigeria's economic crisis in the 1980s, which was partly blamed on the presence of "illegal aliens" in the country. Having identified a source of its economic problems, the Nigerian government expelled "community citizens" it considered "illegal aliens," from the country in 1983. The 1983 national interest-based policy action by Nigeria not only violated ECOWAS protocol, it also exposed a major weakness of the regional efforts—the absence of a unified and verifiable "Community interest." However, Nigeria' s action was consistent with realist assumptions of self-interest and survival—a major characteristic of the international system that tend to constrain cooperation among states. Also, it is this structural constraint, which gives rise to self-help, that may help explain the inability of the Community to unify in defense of Liberia under Doe. In addition, the general economic weakness of the region partly explains the failure of ECOWAS. Thrust into an international capitalist economic system, whose rules were already established, members of the Community can only change the rules if each member is committed to the collective interest of the Community above its individual national interest. However, given the burden of IMF structural adjustment programs in the 1980s, the linkage of francophone African countries' currencies to France's, and Nigeria's violation of ECOWAS protocol for national economic reasons, the community was virtually paralyzed and helpless in pursuing its expressed goals of economic integration and development. Even with the end of the Cold War, ECOWAS is yet to recover from the paralysis of the 1980s. Under the Cold War international system, characterized by major powers' system-wide interest, a successful regional economic development similar to the rapid economic growth in East Asia, required an effective and collective manipulation of the super powers for the interest of the Community.

Such manipulation was necessary as the existing international division of labor and power enhanced the gains of the industrialized western countries at the expense of peripheral states as those in the ECOWAS region. Unfortunately, and contrary to liberal internationalist predictions, the specific interests of the autocratic leaders of various West African States, the cultural and sometimes ideological differences between France and Britain, which were replicated in Anglophone and Francophone African countries made such collaboration impossible. Indeed, the failure of ECOWAS to realize its goals – different states pursuing their national interests in competition with others, the dominance of more capable states in the international system and the absence of an effective enforcement of cooperation between states—are consistent with the general expectations of realism. More specifically, the predominance of Nigeria in terms of GNP and population within the ECOWAS region may have created a perceptual problem for the other members of the Community. On the one hand, Nigeria may have been seen as a potential cushion for the fledgling economies of the smaller states. On the other hand, Nigeria may also have been seen as a potential Leviathan that was to be avoided, especially by the Francophone countries, whose economies benefited from their direct alliance with France. However, Nigeria and the other members of ECOWAS did not anticipate the extent to which Nigeria's reliance on crude petroleum (a finite resource), the control of prices and interest rates by the western industrialized countries would result in its inability to determine the course of its economic development. This is not to suggest that Nigeria or any African country lacks the freedom to design an independent strategy for economic development. Rather, my argument is that a combination of external and domestic factors checkmated the expectations of infinite supply of oil wealth into Nigeria's coffers, thereby forcing it to carry out either the function of helping or dominating member states within the Community. The lack of effective and committed leadership in economic and political arenas remain the most compelling domestic factor for Nigeria's underdevelopment and therefore ECOWAS' failure. Indeed, the general suffocation of civil society, blatant abuse of power, military autocracy, fragmentation of student and labor organizations, the neglect of academic institutions and socio-economic and political infrastructures in Nigeria were replicated in various West African states. Thus, the failure of regional economic development and integration in West Africa is a failure of leadership by Nigeria. With the end of the Cold War, France has delinked its currency from Francophone African states, there is a general lack of interests in West Africa by Britain and the United States, whose interests are now on the former East European Communist States. For peripheral states and regions, this is a rare opportunity to assert themselves and for ECOWAS in particular to regroup under an effective Nigerian leadership.

CONCLUSION

Indeed, the essence of Nigeria's involvement in the formation of ECOWAS cannot be entirely economic. The political undertone and power projection by the Nigerian government in the 1970's is clear from its unwillingness to use the Francophone dominated Communaute Economique de l'Afrique de L'Ouest (CEAO) – The West African Economic Community (WAEC), to advance its desire for regional economic development. As Aaron T. Gana has argued, the formation of a counter economic community to the existing WAEC was consistent with the battle between two schools of thought on the right path to develop Africa. According to Gana, the radicals led by Nkrumah of Ghana "... argued that the only effective way to deal with the problems of under-development and external domination was for Africa to unite under a continental government...." The functionalists or the "... pro-imperialists ... led by Nigeria, ... argued that political realism dictated that unity can only be achieved through gradual functional integration of the continent, and even then this must start at sub-regional levels." It is equally clear that the ideological bipolar struggle between the western and eastern powers affected not only the political conflicts in the Congo, South Africa, Angola, and Ethiopia, but equally the economic development issues in the continent. However, the reality is that politically and economically, Africa lost during the Cold War—largely because African leaders failed to collaborate for effective development of their respective states or regions. The reality of the end of the Cold War for Africa in general and West Africa in particular is that it remains socially fragmented, economically marginalized and politically fragile. Domestic structure of major regional powers like Nigeria is equally characterized by these factors. Indeed, the experience of Nigeria under General Abacha came close to exposing the region to an intolerable level of social, political and economic decay. With the transition to civil rule, Obasanjo's demilitarization and anti-corruption policies, removal of international sanctions and the promise of accountable and transparent governance, Nigeria is at a critical juncture to transition the West African states into a region of peace and economic growth. However, conceptually, ECOWAS has to undergo a paradigm shift from dependence on the goodwill of the international system to a focus on a larger project of regional interdependence. Such a paradigm shift may require the violation of the territorial integrity of states in the region and may result in initial severe economic and political problems. However, to succeed, Nigeria must lead by example in economic growth, a stable political system characterized by public institutional reform and a constitutional government.

Already, the Obasanjo regime has committed itself to reforming public institutions, revising the military constitution to a popularly legitimized constitution for Nigerians as well as open engagement with citizens and associational civil institutions. Economically, Nigeria's foreign economic relations should be framed around economic development in the West African region. The ECOWAS travelers' check- ETC, which was launched in Abuja by the Minister of Finance Adamu Ciroma is a step in the right direction. But institutionalizing a regional economic recovery program in the era of challenging economic globalization is necessary for Nigeria's and regional economic interests. Indeed, the essence of ongoing globalization trends is that no state or government is in control of the international system. Globalization is an equal opportunity hunter—hunting for profits in stable political and economically productive states or regions. It exposes the vulnerability of each state; whether these states are advanced or less developed is irrelevant. Those states or regions that provide efficient infrastructural base for economic investments are likely to benefit more from globalization. Establishing an effective constitutional governance structure in Nigeria and encoraging the same within the Community is likely to result in an accountable political and economic platform for investment by Transnational Corporations. Transnational Corporations are more likely to invest in states and regions where economic and political rules and regulations are clearly formulated and understood. Thus, infrastructural developments such as road and rail networks across the Community, efficient supply of electricity, water and an effective education at all levels are sine qua non in all efforts to accomplish regional economic development. Secondly, collaborative economic development planning should initiate the development of economic development zones across the Community. Such economic development zones would avoid intra-Community duplications and help concentrate industries where access to raw materials allows for economies of scale for specific industries. Thirdly, Nigeria should lead in institutionalizing an effective collective bargaining system with extra-regional enterprises and states. This will potentially reduce transaction costs and increase overall gains for the community. Collective bargaining by the Community, especially with the international financial institutions is the best strategy for dealing with the mounting debts of members of ECOWAS. Finally, the above efforts are likely to result in enhanced status for the community in international organizations and therefore constitute a boost to Nigeria's national interest.

PART IV: WITHER NIGERIA?

The new Nigerian political experiment is the appropriate way forward and for many it is only a way with needed rehabilitation in order to sustain a progressive and responsive but accountable government for the Nigerian people. The 1999 constitution, the bedrock of the present Nigerian republic has been the object of questions because of its origin and lack of effective legitimacy. A review of the constitution is seen as an indispensable process of sustaining the Nigerian democratic experiment. The government in response to these calls has put in place a constitutional review committee to initiate the process and the committees of the national assemblies have also began to evaluate the process of engaging in this critical process of sustaining this democracy. Which way forward? That is the question that preoccupies the mind of many Nigerians today. A question that will continue to reverberate for many generations to come.

Chapter XII

BREAKING RANKS TO BREAK FROM BONDAGE: DEVELOPMENT IN POST-MILITARY NIGERIA

Tope Omoniyi

There seems to be a consensus of opinions in local and international circles that Nigeria has spent enough time in the doldrums during which it was confined to the margins of global economics and politics. Internally, its citizens have suffered depredation and degradation brought on by embarrassingly high levels of mismanagement in spite of an abundance of both top grade human and natural resources. Internationally, the consequence has been the invasion of the West by a broad spectrum of Nigerians, from intellectuals and professionals to crooks and the like seeking either sanctuary or greener pastures. In the process the nation acquired a notoriety that does not augur well for national identity and integrity. While the current experiment at democratic governance is naturally expected to go through a teething period with all the problems associated with this stage of development, the nation can avoid some of the pitfalls that the post-industrial World experienced en route to First World status. The despondency that attended the last years of military 'occupation' must now transform into the positive rage that galvanizes the nation into 'action for development'. It is against this background that we must debate the framework for development in post-military Nigeria. This paper will discuss the legacy of three decades of military rule, with particular reference to the media, education, information technology and the global economy. Secondly, the paper will attempt an appraisal of attitudes to class, culture and civic responsibility all of which I believe weave a web of conflict and thus pose an obstacle to true national development.

BACKGROUND

The attempt in the title of this paper to anchor the discussion to the military as an institution is deliberately intended to spotlight the relationship between the army and the Nigerian nation. This is pertinent if we are to establish the connection between past practice and future possibilities in Nigeria in terms of what we might call desirable development. All over the world, the army is renowned for discipline, order, focus and loyalty thus justifying entrusting national security to it especially in times of crisis or emergency. East Timor, Kosovo, Bosnia, Rwanda, Sierra Leone among others are troubled spots in which the services of the army have been required to put order back into society. These duties are however specific and peculiar in terms of the skills required – fight on the side of Truth and drive the 'bad guys' away, if possible. In every single coup d'etat executed in the course of the last thirty years, lack of discipline, corruption, insensitivity, nepotism among other factors have been cited to gain legitimacy for the incoming regime. Ironically, as the late Vatsa and Fela Anikulapo Kuti both said, 'Soldier go, soldier come' without making the slightest difference to the situation of things. As a matter of fact, the nation's circumstances worsened with each coup. In Nigeria, the crisis that first ushered in the military in the mid-sixties has been documented from several perspectives, but the point that needs to be made is that beyond that initial crisis phase, the army stayed on and in the process its duties and consequently military professionalism became redefined. If the army was the antithesis to civil crisis, taking on civil duties arguably disarmed the army, disorientated it and opened it up to infection by the same viruses and problems it hitherto attempted to provide a panacea for.

First the army became part of the problem and gradually developed into the main problem. The culture of military politicians that emerged, with its tradition of ruler-ship by decrees and edicts destroyed the frail roots of a new nationhood fashioned on democratic principles even if pretentious. It has been said that besides the Major Chukwuma Nzegwu-led coup d'etat of 1966, all others were informed by either sectional or personal rather than national interests. Thus ethnic distrust and suspicion which culminated in the civil war of 1967-1970 and which has been the bane of Nigeria's political development is directly linked to the army even though it may not be solely responsible for it. The politicised military became riddled with lack of discipline, graft and felony including the fabrication of coups in order to slam antagonists within its own ranks. The Late General Maman Vatsa, General Shehu Musa Yar'adua, General Olusegun Obasanjo (rtd), General Oladipo Diya were victims of such odious fabrications.

TACKLING THE PAST

My contention is that a total overhaul of the established disorder is necessary to launch Nigeria's development. There are several perspectives to such an overhaul including the army, national identity and citizenship, social attitudes, foreign relations, the economy and so on. These together paint a picture of Nigeria's gory past.

THE ARMY

President Obasanjo, who himself was a kingpin in Nigeria's nightmarish militocracy, has placed responsibility for the trauma of bad governance and mismanagement on the doorstep of the army. According to him, 'for far too long, our armed forces have been preoccupied with matters for which they have neither training nor constitutional legitimacy. And this trend has been ruinous to the nation as well as the armed forces'. The Nigerian press has been rife with news of retirements in the top echelons of the army, trimming down of the size of the army, allegations, counter-allegations and calls for probes of past military administrators and so on. All of these provide evidence that the military has been an affliction to the nation. The president seized the occasion of the Passing Out Parade of Sierra Leonean Cadets of the Special Short Course Two at the Nigerian Defence Academy in Kaduna to tell cadets to 'shun political ambition and imbibe the culture of loyalty and dedicated service' stressing that their interest as professional soldiers is better served by permanently subordinating yourselves to constitutional authority, instead of subverting it.' This is a first step towards reorientation.

SOCIAL ATTITUDES

But even as the military retraces its steps back to the barracks there is also a need to change established social attitudes and approaches to tackling individual and societal problems. The culture of nepotism, the nest of which has been generously feathered in the span of the last thirty years, must now be done away with in the same way that we are expunging the army as past factors of under development. One difference that is constantly made between Nigeria and other nations in sub-Saharan Africa is the relatively greater political sophistication of Nigerians and their bravery in resisting even in the face of imminent danger. But perhaps the resistance that one calls for now is a philosophical one that guarantees a departure from our old ways. A refusal to be tempted to ask for that 20% cut of the profit for awarding a contract. If that fails, then the courage to lodge formal complaints if such a request is made of one.

Most Nigerian families and communities see the appointment of locals and relatives as their divine access to portions of the national cake. In the process straight folks are weighed down by pressure and eventually budge. This is the reality that makes it not only unfair, but also impossible to blame the nation's predicament solely on the army. Social constructionism would suggest in fact that the army is a consequence of society, so that arguably each society gets the army it deserves. But in order to cause change a number of issues that are basic to the processing renewal need to be addressed, the first of which is national identity.

NATIONAL IDENTITY

The notion of 'nation' is still evolving in Africa since the partition of the continent in the last quarter of the 19th century after which diverse ethnic kingdoms were grafted on to political stems designed by colonial administrations. Within each of the new nations, interethnic feuds have been commonplace and Nigeria had and continues to have its share. Biafra's secession bid in the late 1960s, Major Gideon Orkar's attempt to excise five northern states in the coup d'etat of April 1990 illustrate this fact. More recently, there have been rumblings about marginalization by the Yoruba following the nullification of the June 1993 election results by the Babangida administration, then among the Igbo and the Hausa in the present dispensation. One might argue that these ethnic identities have managed to remain significant simply at the expense of national identity. This again boils down to leadership failure at the centre where individualist and sectionalist philosophies have been dominant.

There is hardly any mono-ethnic nation in the world today. Transnational migration and diaspora movements have put the final nail in the coffin of that kind of social organization. So whether diversity is the consequence of colonial restructuring or, in contemporary times, of displacement or immigration, the fact remains that some governments have managed to design administrative paradigms which efficiently aided the emergence of a national identity. If diversity were so bad, the United States would not conduct the annual lottery scheme, which seeks to admit people from different parts of the world. I shall also cite the example of Singapore at the risk of incurring the wrath of social scientists who would argue that with a population of three million, it does not present as complex a problem as Nigeria. I believe that there is something to be learned there. It is one of the Asian Tiger economies that the World Bank describes as the Newly Industrialised Economies (NIEs). There are four racial groups – Chinese, Malays, Indians and Eurasians with the Chinese accounting for about 70% of the population. Between independence in 1965 and today and without any natural resource, Senior Minister Lee Kwan Yew and his lieutenants have built a nation that anyone can be proud of to a large extent. The workforce which is highly disciplined is continuously challenged to perform better in this meritocratic state, but the real success hinges on the government's ability to manage racial tension through public enlightenment, housing and education policies. The environment is thus rendered convivial for external investors. Consequently, the prosperity has supported the designing and execution of national identity boosting programs. Although people may complain about the government's overbearing presence even in the domestic domain (the Western media delights in this), the material, and hopefully subsequently spiritual, harvest is too desirable to ignore. Comparison to other states in the region puts a chip on the shoulder of every Singaporean.

To return to Nigeria, let us address the passport issue. Fundamentally, the passport is the primary emblem of membership of a nation. It tells the outside world of ones legitimacy of belonging. Acquiring a passport in Nigeria is fraught with problems including the demand for and offer of gratification. National identity is thus commoditized and becomes a material rather than spiritual possession. Resultantly for unscrupulous elements who trade in the nation's passports for clandestine purposes such as drug trafficking, there is already an institutional license. This abuse of the national passport severs all spiritual links to the soul of nation.

CORRUPTION

In June 1998, I was invited to speak at a symposium organized by the Association of Nigerian Asylum Seekers in Ireland (ANASI) in celebration of June 12. On that occasion I drew a contrast between political asylum-seekers and the statesmen and women of the day. The former I described as a crop of patriotic citizens who had undertaken risks in trying to enforce social and political change and in the process become 'enemies' to rogue-leaders whose propensities for personal aggrandizement and enrichment surpass their thought and concern for the states they ruled. In the week following the July 1975 coup d'etat that saw the end of the nine year rule of General Yakubu Gowon, several Nigerian Newspapers went to town with screaming and damning headline stories of the excessive looting that had taken place during the General's stewardship. One of those headlines has stuck vividly in my memory. It was an edition of the Nigerian Herald, the Kwara State newspaper which proclaimed 'CORRUPTION THAT STINKS TO HIGH HEAVENS!' in exposing some of the dirty dealings that had gone on during the period. Although the purpose at the time was to inform the readership of activities that had taken place in the past, for me that headline became a prophecy for in the two decades that followed, military regime after military regime was terminated on account of swinging to the same music.

Nigeria has gone from the self-styled 'Giant of Africa' and 'Santa Claus' of the 1970s to the infamous and debt-ridden 'Black Sheep of Africa'. When the Western media reports that 'Nigeria is one of the most notoriously corrupt countries in the world ...fraud is taught in Nigerian schools. Fraud is actually one of the country's sources of income' (Sunday World of Ireland May 17, 1998, p.6) we realise that we are up against a colossal enemy and only total commitment can ensure victory. In the 1997 British chart for diplomatic misdemeanour, Nigeria came joint-first with Zimbabwe. The panels set up at state and federal levels to investigate allegations of official misconduct and abuse of office are similarly a replay of an old and worn tape. Nothing happened in the past, nothing is likely to happen now is the attitude that most Nigerians have taken and understandably too. However, even if Nigerians let sleeping dogs lie, they must not compromise the future. As the late Afrobeat maestro, Fela Anikulapo charged his student audiences on several occasions in the late 1970s and 1980s 'Aluta Stoppay', that is, 'The Struggle Must Stop! The only way that the struggle can indeed stop is by an insistence on transparent honesty in governance and the inculcation of a new sense of responsibility and duty into the public and private sectors of the society. National renewal, the kind that the National Orientation Agency (NOA) is now calling for can only take place if we begin by acknowledging and resolving the past. We must use the lessons learnt from the past in setting the parameters for evaluating those we put in position of authority today.

Upon inception of the current administration, the governor of Katsina State voluntarily declared his assets to the Katsina State electorate, those who entrusted their interest into his hands for the next four years. Such a step incurs the trust of the citizens and makes accountability and auditing easy at the end of term. If all governors and ministers would do the same, and because they earn fixed salaries it would be easy to stem the miracle wealth of public officials turned millionaires and billionaires in the short space of one term in office. The Tarka and Daboh procedure for cleansing which was popular during the Second Republic of President Shehu Shagari is too individualistic and needs to be given institutional backing. It should be written into the Constitution of the Federal Republic of Nigeria as a requirement for contesting public office.

The role of the press in investigating and making information available to the populace cannot be overemphasised in this regard and Nigeria is blessed with a brave press judging by its stance against the dictatorships of Ibrahim Babangida and Sanni Abacha in the period 1985-1998. However, unless the central government intends more than mere lip-service in its avowed commitment to transparent honesty and eradication of corruption the press is doomed to fail. Alhaji Sule Lamido's, (Foreign Affairs Minister) statement on the problem that the Federal Government faces in pursuing the retrieval of stolen money from overseas account is worrying (Electronic Vanguard, September 2, 1999). If indeed development is to do with coming to terms with the past, the claim that the fear by Western nations in which Nigerian monies are held that the owners of the accounts may sue them must be addressed.

Both the United States and European Union governments have publicly pledged their support for finding and retrieving stolen funds but only if the Federal Government makes a formal request. These declarations conflict with Alhaji Lamido's statement and challenge the government's claim to transparent honesty. The whole idea of a panel of enquiry is to establish that there is evidence of theft of public funds. Once that is established, the basis of any litigation is shattered and as a matter of fact, those concerned can only negotiate as criminals. In the spirit of renewal, no one insists on punishment other than the repatriation of such funds. Nigerian-owned properties and golf courses in Europe only service the economies of the nations in which they are based while the bulk of those deprived through such theft not only suffer abject poverty, but also denigration in the hands of the beneficiaries of their monies.

EDUCATION, MEDIA AND DEVELOPMENT

The role of education in participatory democracy and development cannot be over-emphasised. Karel de Beer, Netherland's Ambassador to Zambia Lusaka remarked that 'there is no development without education' in declaring his country's support for Zambia's Basic Education SubSector Investment Programme (BESSIP). In recognising that certain groups require special attention, the existence of differential levels of educational attainment and general awareness is implied. In the Nigerian context, several claims have been made by commentators to the effect that certain regions and ethnic groups lag behind in educational and basic literacy levels when compared to others. In some communities too, education has shown gender bias in focusing on male education even though this trend may be changing slowly now. Such regional and sociocultural disadvantages need to be addressed in order to optimize the nation's human resource.

It is against this background that the involvement of agencies such as the United Nations Children's Education Fund (UNICEF) in a country like Nigeria assumes great significance. As Minister for Education Professor Tunde Adeniran put it, an illiterate child is a threat to educated ones, and as a matter of fact to the entire nation in the long run. Studies of social exclusion and deviant behaviour consistently demonstrate the dangers of lopsided education policies around the World. In collaboration with the Federal Government, UNICEF through the girl-child project is promoting pre-primary, primary and post-primary education in ten northern states (Sokoto, Kebbi, Zamfara, Yobe, Jigawa, Katsina, Taraba, Bauchi and Kano). Apart from moving the nation towards the kind of equity that reduces suspicion and destructive distrust that damages the national psyche, it would also assist the democratic process of growing a more aware and critical citizenry. In the long run, recognition and regard for civic responsibility is boosted and by that much token is national renewal guaranteed.Dr. Stella Goings, UNICEF's Senior Program Officer in Nigeria, remarked that the organisation 'believes that education is the key instrument for empowering individuals in any society and basic education is the foundation for life-long learning and human development'. All of these together construct the launch pad for national development.

Part of the report of the Transition Monitoring Group which observed the Independent National Electoral Commission's (INEC) conduct of the last election for instance stated that a number of votes were nullified because voters marked their cards wrongly. In some cases, some voters could not even identify the political party of their choice on the electoral documents. The implication is that such people are effectively disenfranchised and the outcome of the election consequently becomes an imposition on such people by the privileged who were sufficiently educated to vote correctly. In this regard, education must be interpreted in its broadest sense. Especially among voting age adults, public enlightenment programmes can be launched to reduce the effect of lack of formal education. Visual rather than orthographic media are likely to make a significant contribution to the process. Such awareness-raising schemes will in the long run also serve to check unscrupulous elements from gaining access into the National Assembly. The impact of the old political dispensation in which money, power and influence rather than honesty, vision and capability decided political victory is evident in the state of the nation today. Mass education should curtail this trend.

As a language scholar and researcher especially in relation to education in multilingual and multicultural societies, I must mention the significance of promoting language policies that are capable of supporting development through education. The over-dependence on English in official circles is both a consequence of inheriting a colonial solely expressed in that medium as well as of a desire for safety net guaranteed by choosing a neutral language. However, several studies have shown that bilingualism or indeed multilingualism is beneficial to individual and society. In the Nigerian case, bilingualism is widespread especially of the type English plus mother tongue. However, government could consider exploring the possibility of establishing what I term 'bilingual education for responsible citizenship'. This project will require that different subjects be taught in two or three languages so that every Nigerian school pupil irrespective of ethnicity learns at least two other Nigerian languages through the years of schooling.

The cultural studies curriculum may be broadened to go hand in hand with the language curriculum so that multiculturalism is encouraged as well as multilingualism. This way, minority groups who account for over 40% of the national population, a substantial percentage, will feel less peripheralized and threatened by the Big Three (Hausa, Yoruba and Igbo) and cultivate a stronger sense of belonging in the nation. What seems to be happening now is that native speakers of the three main languages have no cause to learn any other language besides English, which prepares them for government work. This in itself is narrow and restricts the potential for human resource development. This is evident in the report that Nigerians are not getting appointed to positions in sub-regional organizations due to a lack of French language skills. Internally, speakers of minority languages, by sheer necessity of abode especially in urban areas like Lagos, acquire the language of the immediate community and become trilingual. They are the ideal Nigerians but owing to number politics and its advantage to the Big Three, access to mainstream power remain problematic for these ideal citizens. Multilingualism is growing in Europe and it is institutionally supported. As a result, it is carving out a bright future for the European Union (refer to the Luxembourg Experiment for instance). Investing in language policies that ultimately promote national cohesion will accelerate development.

In the past, public enlightenment has been considered to be a central government responsibility especially because of the old Public Enlightenment Units of Local Government Councils. Such units exist to complement the traditional media in some ways, such as in the dissemination of basic health and hygiene information, civic responsibilities and so on. The problem with this is that in situations where a Council has fallen into the wrong hands such Units may be used to entrench the incumbent regime instead of initiating a change of guard. However, in contemporary times, the nation is blessed with a sophisticated press industry, which is capable of incorporating the business of educating through informing the electorate. The media's embrace of this responsibility is evident in the way it has come alive since the inception of the new regime. Media role in 'outing' dishonourable members of the legislature, judiciary and hopefully eventually the executive in spite of the years of repression under the military may be taken as an indication of hope. Femi Falana, lawyer, human rights and pro-democracy activist, demonstrated the press's awareness and acceptance of the national call to duty when he cited legal backing for the action of his client, The News magazine in publishing the names of forty-nine judges recommended for dismissal in the Justice Kayode Esho report. He argued that the magazine acted in consonance with its constitutional obligation to uphold the responsibility and accountability of government, including its judicial arm to the people and in line with the anti-corruption policy of President Olusegun Obasanjo's administration (my emphasis).

EQUITY

There are several dimensions to the social and economic crises that have befallen Nigeria. Two of these are immediately relevant to my discussion here. The first is agreeing an equitable revenue allocation formula. It is obvious that in the almost forty years history of independence the Niger Delta has been hard done by in the distribution of the nation's wealth in spite of being the source of the fuel on which the nation runs (literally and metaphorically). Ironically, the region is one of the poorest in terms of quality of life in the country. This situation is not peculiar to Nigeria.

The industrial regions of the North and Northeast of England financed massive development in the South. South Africa's goldmines serviced distant towns and cities in the apartheid years. But this does not make the situation any less wrong. Even in those other disadvantaged areas, the quality of life was still better than obtains in Nigeria's Delta region. The welfare system in Britain for instance is a welcome palliative for inhabitants of the industrial North. The crisis which led to the hanging of Ken Saro-Wiwa and the Ogoni Nine in November 1995, and the continuing reports of sporadic kidnappings and killings in the Delta area have not earned Nigeria any respect in international circles but more notoriety. The National Assembly's recent ratification of 13% for mineral producing states is a good starting point. It may be necessary to consider at some point in the future an acknowledgement of the pricelessness of these regions to the nation. Until the problem is resolved development cannot commence in earnest.

The second problem of equity concerns budgetary control and allocation across various sectors. Government needs to also to look closely at the budgeting system that grants priority to armament than to education and health services. Under various military regimes, it is common knowledge that the defence budget superseded that for many other sectors. The embarrassing news of how N361 billion defence vote was spent between January and the May 29 hand-over by the immediate past military administration of General Abdulsalam Abubakar is still being digested in many quarters and the Kolade Panel may yet have to investigate the matter. In the forty years of independence, Nigeria has had one gruesome civil war, which cost the nation dearly in demographic and material terms. This does not justify the amount of money pumped into defence over the years. It would seem that excess money in the kitty could actually have encouraged corruption. No matter how elastic the salary scales of military officers and other public officials are, it is still difficult to understand how any officer/official could end up a millionaire or billionaire. Budgetary control must be revised to place desired emphasis on education, health and infrastructure in line with the demands of the times. Even nations like the United States, Russia and so on have cut down on armament since the end of the Cold War. Any nation that is unable to feed and keep a healthy and sophisticated population cannot raise a decent army even if it spends its entire budget on armament. In other words, investing in education and health is fundamental to building a nation's defense structure and therefore a more strategic approach.

TELECOMMUNICATIONS TECHNOLOGY

On the eve of the new millennium, it is a shame that Africa is saddled with leaders that are content with re-casting their citizens in the continuing saga of 'the wretched of the earth' that Franz Fanon talked about several decades ago. In the same time span the world has witnessed the miraculous transformation of Japan, Taiwan, Singapore, South Korea, Ireland and a host of others too numerous to list here. Apart from Arab North Africa, South Africa, and one or two other nations, the continent remains in dire straits. World development is anchored to telecommunications. In the late 70s and early 80s the Nigerian government joined the bandwagon of nations hooking up for the dawn of the Information Age. Multi-million dollar contracts were signed and that's when the uncrowned president of Nigeria the Late Bashorun MKO Abiola first came to the foreground of national politics, in connection with telecommunication deals with the Murtala/Obasanjo regime (remember ITT).

At least until recently, allegations were made that gratification had to be paid in order for telephone lines to be allocated. Attempts to circumvent that scam through subscription to mobile phone service was stalled by the monopoly that the Ministry of Communications under General David Mark put in place during Babangida's presidency. It is no wonder therefore that in the World Development Report for 1996, out of a selection of 133 countries, Nigeria's GNP per capita was the 19th lowest. On the same league table Cameroon was 47th, Ghana 33rd, Benin 30th, Congo 40th, Mauritania 35th. It is an embarrassment that these countries fare so poorly, but it's even a greater shame that Nigeria presents a relatively more precarious economic situation and therefore grimmer life for its citizens for a nation with its wealth of resources.

The current debates about restructuring telecommunications in Nigeria has revealed that Nigeria has only 700,000 telephone lines to its almost one hundred and twenty million population. This yields one of the world's most ridiculous ratios of one telephone to 17,150 people. Worse still, only 300,000 of the available lines have been allocated, of course, with all the attendant problems of servicing even those few lines. 'NITEL Exchange is temporarily down, please try again later' is the sing-song NITEL's automated responder entertains frustrated clients with regularly. But there is a more fundamental problem, that of attitude. The possession of a telephone line is still regarded as an indication of high social standing. Those in position of authority help to perpetuate such attitudes in their warped re-interpretation of Western capitalism. Unfortunately, to circumvent this official obstacle, those described as 'economic saboteurs' and 'crooks' in officialese set up 'illegal' telephone operations that run on the accounts of some government ministries. In such a situation where does one justifiably lay the blame? Even at the new rate of N20,000 for the installation of a line, telephone ownership still does not become a mass commodity considering that minimum wage is N3000 per month. In other words, over half a year's salary is spent on one facility. In Britain, British Telecom charges £150 connection, which is the equivalent of one week's salary at the very low end of the socio-economic scale. Telephone services are fundamental to appreciation in the quality of life because outside of business transactions, possessing a telephone also means that in cases of emergency people have relatively access to other services such as ambulance services, the fire brigade, and so on. In the exceptional circumstance that there is no telephone in a house, the public phone booths installed by British Telecom and other competing providers serve a useful purpose. The practical problems of vandalism and theft can be closely attended to by law enforcement agencies.

Besides, with global commerce now being increasingly negotiated and conducted on the Internet, immediate upgrading of Nigeria's telecommunications facilities is necessary for any meaningful development to occur. As the Minister of Communications, Mr Arkazi observed, 'the world is currently undergoing a telecommunications revolution and Nigeria cannot be an exception'. Electronic commerce grossed over US$5 billion in 1995. By 1998, this figure had risen fourfold. In terms of Internet connectivity and distribution of telecommunication networks, Nigeria and the rest of sub-Saharan Africa remain consigned to the margins housing only a negligible percentage of global connections. According to reports there are over six million pending applications for telephone installation throughout the country.

FUTURE PERFECT

For true apostles of change, there is only one vision and it must be of Nigeria's permanent rescue from the reins and shackles of tyrannical regimes. Nigeria has potentials not only to sustain itself but also to join the rank and file of the world's donor nations and cease being a recipient of crumbs off Western dinner tables. We have a dream that some day, the miracles of Japan, Singapore, Taiwan, South Korea, and Ireland can be replicated in Nigeria. The immense potentials of the continent feed this hope. It is known that a substantial portion of the world's natural endowment is located on African soil and its territorial waters. It is also known that today large numbers of African intellectuals who brain-drained away from the oppressive systems of their home countries are making significant contributions to the development of nations in the West and across all disciplines too, awaiting the 'come home rally'. All the raw materials are in position for the Nigerian debacle to transform into the Nigerian miracle.

The sub-region

Development in the 21st century must take cognizance of the nation's existence within the sub-region and of the continent as a whole. The early years of the oil boom witnessed Nigeria's assumption of a Tarzanic role, the Santa Claus of the African continent. Some of the measures taken while benefiting sister nations in the region to some extent amounted in the view of some analysts to a misplacement of priority. Basic infrastructure was lacking internally and poverty level rose. The national debt increased and high levels of mismanagement meant economic programmes such as the Structural Adjustment Programme insisted upon by the World Bank and the International Monetary

Fund did not achieve the ends for which they were designed. Coupled with the excessive graft in the system, the need arose for scapegoats and consequently we witnessed the expulsion of Ghanaians during the 2nd Republic of Alhaji Shehu Shagari. The history of the sixteen years that followed that expulsion completely exonerates those expelled.

Nigeria's role in ECOMOG has now repositioned the nation positively within the region. Fresh waves are building to constitute Africa into a strong economic and political block. The notion of an African Union similar to the European Union has been mooted and is being debated. Nigeria will have a role to play in such a union only if it is able to take care of its own problems. In the new political dispensation, the government seems to have realized the importance of good house-keeping. In the process, Nigeria, the sub-region and continent at large stand a better chance of being benefiting if this is followed through successfully. It is in this regard, for instance that the decision to monitor political development in the region but without necessarily frittering away national resource must be understood. President Obasanjo in announcing the phased withdrawal of Nigerian troops from Sierra Leone said, "Both the internal problems and the Sierra Leonean situation are inter-related. They are both important and the problems will be tackled separately." He added that his administration's foreign policy thrust is still on Africa. "Essentially, Africa is our port of call but we are not unmindful of the fact that our world must not start and end in Africa. Our world comprises other regions of the world" (Electronic Guardian News, September 6, 1999). G.G. Darah expressed the same view when he remarked that 'If Nigeria manages to recover from incipient dislocation, it could offer hope for the rest of the continent and Africans in the diaspora' (EGN, September 6).

DIVERSIFYING THE ECONOMIC BASE

Agriculture

Some analysts would argue that Nigeria's problems are rooted in the sudden oil wealth of the 1970s and 80s because it brought about the neglect of the agricultural sector, which had hitherto sustained the economy solely. The get-rich-quick culture was a consequence of that development. However, the problem was less to do it the discovery of oil than with bad leadership and management. A lack of vision and foresight saw Nigeria spending huge sums of money on the importation of food items such as rice and palm oil that had been locally produced. The desire to share in the national cake, which resided in the urban centers led to a mass rural-to urban drift and the abandonment of agricultural land. The Operation Feed the Nation scheme of the first Obasanjo era (1976-1979) lost its focus and soon became the arena for fertilizer scandals. It fed the growth of a middleman culture in which people who had nothing to do with agriculture got the licences for importation and sold them on to practising farmers. Consequently, farmers inflated the price of foodstuff to cover huge investments on procuring fertilizer for better yields. The success of the agricultural sector in places like the United Kingdom and the United States is dependent upon sound agricultural policies, which guarantee that farmers can earn a decent livelihood from the soil. While traditional farmers languish at the bottom of the socio-economic ladder in Nigeria they constitute the rural gentry and powerful lobby group in the West. For instance, in the US, potato farmer P.J. Taggares was nicknamed or renamed of Mr. Potato Head for 'receiving a record $52,000 fine from the PDC for his illegal contributions to Republican gubernatorial candidate Dale Foreman in 1996'. The fortune of the Nigerian farmer is buried beneath piles of State rubble and needs to be freed for the benefit of all and nation. The following song taught to primary school children in Yoruba-speaking areas of the country bears testimony to the significance of this sector of the economy.

Ise agbe n'ise ile wa
Eni ko sise yio ma ja'le
Iwe kiko lai si oko ati ada
Ko pe o, ko pe o.

Farming is our heritage occupation
Whoever does not farm will steal
Education without the hoe and machete
Doesn't pay, doesn't pay.

Obviously, people's attitudes have since changed. It is almost considered a curse to wish farming on any school-going kid today. As a matter of fact parents construct monstrosities of farmers and farming in trying to encourage their children to work hard at school in order to avoid ending up on a rural farm. This coupled with an educational system that seems to encourage people to see office work as the 'end', have done agriculture a bad turn.It is disheartening to note that improved palm kernel seedlings were taken from the International Institute for Tropical Agriculture (IITA), Ibadan in the mid-sixties to Malaysia. Today, while Malaysia is a leading world exporter of palm oil, Nigeria imports the commodity because not enough to meet internal consumption is produced locally.

Growing up in Makurdi in the 1960s, I remember the proliferation of cashew and other fruit trees – mango, guava, oranges, breadfruit, black currants etc. Some of these actually grew in the wild and had no owners to tend them, yet they flowered and yielded fruits. When these fruits were in season, people animals and insects had one endless festival and a lot went to waste. The situation is still very much the same today. It is also ironical that the nuts we discard after eating the flesh of cashew are worth a diamond in Europe. Europe's major supermarket stores carry processed fruits in cans and packets with various developing countries' insignia or names. South African wines, grapes, and other items, for instance, are a common sight in these stores. Preservation needs to be seriously addressed and government and big industrialists should invest in setting up storage, which can serve as distribution centers to which small-scale farmers can take their excess produce. Small family farm holdings have been abandoned as folks moved to the economic fringes of cities and towns, convinced that farming could not sustain them, especially with the onslaught of inflation in the 1980s. The harvests from the American prairies demonstrate how to turn Nigeria's wastelands into productive use. The nation is obviously blessed with good arable land and a climate that most other nations would give anything to have. Mechanized farming can be achieved with state support. As a matter of fact, state investment in agricultural production will not only solve the problem of food scarcity but it will also reduce the unemployment figure drastically and in the process solve some of the social problems of unemployment such as urban congestion, crime and the like.

Retraining of demobilized soldiers could prepare them for entry into another productive sector of the economy. This definitely is preferable to the rising rate of armed robbery allegedly traced to frustrated unemployed former soldiers who still have to carry the responsibility of breadwinners for their respective families. The National Youth Service Corps scheme can also be redesigned to serve the agricultural sector. According to the World Bank Report for 1996, Nigeria's urbanized population is a meagre 27%. In other words, the concentration of infrastructure in the urban areas is done at the expense of development in the rural areas and consequently against the current of all efforts geared toward national development. For one thing it encourages rural-urban drift creating the abandonment of the agricultural sector of the economy. For the cities, the problem of congestion leads to an over-stretching of available resources and with a poor maintenance culture and poor management all soon grinds to a halt. The economy's over-dependence on oil revenue means that the nation is gravely susceptible to downturns in the oil market.

Iron and Steel

Many would have seen the establishment of the Ministry for Iron and Steel in the Shagari era as paving the way for Nigeria's eventual entry into the industrial age. Unfortunately, it turned out to be a white elephant scheme both in its planning and execution. In the end, it became one of the major routes for emptying out the national treasury supervised by the late Minister Alhaji Ali Maman Makele. The general absence of any sense of probity grounded the project. Two decades later, the new minister in charge of the ministry, Chief Bola Ige is designing a framework for revamping the project.

His pronouncements though appear reassuring, his success will depend hugely on the successful re-orientation of those through whom he will have to translate his visions and plans into reality. In other words, the point made earlier about a need for change of attitudes has wide-reaching implications for Nigeria's future development.There was too much talk-shopping in the 80s about technology transfer that was not backed with concrete action. Indigenous technology needs to be encouraged. It was only a short while back that Taiwan-made motor parts and other goods were regarded as second rate, today Taiwan is one of the four Asian tigers and the World Bank's newly Industrialised Economies. Korean goods equally attracted the same reaction among Nigerians and South Korea is the fourth Asian tiger and NIE member-state. The expressions Aba-made and Onitsha-made may be the indication that these goods will some day hit the international market too. But in the case of the Asian nations, conscious institutional effort was made to promote these developments. Towards the close of the civil war in 1970, information emerged that the Biafran Army had invented an indigenous bomb, the 'Ogbunigwe'. Three decades later, there is no reason why between the National Academy of Science, The Nigerian Society of Engineers, and the Federal Ministry of Science and Technology, that invention has not been explored further, improved upon and patented. Unless government desire and commitment to development becomes evident, the nation will continue to frustrate its creative minds and drive them into the waiting hands of Bill Gates and his Western cohorts.

According to the Chief Ige, Iron and Steel constitute the backbone of development while electricity is its lifeblood. These resources if properly managed and exploited will provide the breather needed by the petroleum sector. Investments in gas exploration should also boost the economy considerably. However, those who negotiate on behalf of government especially with external firms need to demonstrate extreme shrewdness and patriotism to the nation. It is obvious that the wastes of the past three decades have been perpetrated with the assistance of some of these companies and firms. The ease with which large sums of government money were transferred into foreign accounts is a possible indication of external involvement in the graft that consumed the nation. It must be borne in mind that the primary loyalty of these firms is to their businesses and the nations in which they are registered. It is ironical that starving Nigerians should end up as second class citizens in the countries that have benefited from its wealth.

CONCLUSION

To borrow President Bill Clinton's quotation from his 1992 and 1996 campaign speeches in the US, 'I still believe in a place called Hope'. The past has been nightmarish, the present is no better, but Nigeria still has the wherewithal to make the necessary turn around in its fortunes. The future cannot be compromised or the repercussions will be grave. In fact, unless that turn around happens, the disintegration of the nation along lines of ethnicity and religion cannot be guaranteed. First and foremost public enlightenment and education are an absolute necessity for jump-starting the nation's development. Not only will the increased literacy level create a more sophisticated electorate needed to sustain democracy but it will also in the long run ensure better quality of life and higher standards of living. Diversifying the nation's economic base will reduce the stress of over-dependence on an unpredictable oil market. If corruption is permanently contained the image of the nation will improve and thus will the integrity lost during the wasted years of military rule be reinstated.

In closing, we must break ranks in order to break from the bondage of past disorderliness, endemic corruption and rot. In reconstituting ourselves for citizenship in the new Nation that we envision, transparent honesty, patriotism which ensure that we always put the interest of nation over and above our personal interests are the targets to aim at. Development needs these for a stable foundation to stand on.

Chapter XIII

MANAGING MULTI-ETHNICITY: LESSONS FROM NIGERIA

Kasirim Nwuke

1. INTRODUCTION

"An Igboman lives here" declares a statement scrawled across a door of a house in Ajegunle, a suburb of Lagos. "Hausa house" declares another. Occupants of these homes were compelled to declare their ethnic identity by the efflorescence of inter-ethnic violence between the Yoruba and Ijaw ethnic groups in the Lagos suburb in early November 1999. In another part of Lagos, Ketu, on the 24th November 1999, yet another violence broke out between the Yoruba and Hausa ethnic groups. The immediate cause of the violence appeared to be an attempt by the some Yoruba elements to have one of their own as the leader of a very prosperous market association, Shukura Yam Sellers Association of Nigeria (SYSAN). The market, the largest yam market in Nigeria, was founded by Hausa and Igbo traders and has few Yoruba traders and as members of the sellers association. The leadership of the association since its, since its inception, has always come from the North. The violence lasted for 2 days, left about one hundred persons dead and forced the President of the country to order the arrest of members of a Yoruba nationalist group, Oodua Peoples' Congress, (OPC), believed to be behind the violence and most of the violence in the south-west of the country. Any member of the OPC resisting arrest was to be shot-on-sight. In the aftermath, truckloads of Hausas have left Lagos in the southwest for the North.

In almost all parts of the country, there is one form of conflict or the other - ethnic or inter-ethnic. A very quick census might help illustrate the pervasiveness of the problem. The Niger Delta continues to boil. In October, twelve police officers sent to put down one of the conflicts in the town of Odi were kidnapped and killed by militant members of the Ijaw ethnic group. In the third week of November, the President ordered a punitive military expedition to Odi, ostensibly to apprehend the killers of the police officers. The town was razed to the ground, civilian casualties were high but the killers of the police officers are yet to be apprehended. In other parts of the Niger Delta, we can count the following conflicts: Ijaw/Itsekiri, Isoko/Isoko, Itsekiri/Urhobo. In the southwest we can count the Agbowo-Ijaw/Ilaje, Ife/Modakeke, Ijaw/Yoruba, Yoruba/Igbo, and an earlier Yoruba/Hausa conflict in Sagamu (which prompted reciprocal violence in Kano, Northern Nigeria, against Yoruba.) In the far north of the country, the governor of Zamfara, the poorest state in the Federation, has stoked the embers of religious and ethnic conflict by adopting the Islamic system of jurisprudence, Sharia. In the Northwest, there is conflict between the Takum and the Kuteb. So numerous are the conflicts that the government has deployed over 22,000 soldiers across the country in an effort to maintain the peace. In light of the efflorescence of ethnic and inter-ethnic, one can justifiably wonder if the Nigerian experiment is on the brink.

Nigeria is not new to ethnic and inter-ethnic conflict. It has over the years developed a tool kit for managing her diversity so as to reduce the incidence and intensity of conflict. It is a federation in which the constituent units exercise some reasonable degree of autonomy over their own affairs. The police force is organized as a federal rather than as a regional institution. The salary structure was until recently unified. It has a system of proportional representation in the civil service and the armed forces. The increase in the number and intensity of conflicts in the past several years, in spite of the existence of this tool kit, create the impulse for and provide an incentive to look anew at these tools. The central claim of this paper is that the instruments that Nigeria has used to manage her multi-ethnicity have themselves become a factor responsible for the increase in the number and intensity of conflict. Hence, efforts aimed at reducing the incidence and intensity of ethnic and inter-ethnic conflict must of necessity include a complete overhaul of these instruments. The importance of understanding the nature and causes of conflict arise from the basic fact that conflicts impose real economic costs on the country. First, they are costly to manage. Resources that could otherwise be used to increase the country's productive base have been dissipated in efforts to contain the conflicts. For example, the punitive expedition to Odi cost N500 million (The Guardian). Second, conflicts produce physical destruction of assets. Third, they disrupt transactions. They do this directly and indirectly—directly through the physical destruction of institutions that intermediate transactions and indirectly by eroding the basis for mutual trust among contracting parties, thus raising the cost of collective action across groups. Many economic activities cease in conflict-characterized environments. Conflict may also affect the consumption/saving decisions of households in the regions of the country most prone to conflict. Households may dissave out of fear that their savings may be destroyed in the next round of violence. Businesses may move out of the conflict-prone regions especially if there is no insurance. Ethnic conflict may also result in decreased in-flows of foreign direct investment and the flight of domestic capital—and out-flow of human capital through emigration. All of these consequences have growth reducing effects. It is thus evident that understanding the sources of domestic conflict—its causes—and crafting appropriate instruments for its effective and efficient management may have growth enhancing effects.

The rest of this paper is organized as follows. The next section (2) reviews the emerging economics literature on the growth effects of ethnic fragmentation. Section 3 provides a historical background to the management of ethnic conflict in Nigeria. Three instruments – creation of states, the Federal character principle, and the system of revenue allocation - used in Nigeria to manage the country's multi-ethnicity are analyzed in Section 4. Section 5 concludes.

2. PREVIOUS RESEARCH

Much has been written on the subject of ethnic conflict in the non-economics literature that it will be futile for me to attempt to discuss that literature. I shall therefore restrict myself to a brief discussion of the emerging economics of conflict literature. It was argued in the preceding section that the way in which a multi-ethnic country manages her multi-ethnicity may have implications for economic growth. The claim that ethnic fragmentation and conflict often associated with it may have fettered economic growth is not new in the literature. Early studies by Adelman and Morris (1967), Huag (1967), and Reynolds (1985) suggested that ethnic, religious, or linguistic diversity may fetter economic growth. Adelman and Morris (1967) hypothesized that "less developed countries that are relatively homogenous are less hampered in the achievement of social and political integration and in the initiation of continuous economic growth". Based on the analysis of limited time series data on language, religion, and ethnicity, from 74 countries for the period 1957 to 1962 they found that homogenous countries typically had higher economic growth rates. Huag (1967), a cross-section study based on the analysis of a 1963 data set from 114 countries, found an inverse relationship between ethnic diversity and per capita GNP – low levels of ethnic diversity were associated with higher levels of per capita GNP.

The observed widespread differences in recent times in economic growth rates across countries and regions and the persistence of low and negative growth rates in some countries, after corrections have been made for those factors that economists generally associate with growth, have kindled economists' interest in the role of "non-economic" factors as additional factors explaining a country's growth performance. Variables explored in this exercise include democracy (or a country's political regime), cultural diversity, ethnic and political fragmentation. With respect to developing countries in general and Africa in particular, attention has been focused on the growth effects of ethnic/group diversity. The widely held view is that countries that are ethnically and culturally heterogenous are vulnerable to slow growth rates. This conclusion is usually attributed to the variety of competing demands on political and economic capital that must be met or low level of social capital due to the difficulty disparate groups have in communicating or cooperating with each other.Recent findings (Reynolds (1985), Easterly and Levine (1997) lend credence to this view. Reynolds used data from 37 countries for the period 1950 – 1980 to explore the relationship between cultural diversity and economic growth. Again the hypothesis was confirmed: ethnic and cultural diversity leads to lower growth rates. He suggested that this result can be attributed to dichotomy between different peoples. Easterly and Levine (1998) set out to investigate the factors responsible for "Africa's growth tragedy". Using Barro-type regressions they found that at the aggregate level diversity significantly reduces the growth rate of the economy. They also argued that ethnic fragmentation may account for about 40% of Africa's poor growth performance. But Easterly and Levine provide no explanations as to why diversity may be detrimental to economic growth. Ethnic diversity constrains economic activity in different ways. For example, Alesina and Easterly (1997) found that the public sector performs poorly in very ethnically diverse societies while Collier and Garg (forthcoming) found patronage and rent-seeking to be especially common in ethnically diverse societies.

Collier (1998), unlike Easterly and Levine, found that that the effect of ethnic diversity on economic growth was very sensitive to the political environment. Put differently, ethnic diversity by itself is not a fetter on growth, it is political regimes that convert multi-ethnicity into constraints on growth. Ethnic fragmentation, Collier concluded, was damaging to economic growth in the context of limited political rights, but not in democracies. Collier also reports a non-monotonic relationship between ethnic diversity and violent conflict – societies most at risk of ethnic conflict, he found, were those in the middle of the range of diversity. Another important study is Roderick (1998) which studied differences in cross country growth rates between 1960 – 75 and 1975 – 89 and found that countries that experienced the sharpest drops in growth after 1975 were those with divided societies and weak institutions of conflict management.

In Roderick's world, conflict by groups over diminishing resources following an adverse external shock explained persistence in poor economic performance. However, ethnic conflicts need not however arise solely during periods of economic distress. Economic prosperity and declining inequality among ethnic groups can also release the forces of competitive exclusion and conflict. Ethnic groups compete in the same labor market and have access to similar sets of economic and political and social resources whose quantity is fixed. As the capacity of the economy to satisfy the increasing claims is exhausted, ethnic conflicts may result from niche overlap as groups struggle to protect that which they consider to be theirs. There is another problem with Roderick's analysis. It implicitly assumes that groups have an identifiable common utility function which they seek to maximize by engaging in collective actions and concludes therefrom that effective management of the inter-group conflict could have attenuated the growth reducing effects of the adverse external shock. If that is true, one would expect rational groups to make the instruments of conflict management an argument of their utility function.

From this brief review of the literature, it is clear that there is thus an economic component to ethnic conflict and that through various channels a connection between ethnic conflict and economic growth exits. Nonetheless (although not important for our purposes) these studies suffer from a number of shortcomings. First, they assume that all fragmented societies are conflict prone and that all homogenous societies are peace prone. But as Harris (1997?) has pointed out, conflict does not characterize all multi-ethnic countries neither is conflict the monopoly of multi-ethnic countries. Kazakhstan has over 102 nationalities or ethnic groups, none of which has yet entered into conflict with the state or with each other. The country of Yemen, which by all accounts is ethnically homogenous, was reported to have 46 political parties (Ibrahim, 1993). Yemen is relatively at peace while similarly homogenous groups (e.g. Somalia) are in pieces. The second problem with these studies is that they make use of highly aggregated data, and there are no country-level studies. Reynolds, for example, studied only 37 countries while Adelman and Morris used data for only 6 years and focused exclusively on developing countries. Huag used data for only one year although a time series analysis would have been more appropriate. The common methodological weakness of these studies, except Roderick, is that although they emphasize ethnic diversity they provide no compelling theoretical basis or rationale why and how ethnic fragmentation can be an additional factor explaining differences in growth performance. Finally, in none of the these papers is discussed the idea that the instruments of managing inter-group conflict can themselves be generators of conflict and retardants of growth.

3. BACKGROUND TO THE STUDY*

A sketch history of Nigeria is worthy of documentation in order to provide context for the issues discussed in this paper. The modern history of the country now known as Nigeria goes back to 1898. At that time, Britain controlled three contiguous territories: a) the Colony of Lagos with its Yoruba which was administered by the Colonial Office, b) the Niger Coast Protectorate consisting of the Bights of Benin and Biafra and their hinterlands which was administered by the Foreign Office, and c) the territory that later became known as Northern Nigeria which was under the Royal Niger Company.

The need to save on administrative costs forced Britain to consolidate these possessions. By 1900, administrative responsibility for these territories was consolidated in the Colonial Office. The Colony of Lagos became the Colony and Protectorate of Lagos, the Niger Coast Protectorate became the Protectorate of Southern Nigeria and the territory now known as Northern Nigeria became the Protectorate of Northern Nigeria and also came under the supervision of the Colonial Office. As can be seen from the foregoing, the need to exploit economies of scale (in London) was the compelling reason for bringing these territories. Further economies were achieved in 1906 when the two southern protectorates were amalgamated into the Colony and Protectorate of Southern Nigeria in 1906. The North and the South were administered as separate units until January 1st, 1914 when the Colony and Protectorate of Southern Nigeria was amalgamated with the Protectorate of Northern Nigeria to create the country today known as Nigeria. The British saw this "loose federation" as two cultural worlds (Afigbo, 1987). While, in the British view, the south was pagan, barbarous, unruly and unmanageable; the North was organized, Moslem and monotheist. It was a stratified society consisting of a ruling aristocracy and a peasantry, with a reasonable degree of social immobility. Because the south was "pagan and primitive", the British unleashed Livingstone's three C's – Civilization, Christianity, and Commerce – on the territory. Consequently, over a short period of time the south became covered with schools and churches as a result of the activities of the missionaries allowed into the territory. The North on the other hand, the British protected from the influence of missionaries, western commercialism, and the pagan southerners. The British were sensitive to the sensibilities of the ruling northern aristocracy who they soon co-opted into the system of native administration known as Indirect Rule. The provision of infrastructure in the North was undertaken at a relatively slower pace in order not to upset the Northern status quo and when efforts to dispense with southern labor failed, the British segregated southern migrants to the North in townships called Sabo-ngari. Until 1946, there was very little political contact between the north and the south.

There are three identifiable consequences of this deliberate British policy. First, it slowed the involvement of the North in western education and created disparities between the North and the South in terms of education and infrastructural development. These disparities, especially in education persist today. Second, it led to the emergence of ethnic awareness. Southern migrants segregated in the townships and the northerners locked behind their walled cities became aware of their "distinctness." Third, it awakened ethnic conscious and led to the creation of stereotypes – most of them negative. To the northerner, the southerner was primitive, an unbeliever; and to the southerner, the northerner was backward, lazy, indolent, uneducated and very amenable to British control. The process of awakening ethnic awareness and consciousness was further helped by increasing urbanization. For many migrants to the new commercial centers in search of modern sector jobs, the urban environment was risky, alien, and insecure. The jobs open to Africans were limited in number and the incidence of destructive competition for them high. In the uncertain and risky urban environment, many migrants sought security in ethnic and clan associations. Only in such associations were they confident of mutual trust, useful communication, and mutual aid. They thus served to ameliorate the pervasive insecurity of urban life and to enhance the migrant's chances of getting a job. These organizations also served as buffers for those who had lost their jobs. In due course, they began to serve as cells for political agitation aimed at advancing the political interest of the specific ethnic group.

Britain's two-pronged approach to governing was an important determinant of the future constitutional structure of Nigeria. As the struggle for independence, led mostly by nationalists from the south intensified, the British began to search for ways to secure the interest of the North in an independent Nigeria. The geographical map of Nigeria had already been drawn in a way that made the North bigger than the south. In 1939, the south was re-divided into two, East and West. The River Niger was used as the natural boundary. This new arrangement led to the emergence of new stereotypes. The West became synonymous with Yoruba, the East with Igbo, and the North with Hausa-Fulani. But "these images corresponded not with the cultural and sociological realities but with demographic reality" (Afigbo, 1987). Believing that each administrative unit was a homogenous political and cultural entity that could operate as an organic unit within a loose federal structure, the British began to consider the possibility of a federal system for Nigeria. A federation, it was argued, would permit each of the groups of provinces to enjoy its distinct cultural and political traditions and to develop at its own pace. The 1946

Richards (Milverton) Constitution pointed to the possibility of political development along the lines of three regions. And by the constitutional arrangements of 1951 and 1953-4, a federal pattern of development was firmly established. Political thinking thereafter amongst influential sections of the Nigerian nationalist movement began to speak the language of ethnicity and, reacting to the new constitutional and office-holding opportunities that arose, intensified withdrawal into the region. In each region, the dominant ethnic group became the ultimate source of power, influence and advancement.

It can thus be seen from the foregoing that deliberate British policy created a tripartite conflict which to a large extent, determined the nature of Nigerian politics and the allocation of resources and access to economic resources. It can also be seen that this policy created another challenge for the emerging country – what to do with other ethnic groups, members of whom had become suspicious that independence from the British would result in their domination by the large ethnic groups. These ignored groups began to clamor for regions of their own. Sensitive to the need to assuage the fears of these newly emerged ethnic minorities, the British set up a Commission in 1957 - the Willink Commission - to examine the desirability of further division of Nigeria into more states. Intriguingly, most of the demands for new regions came from the majority ethnic groups, not from the minority ethnic groups. Only one demand came from the North. The Commission rejected each one of the demands and gave preference instead to constitutional guarantees of individual rights. It also recommended ad hoc Development Boards and Councils for areas that were in need of special attention such as the Niger Delta. But this was not sufficient to stem the demand and clamor for new states.

4. DEALING WITH MULTIPLE ETHNICITY

Immediate post-independence Nigeria was characterized by the unequal distribution of political power on a regional and ethnic basis. In the Regions, the dominant ethnic groups dominated political power and access to scarce economic resources. At the Center, a coalition of the East and the North dominated power. Large indigenous capital was absent or non-existent. The governments – Federal and Regional – controlled almost all the resources and the means of production. The implication of this was obvious - government, whether at the center or in the regions, was going to be the prime engine for and of change.

Consequently possession by a party (and by extension, an ethnic group) of the levers of government would guarantee control of the allocation of the scarce economic resources which could be used to transform the social and economic conditions of its ethnic group.Against this reality, the minority ethnic groups intensified their agitation for regions of their own but none of the three dominant ethnic groups wanted its power diluted by the creation of a new state out of the region that it controlled. It was not until 1963 that the coalition government of the East and North at the Center created the Midwest Region out of opposition controlled Western Nigeria.

No further attempts were made to manage Nigeria's multi-ethnicity through this instrumentality until the military take over of power in January 1966. The new military government, aware of the destabilizing influence of regionalism, abolished the regions by Decree No. 34 of May 1966 and reconstituted Nigeria into a unitary state. It also prohibited ethnic unions and associations. The hope of the military administration was that a unitary system, by removing the majority/minority dichotomy, will extirpate the scourge of ethnic politics. Subsequent military regimes have taken other concrete actions to de-emphasize the structural and institutional basis of assertive competition arising from ethnic consciousness. These attempts include the creation of states, the introduction of the National Youth Service Corps, the Unity Schools, a Central Police Force, Federal Character system, and a host of other instruments. In the sections that follow, I review three of the instruments used to manage ethnic conflict in Nigeria: a) the creation of states, b) and the Federal Character Principle, and c) revenue allocation.

Creation of States

Few policies better illustrate the dynamics of the management of ethnic competition in Nigeria than the creation of states and the changes it has produced in the consolidation of ethnic and individual identity. As noted elsewhere in this paper, British policy set in motion the process of the "transformation of the ethnic-group-in-itself into the ethnic-group-for-itself." (Nnoli, 1980). As already discussed, the "exclusionary" politics of the newly emerged ethnic majorities both at the center and in the regions forced the newly emerged ethnic minorities to begin to agitate for their own states. In 1966, the military administration committed itself to the creation of states based on principle that no one state should be in a position to dominate or control the central government. On the eve of the civil war in 1967, the Military government divided up the country into twelve states based on the principle that "no one state should be in a position to dominate or control the central government." As Afigbo (1987) has noted, this "was an essential measure in the context of the confrontation between the East and North."

It was necessary that "the secession be seen, not as that of the whole of Eastern Nigeria against the North but as that of the majority in one state - East Central State, trying to secede from the Federation of twelve." But it was an ad hoc solution to a long festering problem. There were no consultations among the federating units and the units were very unequal in size. Therefore, not unexpectedly, the agitation for states continued. Seven more states were carved out in 1976. Today, there are thirty six states. Within each of these states, new majorities have emerged as have new minorities.Yet, the agitation for states continue. Why? There are two explanations for this phenomenon. First, state creation has become an institutionalized way of distributing rents, especially among the dominant ethnic groups because States are the basis for the distribution of national resources.

The majority ethnic groups have clamored for and have been subdivided into very many states. This has increased their share of revenues distributed from the Federation account. Consider the two main ethnic groups in the South. In 1975, when all the Yorubas were in one state – Western State, their share of the majority of revenue from the Federation account was 10.8%. The Igbo who were all in one state at that time, East Central State, received 10.32%. In 1977/78, after the Yoruba had been divided into three new states, their share of the Federation account rose to 14.55%, while the Igbo then in two states received 11.46% of the Federation account. In 1996 (Table 1), the share of the Yoruba, now in five states, (excluding Lagos) out of the Federation account stood at 11.88%, the share of the Igbo (now in 5 states) stood at 9.29%. Contrast this with the share of revenues received by the two minority states – Rivers and Bendel who produce much of Nigeria's oil. In 1975, Rivers State's share was 10.72% while Bendel's was 12.90%. In 1996, River's share had fallen to 3.86% while Bendel's fell to 3.40%. Put bluntly, state creation in Nigeria has meant the redistribution of resources from the minority ethnic groups to the majority ethnic groups. This has has created anger and discontentment in the oil producing region where the view is widely held that resources from the region are used, figuratively speaking, to irrigate other parts of the country while leaving the Delta region dry.

The second explanation for the persistent clamor for states is the federal character principle (to be discussed in the next section). This principle requires proportional representation of all states in all institutions of the Federal government. The effect of this mandate on the agitation for new states is captured in this statement by Ayida (19***):

"The inevitable division, in the long run, of Bendel state into three or four states is in the interest of future Bendelites given the current morally indefensible quota system of admission into Federal Unity Schhols and colleges and the adverse consequence of reflecting "Federal character"in appointment in the Federal Public Service."

A perverse consequence of the Nigerian type of federalism is that the primary motive for a devolution of powers and responsibilities is not the need to bring government closer to the people, gains each of the federating units will get from a federal structure. The struggle for the spoils of the federation among the ethnic groups-as-states has thus become a source of conflict.

One of the major shortcomings of the state creation process in Nigeria is that very little attention was paid to the viable of the new units. Created largely on ad hoc basis or as Soyinka (1999) has submitted "as a birthday present to an importuning military Head of State's spouse or as a bribe to one constituency or the other", most of the states are not economically viable. Their non-viability is reflected in their poor fiscal positions. The revenue base of almost all the states is shallow. Only two states, Lagos and Rivers, consistently generate substantial revenues internally (see Table 2). Almost all depend on the Federal government for at least 80% of their revenues. Taken together, the states do not contribute up to 10% of the combined revenues of the Federal and State governments (see Table 3). Consequently, the fiscal operations of the state governments have been characterized by growing deficits. The combined deficits of the States rose from N81.9

million in 1990 to N5,564.7 million in 1995 (CBN). Most of the states are not in a position to provide public goods and social services.

Most have difficulties meeting their payrolls on a monthly basis and their ability to engineer economic growth has been constrained by the fact that almost all their expenditures are concentrated on recurrent expenditures at the expense of capital programs that would naturally enhance economic growth. The inability of the State governments to fulfill their statutory obligations has raised social and ethnic tension.The Federal government has on several occasions bailed the states out. The accumulating fiscal deficits of the State governments have macroeconomic consequences since they reduce the amount of funds that could be lent to the private sector. Although the fiscal deficits of the States can be interpreted as a proxy measure of the cost of the use of state creation as a tool for managing multi-ethnicity, the full measure of the cost must include the value of the services not provided, the social tensions generated by their inability to provide basic services, and the cost of containing the conflicts consequently generated.

Revenue Allocation Formula

Successive Nigerian governments have used the system of redistributing fiscal capacity among the constituent units of the country as an instrument for promoting national unity. The goal is to ensure that a situation would not arise where a state's or a region's fiscal capacity could be greater than the Federal government's or where disparities in fiscal capacities among the regions (horizontal imbalance) could threaten the continued existence of the country. Consequently, over several years and after several iterations, the federal government came to concentrate most revenue generating resources in her hands. This has created the need to redistribute fiscal capacity to the states and local governments. In doing so, the Federal government seeks to use as an instrument to: a) ensure balanced development across different parts of the country, and b) equalize resources among the constituent units of the Federation, and c) promote national unity.

Revenue sharing has been a thorny and contentious issue in Nigeria. On this subject alone, between 1946 – when Nigeria formally adopted the regional structure - and 1988, Nigeria has had nine fiscal commissions, six military decrees, and one Act of Parliament. Almost all of these revenue allocation commissions, decrees, or Act of Parliament have been correlated with a change in government, reflecting a change in the balance of power between the ethnic groups. Revenue sharing was an important issue in the Richards constitution 1946 because it was the critical variable upon which the subsequent distribution of responsibilities between the National and the regional governments was based. From 1946 to 1969, three main principles - derivation, national interest and need - governed the distribution of revenue among the various administrative units in the country. To these were added at various times the principles of even development, fiscal autonomy and continuity of government services. In 1970, the structure of the Nigerian economy changed. Oil, found largely in the minority Niger Delta became the country's main revenue earner. The Federal government abrogated the principle of derivation and directed that the Federation Account should be shared on the basis of population (50%) and equality of states (50%). Only two percent of Federally collected revenue was set aside to be shared among the "minerals" producing states on the basis of derivation. Several Commissions and many military decrees, later the Federal government in 1999 retains 50% of all federally collected revenues collected.

Thirty percent is shared among the States on the basis of: a) equality of states (40%), b) population, 30%, c) social development factor 10% (education 4%, health 3%, water 3%), d) land mass and terrain (10%), and e) internal revenue effort - 10%. Of the remaining 20%, Local governments receive 15%, and the Special fund 5% (Federal Capital Territory, 1%, stabilization 0.5%, derivation 1%, development of oil producing areas 1.5%, and general ecology, 1%.)

Much of the conflict in the oil producing Niger Delta is attributable to anger over the manner in which the revenue is allocated amongst the constituent units of the federation. As was noted earlier the creation of additional states out of the twelve initially created in 1967 has been at the expense of the two major oil producing states of Rivers and Bendel. Much of the financing of these new states was made possible only through proportionate reductions in their share of revenue from the federation account. This has resulted in a substantial decrease in the fiscal capacity of these two states making it difficult for them to carry out the developmental activities in the Niger Delta. The use of population and land mass as redistributive principles resulted in the further reduction of their share of Federation account accruing to the oil producing minority states. On a per capita basis non-revenue producing states received such as Yobe, Kwara, Niger, and Adamawa, in 1996 (see Table 4) received almost twice as much as Rivers and Delta States from the Federation account. This redistribution of fiscal capacity away from the revenue producing states to the non-revenue producing states led Soyinka (1999) to the conclusion that "the oil producing states have been treated as vassals to a remote and avaricious center". It is the perceived unfairness of the principles upon which the search for horizontal equity is based that explains the wide spread revolt against the Federal government and her agents in the oil-producing region.

There is another sense in which the revenue allocation formula generates conflict. The concentration of fiscal capacity in the hands of the federal government even as greater fiscal responsibility is being shifted to the state and local governments makes the center the object of contest amongst dominant groups. Control of the central government will enable them to allocate albeit in the right way through the location of projects, additional scarce resources either to their states of origin or the benefit of their ethnic group. This in turn makes the center an agent of conflict as it becomes an instrument of struggle for control of the ethnic group in power. It is against this backdrop that the brutal suppressions of protest in the Niger Delta carried out by successive regimes can be understood.

5. Conclusion

The discussion thus far has tried to show that the three main instruments used by Nigeria to manage her multi-ethnicity have become conflict-generators, not conflict-pacifiers. In this section we try to draw some policy lessons. In the real world of Nigerian politics, the situation is more complex. The ambitions and egos of ethnic leaders and politicians are probably not amenable to policy prescriptions. The government should work towards an incentive structure that can induce disaffected communities to patch up. The Federal character principle should be reviewed – perhaps it should not be a constitutional provision and there should be a date certain when it will no longer be used in hiring and appointments in the Federal Services.

Further, an arrangement should be worked out to wind down States that are not economically viable as they have become a drain on national resources. In addition, the derivation should be brought back as a one of the principles for the sharing of the Federation of account.

Chapter XIV

Constitutional Authenticity: Constructive Incorporation of Traditional Institutions into the New Nigerian Experiment

Bamidele A. Ojo

Prior to the coming of the Europeans to our shores, we lived in our respective communities and shares certain values and in many cases different from neighboring groups and thereby resolves our differences and in competition according to unique and local norms. The Europeans in its colonizing mission rendered obsolete and undermine these norms and values. The result is the dissolution of our norms, institutions and values. Today, we suffer encore from the absence of and the ineffectiveness of these values and norms, which renders our culture in complete and totally at odd with our new found imported values and norms. Central to this entire imbroglio is our relationship with our environment and perceptions of our obligations toward one another and existing institutions. Many people cringes from the questions of religion and their impact on contemporary culture in our society today. Like many societies, religion constitute the bedrock of social formation and intra and inter community interaction. It is also valuable to consider the impact of religion on institutional building and social interaction in our society. The problems of contemporary Nigerian society like many other African societies cannot be divorced from the legacy of colonial disruption of pre-colonial ethnic societies as well as the termination and disruption of existing ethnic religions. The post colonial decay we are experiencing cannot be divorced from the confusion resulting from a lack of a firm tradition and religious foundation that recognizes our unique environment and that which form the basis of our very own society. The alien religion thereafter imposed and instituted in our societies constitute therefore a major obstacle to socio-political development, wherein a people is linked to its root and from whence it develops its identity. We remain therefore a people in a flux, unsure and unable to sustain the necessary socio-political growth because of an absence of a linkage to our own heritage.

The attempt to adopt alien values and norms creates therefore a traumatic and incomplete process of nationbuilding and socio-political development.

Why else do we think that, what form the basis of the "people" is irrelevant to the process through which we evaluate our intra-and inter societal responsibility. Why do we think that eliminating the linkage to our heritage and norms is irrelevant to the process of nation building and agenda setting in a competitive environment whereby we have to adapt to others values in order to be able to compete with that "other" within its own socio-culturally determined environment, wherein we are at a disadvantage because of our inauthenticness in their norms and tradition. This is not an attempt to propose that the reason why the state has failed in Nigeria or every where else in Africa is because we have abandoned our tradition and embraced western values and culture. We could have embraced these values and still be successful at statebuilding, if we have integrated some of our values and adapt these alien institutions to our unique environment. We have not done that and therefore lack the raison d'etre as a people in the process of socio-political development. Since independence, we have constantly promoted a colonial agenda, which reinforces western values and tradition as against traditional African cultures.

In many Nigerian (and in many other African countries) schools, the curriculum is developed with the aim of making students responsive to, while promoting colonial civilization and therefore knowledgeable about the western world rather than facilitate an understanding of their respective ethnic and national tradition and civilization. Many Nigerians went through a socialization process akin to that in existence in many western societies. For instance, speaking of any Nigerian languages in high school is unacceptable and the use of Nigerian languages as business and official medium of expression is just gaining ground. English and other foreign languages are compulsory in our elementary and high school curriculum while Nigerian languages do not command such respect. The history of our people or our literature or philosophy do not command the same recognition as those of western Europe. Aristotle and Plato are of more significance as well as Shakespeare than the thoughts of leading Hausa, Ibo or Yoruba historical figures. Even at the University, it remain the same and many young Nigerians have no choice but to embrace these new western values. Many Nigerians today could hardly speak their own languages with clarity and efficiency and many more could hardly remember any historical figure in their past and neither could they decipher what their ancestral beliefs were. This is a painful process which include a deliberate elimination of whatever might have survived the traumatic years of colonization such as some traditional religions and institutions, such as that of the rulership in many part of Nigeria. While I respect the right of people to profess whatever religion that they may hold dear to their heart I wonder why, in a continuation of the colonial modus operandi, we have effectively undermine the relevance of many of our traditional religions and institutions, thereby disrespecting our traditional values instead of using it as a vehicle for promoting the well being of our people. Like any religion, we could have effectively adapted our traditional religion to changing environment. But if one look around today, one is more likely to conclude that we have always been Christians and Muslims. All our holidays and activities presents these false sense of identity and that is why today the traditional institutions have become ineffective and getting obsolete.

In the realm of politics, there has been a unique recognition of the important role of the institution of the Oba and traditional rulership. It remains the most authentic link to our heritage. This fact is never lost on the politician as he or she seeks recognition and the blessing of the traditional ruler and eventually its people and voters. The politicians sees nothing wrong in seeking the protection of the Ifa oracle or Sango as he compete for the political office. Today, Nigerian are all preoccupied with chieftancy titles as they seek political recognition and at the same time they fail to acknowledge the relevance of these symbols and institutions to our political system. We know why the Europeans eliminated these institution in the past because, it constitute at that point in time the most important resistance to colonial rule. Its divine authority and spirituality allows people to respect its very existence but it co-exist today inspite of the growing domination of modern religions. It is the premise of this piece that, it is important to incorporate these traditions into the contemporary political experiment. It is a process that must receive popular support and our curriculum at all levels of education should acknowledge the existence of our unique values and religions, which will make it easier for social transition as we come together as a people. This is not an anti- Christian or anti-Muslim proposal but it is a proposal that acknowledge and condemns the inhuman and unfair destruction of these institutions in the hands of earlier missionaries, colonial government and jihadist while they prosecuted many adherent of traditional religions.

We must therefore give some credence to their existence and allow people to freely choose their form of spiritual aspiration in the spirit of the fundamental right to practice any religion. While the constitution proclaims a secular state, governments at all levels should desist from sponsoring religion activities and pilgrimages. There is a need to depoliticized religion at all levels in Nigeria and allow voluntary social and religion association to operate freely through an independent commission that has nothing to do with any levels of government. The commission should acknowledge all religious practices in the country and should treat them as equal while helping to promote them. Obviously some will be powerful than the other but special assistance should be given to encourage endangered traditional activities that could help to inform and rehabilitate many of our traditions and norms that have suffered centuries of abuse and humiliation.

At the political level, traditional institutions should be incorporated into the new Nigerian political experiment as a means of facilitating its integration in our social and political milieu. The traditional rulership can play important roles in our political infrastructure as we did earlier in our political history. We could involve them as part of a legislative or executive process at all levels of government. We should also encourage their judicial role as a means of building the foundation for a more viable and authentic democratic society. Democracy is a way of life and involves a covenant between the ruled and the rulers to create within the community mutual respect for all citizens and a collective responsibility for everybody's political and material survival. Everybody, including the traditional elite (such the Obas, Obis, Emirs) should participate fully in the running of the community affairs. The Chiefs or the Obas, or the Obis, or the Emirs, etc could play primary role in our new democratic experiment. As is the case in Botswana's democratic experience, the traditional elite should be the moderator for their people. They should provide leadership and help to decide whether to modify, develop or abolish certain practices and traditions. They should, in this new experiment concern themselves with the protection of fundamental rights. By being the protector of people's right, they would facilitate a gradual integration into the new experiment. The Chiefs and their contemporaries remain therefore the most important promoter of democracy. Their functions should be the democratization of existing institutions within their community and as part of the ruling class, they remain the most viable agent for democratic institution in Nigeria.

CONCLUSION : SUSTAINING DEMOCRACY IN NIGERIA

The task ahead in Nigeria now is to sustain the current political experiment and that will take years of socio-political stability and economic development. In order to realize the intrinsic value of democracy within which lies the idea of liberty, equality, freedom and the government of, for and by the people, and given Nigeria recent history, it becomes necessary to create the conditions necessary for sustaining the current democratic process as an avenue toward enhancing the process of nation building. What has become obvious since the present leadership assume office, is that they are in need of political education, that would allow them to appreciate their role as democratic leaders in this new dispensation. We have seen witch hunting, abuse of both legislative and executive powers at both the local, state and national levels and a level of ignorant of their responsibility that is very scary. The result of this uncertainty has manifest itself in the lack of response to some critical development since May 29th, 1999. There might be a tendency to give some lee -way to slow response to the killings and chaos caused by the ethnic and religious crisis that has been taking place in Nigeria but one must wonder about the non- prosecution of some current political actors who have contributed to the pillaging of the Nigerian economy in the last decades.

Since the inauguration of the current elected representatives and given the absence of existing democratic tradition(given), there has also been a disconnect between leadership responsibility and their respective constitutional obligations(a manifested lack of coordinated and organized adherence to democratic and constitutional requirements of the new Republic). Legislators at both the national and state levels do not understand what their roles should be, what is required of them, what their rights are and the functioning of their respective institutions. While the level of ignorance may not necessarily be as a result of a lack of desire to do otherwise, it is apparently a dangerous trend which may undermine the current political experiment in Nigeria. Many of our representatives do not understand the diversity existing outside their constituencies. For example, it is extremely difficult for a senator or a member of the house of representative from Sokoto state in north western Nigeria, who has never been to Delta State to fully appreciate a legislative issue bearing on the current ethnic conflict in that region. This is where many of the mushrooming non-profit human rights organizations and AID organizations will become a very viable actors in Nigeria political development. Many of which, thanks to grants from many international organizations and governments, have been involved in political education of the leadership as a means of addressing this particular problem.

The current climate in Nigeria is very tenuous but it is a valuable test for a young democracy and the ability to resolve this and many others will be very important in the process of sustaining it. The inter-ethnic crisis all over Nigeria, coupled with the religious strives are obstacles to democratization but in order for Nigeria to build a sense of nationhood, it must find a way to resolve them within the context of the constitutional provision and the rule of law, thereby developing in the mind of the people, a sense of security and common identity within their respective communities.

The Obasanjo administration must show its commitment to rid the country of the epidemic corruption that has become the culture under the past administration and this must be done by making it obvious to every Nigerians, that bribery and corruption will no longer be acceptable. It must demonstrate its commitment by showing leadership and its choice of policy and actions taken against past individuals who have pillage the Nigerian economy. This process must be just and within the rule of law. In resolving the crisis in Nigeria today, a special federal commission is needed to serve as a bridge builder between all communities and to help in conflict resolution and peace making between warring factions. All hands need to be on deck in helping Nigeria navigate the present transitional period. That is why, this exercise is put together and very timely in voicing a generational perspectives on the Nigerian experiment. There are millions of Nigerian experts and scholars outside the country and the new leadership must find the appropriate incentive, to enable the country benefit from their knowledge and expertise. Effort must be made to facilitate the home-coming of all the brains that have left our shores during the hey days of the military. Contrary to some view that many of these people have abandon the country, many of them have given a lot to this country before they traveled out and many did so, in fear for their lives. We need every one to come together to work for the renaissance of the giant of Africa. For Nigeria needs all Nigerians and Africa needs Nigeria even more.

ENDNOTES

CHAPTER I:

1. Ronald Reagan, quoted in *New York Times,* (May the 7, 1987), p.14.
2 Nigerian (Constitution) Order in Council, S.I 1960 no. 1652.
3. See Frederick Rotimi Williams. The Making of The Nigerian Constitution. *Constitution Makers on Constitution Making: The Experience of Eight Nations.* Robert A. Goldwin and Art Kaufman, eds. (Washington D.C.: American Enterprise Institute for Public Policy Research, 1988), p. 433.
4. Ali Mazrui, The Blood of Experience: The Failed State and Political Collapse in Africa, Paper Presented at the Cairo Consultation on The OAU Mechanism on Conflict Prevention, Management, and Resolution, sponsored by the Organization of African Unity, the Government of the Arab Republic of Egypt, and the International Academy, May 7-11, 1994.
5. Myron Weiner Empirical Democratic Theory and The Transition From Authoritarianism to Democracy. *Political Science,* 20:4, (Fall, 1987) p.866.
6. Robert A. Goldwin and Art Kaufman. eds. *Constitution Makers on Constitution Making: The Experience of Eight Nations.* (Washington D.C.: American Enterprise Institute for Public Policy Research, 1988), p. vii.
7 ibid, p.1.
8. Two distinguished studies which trace the evolution of modern constitutionalism are Charles H. Mcllwain, *Constitutionalism: Ancient and Modern.* (Ithaca: Cornell University Press, 1983); and Edwin C. Corwin, *The Higher Law Background of American Constitutional Law.* (Ithaca: Cornell University Press, 1979).
9 As a noted legal authority has observed, the former Soviet Constitution does not provide for judicial review to check the power of the Supreme Soviet. See Louis Henkin, *The Rights of Man Today.* (Boulder, Co.: Westview Press, 1978), pp.66-70.
10. For a fuller discussion of these claims, see Henkin, *The rights of Man Today,* pp.31-35.
11. For a full discussion of this, see Herber Butterfield, *The Whig Interpretation of History.* (New York: Norton, 1965).

12. For a clear statement of this view, see Immanuel Kant, AWhat Is Enlightenment? in Terrence Ball and Richard Dagger, eds. *Ideals and Ideologies: A reader*. 3rd ed. (New York: Longman, 1999), selection 17.

13. Nosa Omoigui, Identifying and Eliminating The True Causes of Nigeria's Malaise. distributed by NOSAO@EXCHANGE.MICROSOFT.COM, June 23, 1999.

14. Alan S. Rosenbaum, ed. *Constitutionalism: The Philosophical Dimension.* (New York: Greenwood Press, 1988), p.4.

15. For a thorough discussion of this, see Julius O. Ihonvbere, The 1999 Constitution of Nigeria: The Limitation of Undemocratic Constitution Making. Paper presented at the Conference on The 1999 Constitution and the Future of Democracy in Nigeria: Bridging the Gap Between the State and Civil Society, organized by the Centre for Democracy and Development (CDD), Abuja, Nigeria, June 29-July 3, 1999. See also, Issa G. Shivji, AState and Constitutionalism: A New Democratic Perspective, in Issa G. Shivji, ed. *State and Constitutionalism: An African Debate on Democracy.* pp.27-28.

16. Evod Mmanda Debate on Constitutional Reform in Tanzania: Which Way to Effect Democratic Reforms? Paper presented at the workshop on The Process of Constitution Making in Kenya with Experiences From Uganda and Tanzania, Organized by Kituo Cha Katiba (Centre for Constitutionalism), Mombassa, Kenya, pp.19-20, November 1998.

17. John Mbaku. Private conversation on reactions to the 1999 Nigerian Constitution, May 25, 1999.

18. See the discussion provided by Amos Sawyer on Making the Nigerian Constitution in *Constitution Makers on Constitution Making: The Experience of Eight Nations.* ibid. pp.436-437.

19. Rotimi Williams, ibid. pp.434-435.

20. See Victor Aikhionbare and O.Jay Umeh, ARedefining the Role of the Military in the Third World: The Case of Nigeria, paper presented at the 23rd Annual Third World Conference, March 19-22, 1997, Chicago, Illinois. For a thorough discussion of this role, see Talukder Maniruzzman, *Military Withdrawal From Power*, (Cambridge: Ballinger Publishing company, 1987).

21. Karl Von Clausewitz. *On War* (New York: Modern Library, 1943, Vol I and II).

22. This point was made unequivocally by leaders of the United Democratic Front of Nigeria (UDFN) in a meeting with General Abdusalami Abubakar during his visit to New York in 1998.

23. For a discussion of the non-federal nature of Nigeria, see Chris Ebhote, The New Constitution, *The Guardian* (April 19, 1999). See also, Kofo Awosika, The Fiction of Democracy in Nigeria, *The Guardian* (April 17, 1999).

24. Charles Hauss, *Comparative Politics: Domestic Response to Global Challenges.* (New York: West Publishing company, 1994) p.443.

25. Jide Ajani, The Imperatives of a State Police Force, *Vanguard* (September 10, 1999). Distributed by DEFSEC@EGROUPS.COM, September 10, 1999.

26. ibid.

27. Nosa Omoigui, ibid.

28. Martin Edelman. *Democratic Theories and The Constitution*. (Albany: State University of New York Press, 1984), p.35.

29. See Morton White, *Philosophy, The Federalist, and The Constitution*. (New York: Oxford University Press, 1987), p.97-99.

30. Chinua Achebe, AAchebe to Nigerians: We're on the Right Course, *The Guardian* (August 25, 1999).

31. Alan S. Rosenbaum, ibid, p. 4.

32. ibid.

33. Paul H. Dunn, *Look at Your World*. (Salt Lake City: Bookcraft, 1978).

34. See *The Political and Miscellaneous Works of Thomas Pain* (London, 1819).

CHAPTER II:

1. An earlier version of this article was presented at the 41st Annual Meetings of the African Studies Association, Chicago, Illinois, 29 October-1 November 1998. I have benefited from valuable criticisms and insights of Professor Helen Desfosses, Professor I. Crawford Young, and Professor Joseph F. Zimmerman. Mistakes are, of course, mine alone.

2. It should be stressed that none of the original three regions is culturally or religiously monolithic. The so-called "north," for instance, includes the Middle-Belt which is heavily Christian, as well as many Christian enclaves in the far north.

3. There are no reliable figures for Christian/Muslim population among the Yoruba. Some have estimated that adherents of the two World religions are equally divided, representing about 80 percent of the Yoruba, while the rest is comprised of traditional believers. For instance, see Simeon Ilesanmi, Religious Pluralism and the Nigerian State (Athens: Ohio University, 1997), Philip M. Parker. Ethnic Cultures of The World: A Statistical Reference (Westport, CT: Greenwood Press, 1997), and Encyclopedia of World Cultures Vol. XI Africa and The Middle East (Boston: G. K. Hall & Co., 1995).

4. Wole Soyinka, "Nigeria's Long, Steep, Bloody Slide," The New York Times, August 22, 1994, p. A13.

5. Arend Lijphart identifies 4 elements of consociational democracy which distinguish it from majoritarian democracy as:

(1) government formed by a "grand coalition" of major groups in a plural society; (2) guarantee of vital minority interests through "mutual veto;" (3) proportionality in political representation, revenue sharing and public appointments; and (4) sufficient segmental autonomy. David Apter is said to have been the first to use the term "consociational" in reference to Nigeria. Lijphart, however, contends that while Apter may have been right because of the grand coalition of the three regionally based political parties in the pre-independence federal cabinet in 1957, the same cannot be said after independence--1959-66. The central government was a coalition of a northern-based NPC and eastern--based NCNC at the exclusion of the western AG.

See Arend Lijphart, Democracy in Plural Societies: A Comparative Exploration (New Haven: Yale University Press, 1977)pp. 25-52 & 161-164.

6. Daniel J. Elazar, Federal Systems of The World (Harlow, U.K.: Longman Group Limited, 1994), p. 175.

7. Report of The Political Bureau (Lagos: The Directorate For Social Mobilisation, 1987), p. 86.

8. L. Adele Jinadu, "Federalism, The Constitutional State, and Ethnic Conflict in Nigeria," Publius: The Journal of Federalism, (Spring 1985), p. 72.

9. Adiele E. Afigbo, "Background to Nigerian Federalism: Federal Features in the Colonial State," Publius: The Journal of Federalism, 21 (Fall 1991), p. 13.

10. Since the return of democratic rule in May 1999 and the first Yoruba-Olusegun Obasanjo-to be elected president of the country, Hausa and Igbo elites have persistently accused his administration of marginalizing the north and the east. To an informed observer, this is an eerie reminder of the pre-Civil War Nigerian politics. See for instance, "Sultan asks Obasanjo to adhere to federal character principle," http://www.afbis.com/vanguard/. July 7 1999; "Obasanjo probes self: denies marginalization," http://www.afbis com/vanguard/, July 22, 1999; and "Lawmaker slams Obasanjo over Marginalization of southeast," http://www.postexpresswired.com/postexpre, July 29, 1999. Alex Gboyega has also noted the continuing salience of ethnoregional cleavages. "No matter into how many states the original three have been subdivided, the tripartite regionalization effected by the colonizer [will continue to have political relevance]... These units are not ethnic but rather 'super-ethno-regional' constructions whose longevity is ensured by the fact that they have become competing teams. Along with cheering fans, they fight for the trophy, both symbolic and tangible, of the right to rule." "Nigeria: Conflict Unresolved," in I. William Zartman, ed., Governance as Conflict Management (Brookings Institution Press, 1998), p. 149.

11. Daniel J. Elazar, "International and Comparative Federalism," PS: Political Science & Politics, (June 1993), p.190.

12. B. 0. Nwabueze, The Presidential Constitution of Nigeria (London: C. Hurst & Company, 1982), p. 37.

13. Daniel J Elazar, ed., Federal Systems of The World (Harlow, U.K.: Longman Group Limited, 1994), p. xiii.

14. Uma 0. Eleazu, Federalism and Nation-building: The Nigerian Experience 1954-1964 (Elms Court: Arthur H. Stockwell Ltd., 1977) p. 9.

15. K. C. Wheare, Federal Government (London: Oxford University Press, 1953), pp. 35-36.

16. Ibid., pp. 37-39.

17. Ibid., p. 36.

18. Uma 0. Eleazu, Federalism and nation-building: The Nigerian Experience (Elms Court: Arthur H. Stockwell Ltd., 1977), p. 72.

19. Ibid., p. 90.

20. Thomas M. Franck, "Why Federalism Fail," in Thomas M. Franck, ed., Whv Federations Fail: An Inguirv into the Requisites for Successful Federalism (New York: New York University, 1968), pp. 171-74.

21. Ibid.

22. Ibid., p.173.

23. John Coakley, ed., The Territorial Management of Ethnic Conflict (London: Frank Cass & Co. Ltd., 1993), p. 15

24. I am grateful to Professor Crawford Young for alerting me to these differences.

25. John Coakley, ed., The Territorial Management of Ethnic Conflict (London: Frank Cass & Co. Ltd., 1993), p. 15

26. Ibid., p. 16.

27. Daniel J. Elazar, "International and Comparative Federalism," PS: Political Science and Politics, June 1993, p.194.

28. See John W. Kingdon, Agendas, Alternatives, and Public Policies (New York: Harper Collins, 1995).

29. Ibid., p. 118.

30. Ibid., p. 165.

31. Ibid.

32. Ibid., p. 94.

33. Ibid., p. 90.

34. Ibid., p. 95.

35. Ibid., p. 116.

36. Ibid., p. 131.

37. Ibid., p. 132.

38. Ibid., p. 138.

39. Ibid., p. 146.

40. Ibid., p. 153.

41. Ibid., pp. 165-82.

42. Paul Fordham, The Geographv of African Affairs (Middlesex: Penguin Books Ltd., 1965), p. 103.

43. Mahdi Adamu, The Hausa Factor in West African Historv (Oxford: Oxford University Press, 1978), pp. 25-26. See also Simeon Ilesanmi, Religious Pluralism and the Nigerian State (Athens: Ohio University, 1997).

44. Paul Fordham, op. cit., p. 105.

45. Joseph C. Anene and Godfrey N Brown, eds., Africa in the Nineteenth and Twentieth Centuries (Ibadan: Ibadan University press, 1966), p. 281.

46. Adiele E. Afigbo, "Background to Nigerian Federalism: Federal Features in the Colonial State," Publius: The Journal of Federalism, 21 (Fall 1991), p. 13.

47. See, for instance, Ibid., pp. 13-29., and Jeremy White, Central Administration in Nigeria 1914-1948 (Dublin: Irish Academy Press, 1981).

48. Adiele E. Afigbo, op. cit., p. 20.

49. Ibid., p.22.

50. Ibid.

51. See I. M. Okonjo, British Administration in Nigeria 1900-1950 (New York: NOK Publishers, 1974).

52. Ibid., p. 33.

53. Ibid., pp. 34-35.

54. Helen Chaplin-Metz, Nigeria: A Country Study. 5th edition (Washington, D.C.: U.S. Government printing Office, 1992), pp.37-38.

55. Ben Nwabueze, A Constitutional History of Nigeria (London: C. Hurst & Company, 1982), p. 42.

56. Ibid., pp. 44-45.

57. Ibid., p. 53.

58. Billy Dudley, An Introduction to Nigerian Government and Politics (Bloomington: Indiana University Press, 1982), P. 52.

59. Ibid., p. 54.

60. Ibid., p. 57.

61. R.T. Akinyele, "State Creation in Nigeria: The Willink Report in Retrospect," African Studies Review 39, 2 (September 1996), p. 76.

62. A. H. M. Kirk-Green, Crisis and conflict in Nigeria Volume I (London: Oxford University Press, 1971), p. 12.

63. Ibid., p. 11.

64. See ibid.

65. Billy Dudley, op. cit., p. 57.

66. Ibid., p. 60.

67. Uma 0. Eleazu, Federalism and Nation-building: The Nigerian Experience 1954-1964 (Elms Court: Arthur H. Stockwell Ltd., 1977), pp.86-89.

68. Ibid., p. 87.

69. Ibid., p. 89.

70. Ibid.

71. Ibid., p. 90.

72. See A. H. M. Kirk-Green, Crisis and Conflict in Nigeria, Volume I (London: Oxford University Press, 1971) and R. T. Akinyele, "States Creation in Nigeria: The Willink Report in Retrospect," African Studies Review 39, 2 (September 1996).

73. R. T Akinyele, op. cit., pp. 73-74.

74. See Donald L. Horowitz, "Self-determination" Politics, Philosophy, and Law," in Ian Shapiro and Will Kymlicka, Ethnicity and Group Rights, eds., (New York: New York University Press, 1997), p. 430. Secessionist overtures marked the relationships among the three regions at this time. In fact, as Horowitz (above) points out, the north had wanted to secede when power was wrested from its leadership at the federal level. Similarly, the leadership in the west openly threatened to secede even as the civil war was being prosecuted. See A. H. M. Kirk-Green, Crisis and Conflict in Nigeria, Volume I (London: Oxford University Press, 1971), pp.92-3.

75. Jonas Isawa Elaigwu, "Federalism and National Leadership in Nigeria," Publius: The Journal of Federalism 21 (Fall 1991), p. 128.

76. Ibid.

77. Daniel C. Bach, "Indigeneity, Ethnicity, and Federalism,"in Larry Diamond et al, eds., Transition Without End: Nigerian Politics and Civil society Under Babangida (Boulder: Lynne Rienner, 1997), p. 334.

78. Nereus I. Nwosu, "The Politics of State Creation in Nigeria," African Studv Monographs 16, 1 (1995), pp. 4-5.

79. Report of The Political Bureau (Lagos: The Directorate for Social Mobilisation, 1987). p. 33.

80. Ibid. See also Rotimi T. Suberu, "The Struggle for New States in Nigeria, 1976-1990," African Affairs 90(1991), pp.500- 502.

81. Daniel J. Elazar, "International and Comparative Federalism," PS: Political Science & Politics, June 1993, p. 194.

82. Sam Egite Oyovbaire, Federalism in Nigeria: A Studv in the Development of Nigerian State (New York: St. Martin's Press, 1984), p. xv. See also Ibid.

83. Sam Egite Oyovbaire, op. cit., p. 19.

84. Ibid., p. 15.

85. Ibid., pp. 14-17.

86. Ibid., pp. 14-15. See also Joseph F. Zimmerman, Contemporary American Federalism: The Growth of National Power (Leicester: Leicester University Press, 1992).

87. Ibid., p. 17.

88. Ibid.

89. Ibid.

90. Ibid., p. 11.

91. Daniel J. Elazar, op. cit., p. 194.

92. K. C. Wheare, Federal Government (London: Oxford University Press, 1953), p. 53.

93. See, for instance, Dele Olowu, "The Literature on Nigerian Federalism: A Critical Appraisal," Publius: The Journal of Federalism, 21 (Fall 1991), pp. 158-61.

94. Quoted in Izevbuwa Osayimwese and Sunday Iyare, "The Economics of Nigerian Federalism: Selected Issues in Economic Management," Publius: The Journal of Federalism, 21 (Fall 1991), p. 91.

95. Nereus I. Nwosu, "The Politics of State Creation in Nigeria," African Studies Monographs, June 1995, p. 15.

CHAPTER III:

The Constitution of the Federal Republic of Nigeria, 1999(Abuja, Nigeria: The Government Press)

Ojo, Bamidele A(1999) "The Military And The Democratization Process In Africa" In, Bamidele A Ojo(editor), Contemporary African Politics: A Comparative Study of the Political Transition To Democratic Legitimacy(Lanham, MD: University Press of America) "The Military And national Integration In Nigeria" in, Bamidele A

Ojo(editor),(1998) *Nigeria's Third Republic: The Problems And Prospects Of Political Transition To Civil Rule*(Commack, NY: Nova publishers)

CHAPTER IV:

Obafemi Awolowo, *Path to Nigerian Freedom*(London: Faber and Faber, 1947).

Abubakar Tafawa Balewa, *Legislative Council Debates*(Lagos, March 4, 1948).

Olayiwola Abegunrin, *Nigeria and the Struggle for the Liberation of Zimbabwe: A Study of Foreign Policy Decision Making of An Emerging Nation*(Stockholm, Sweden: Bethany Books, 1993).

_____, and Franklin Vivekananda(editors) *The Political Economy of South-South Cooperation: Towards A New International Economic Order*(Stockholm, Sweden: Bethany Books, 1998).

_____, *Federalism and Political Problems in Nigeria,* Unpublished M.A. Thesis, Department of Political Science, North Texas State University(Denton, Texas, 1975).

John de st. Jorre, *The Brothers' War: Biafra and Nigeria*(Boston,MA.: Houghton Mifflin Company, 1972).

P.N.C. Okigbo, *Nigerian Public Finance*(Evanston, IL.: Northwestern University Press, 1965).

Margery Perham, *Native Administration in Nigeria*(London: 1937).

Ralph Uwechue, *Reflections on the Nigerian Civil war*(New York: Africana Publishing corporation, 1971).

P.H. Odegard and E.A. Helms, *American Politics 2nd Edition*(New York, Harper and Row Publishers, 1947).

A.O. Olukoshi(editor),*The Politics of Structural Adjustment in Nigeria*(London: James Currey, 1993).

_____, The Politics of Structural Adjustment in Nigeria in

Mkandawire and Olukoshi, eds., *Between Liberalization and Oppression: The Politics of Structural Adjustment in Africa* (Dakar: CODESRIA, 1995).

Eghosa E. Osaghae, *Crippled Giant :Nigeria Since Independence* (Bloomington, IN.: Indiana University Press, 1998).

Central Bank of Nigeria Annual Report (Lagos, 1992)

P.O. Agbese Demilitarization and the Prospects for Democracy in Nigeria, *Bulletin of Peace Proposals,* (Volume 22, 1991).

Africa Today(London, August 1998).

Frederick A. O. Schwartz, *NIGERIA: The Tribes, the Nation, or the Race-The Politics of Independence* (Cambridge, MA.: M.I.T. Press, 1965).

Daily Times(Lagos, March 1992).

BBC New Report(London, July, 1998).

National Concord(Lagos, 1992).

Isokan Yoruba Magazine(Volume 3, No.3, Summer 1997).

Nigeria Roundup,(New York: Consulate-General of Nigeria, Information Division, 1970).

The Washington Post (Washington, D.C., 1998, and 1999 issues).

West Africa (London: June 1966).

CHAPTER VI:

1. Dubinsky, E & Kaput J.J.(1994). Research Issues in Undergraduate Mathematics Learning. MAA Notes (33).

2. Egbagha, H. (1999). Education- Casualty of Military Rule. (Guardiannews.com, 1999).

3. George D. M. (1996): Shaping the Future: New expectation for undergraduate Education in Science, Mathematics, Engineering, and Technology. NSF -(Review of Undergraduate education) Report.

4. Leitzel J.R., Fisher P.O. (1996): Making the Change: Pioneering Attempts in Implementing Reform in Mathematics Education. University of Nebraska-Lincoln.

5. Okonkwo Z, Maryland W, Jr., & Crawford B.: Curriculum Innovations and Emerging Careers In The Mathematical Sciences. Technology Education Review, Vol. 1 (2) (1998), 8-16.

6. Toombs W., Tierney W. (1991): Meeting the mandate, Renewing the college and departmental Curriculum. ASHE-ERIC Higher Education Report 6. Clearing House on Higher Education. Chapter X

CHAPTER VIII:

Abegunrin, Olayiwola, Nigeria and the Struggle for the Liberation of Zimbabwe: A Study of Foreign Policy Decision Making of An Emerging Nation (Stockholm, Sweden: Bethany Books, 1992).

_____, Federalism and Political Problems in Nigeria Unpublished M.A. Thesis, Department of Political Science, North Texas State University, 1975

Agbese, P. O. *Demilitarization and the Prospects for Democracy in Nigeria*, Bulletin of Peace Proposals, Vol. 22 (1991).

Akinyemi, A. B., Foreign Policy and Federalism: The Nigerian Experience (Ibadan: University Press, 1974).

_____, *Muhammed/Obasanjo Foreign Policy*, in Oyeleye Oyediran, ed., Nigerian Government and Politics Under Military Rule, 1966-1979 (Lagos: Macmillan Press, 1979).

_____, *The Colonial Legacy and Major Themes in Nigeria's Foreign Policy* in A. B. Akinyemi et al., eds., Nigeria Since Independence: The First 25 Years, vol. X: International Relations (Ibadan: Heinemann, 1989).

Aluko, Olajide, *Essays on Nigerian Foreign Policy* (London: George Allen and Unwin, 1982).

_____, *The Civil War and Nigerian Foreign Policy*, The Political Quarterly, Vol. 42, No. 2 (April-June, 1977).

Awa, Ewe O., Federal Government in Nigeria(Berkeley: University of California Press, 1967).

Babawale, T., *Nigeria's Foreign Policy*, in S. Adejumobi and A. Momoh, eds., The Political Economy of Nigeria Under Military Rule: 1984-1993 (Harare: SAPES Books, 1995).

Daily Times(Lagos), Various issues, 1960-1967.

Forest, T., Politics and Economic Development in Nigeria (Boulder, CO.: Westview Press, 1993).

Gambari, Ibrahim A., Theory and Reality in Foreign Policy Making: Nigeria After the Second Republic (Atlantic Highlands, NJ.: Humanities Press International, 1990).

Gana, T. A., *Nigeria, West Africa and the Economic Community of West African States*, in A. B. Akinyemi et al., eds., Nigeria Since Independence: The First 25 Years, Vol. X: International Relations (Ibadan: Heinemann, 1989).

Idang, Gordon J., Nigeria: Internal Politics and Foreign Policy, 1960-1966 (Ibadan: University Press, 1973).

Garba, Joseph M., The Time Has Come....Reminiscences and Reflections of a Nigerian Pioneer Diplomat (Ibadan: Spectrum, 1989).

King, Mae C., Basic Currents of Nigerian Foreign Policy (Washington, D.C.: Howard University Press, 1998).

Klein, A. *Trapped in the Traffick: Growing Problems of Drug Consumption in Lagos*, Journal of Modern African Studies, vol. 32, no. 4 (1994).

Lerche, Charles O. and Said, Abdul A. Concepts of International Politics (Englewood Cliffs, NJ.: Prentice-Hall, 1970).

Lewis, P. M., *Endgame in Nigeria? The Politics of a Failed Transition Programme*, African Affairs, Vol. 93 (London: 1994).

Nwolise, O.B.C., *The Internationalization of the Liberian Crisis and its effects on West Africa*, in M.A. Vogt, ed., Liberian Crisis and ECOMOG: A Bold Attempt at Regional Peace-Keeping (Lagos: Gabumo Publishers, 1992).

Ofoegbu, R., *Foreign Policy under Military Rule*, in Oyele Oyediran, ed., Nigeria Government and Politics Under Military Rule, 1966-79 (Ibadan: Macmillan Press, 1979).

Okolo, A., *Nigeria and the Superpowers*, in A.B. Akinyemi et al., eds., Nigeria Since Independence: The First 25 Years, Vol. X: International Relations (Ibadan: Heinemann, 1989).

Okolo, Julius E. *Nigeria: Aspirations of Regional Power*, in Stephen Wright, ed., African Foreign Policies (Boulder, CO.: westview Press, 1999).

Olukoshi, Adebayo O. ed., The Politics of Structural Adjustment in Nigeria (London: James Currey, 1993).

_____, *The Politics of Structural of Adjustment in Nigeria*. in T. Mkandawire and A. Olukoshi, eds., Between Liberalization and Oppression: The Politics of Structural Adjustment in Africa (Dakar: CODESRIA, 1995).

Osaghae, Eghosa E., Crippled Giant: Nigeria Since Independence (Bloomington and Indianapolis: Indiana University Press, 1998).

Otubanjo, F. *Introduction: Phases and Changes in Nigeria's Foreign Policy*, in A. B. Akinyemi et al., eds., Nigeria Since Independence: The First 25 Years vol. X: International Relations (Ibadan: Heinemann, 1989).

Polhemus, James H. *Nigeria and Southern Africa: Interest, Policy and Means*, Canadian Journal of African Studies, Vol. 11, no. 1 (177).

Rupert, James The Washington Post (Washington, D.C.: 1993, 1997, 1998, and 1999).

Schwarz, Frederick A.O.., Nigeria: The Tribe, The Nation or the Race: The Politics of Independence (Cambridge, MA.: M.I.T. Press, 1965).

Tijani, Aminu and Williams, David, eds., Shehu Shagari: My Vision of Nigeria: Selected Speeches (London: Frank Cass, 1981).

The Military Balance 1977-1978, West Africa (London: October 24, 1977).

Vogt, Margaret A., ed., Liberian Crisis and ECOMOG: A Bold Attempt at Regional Peace-Keeping (Lagos, Gabumo Publishers, 1992).

Wachuku, Jaja, *Nigeria's Foreign Policy,* Toronto University Quarterly, Vol. XXXI (October 1965).

1* *Head of State Addresses the Nation on Domestic and Foreign Policies,* Nigeria (Washington, D.C.: Embassy of Nigeria, Information Division, July 1976).

CHAPTER IX:

1. Kup A.P. A HISTORY OF SIERRA LEONE, 1400-1787. Cambridge University Press, 1961

2. Fyfe C: A HISTORY OF SIERRA LEONE. Oxford University Press, 1962

3. Hibbert Christopher. AFRICA EXPLORED: EUROPEANS IN THE DARK CONTINENT 1769-1889. Norton and Co. 1983.

4. Gunther John. INSIDE AFRICA. Harper & Brothers, New York 1953

5. Foreign Policy Reports, March 15, 1948 (Role of Freetown during WW2)

6. Lynch H. R. SIERRA LEONE AND LIBERIA IN THE NINETEENTH CENTURY In: JF Ade Ajayi and Ian Espie (Eds): A THOUSAND YEARS OF WEST AFRICAN HISTORY. Ibadan University Press/ Nelson 1965

7. Ajayi, JF. CHRISTIAN MISSIONS IN NIGERIA 1841-91: THE MAKING OF A NEW ELITE. Longmans 1965.

8. Pakenham Thomas. THE SCRAMBLE FOR AFRICA. Random House New York 1991

9. Hargreaves JD: THE ESTABLISHMENT OF THE SIERRA LEONE PROTECTORATE AND THE INSURRECTION OF 1898. Cambridge Historical Journal. XII. I. 1956. 56-80.

10. Crowder Michael. WEST AFRICA UNDER COLONIAL RULE. Hutchison/Ethiope Publishing Corporation 1968.

11. Coleman JS and Rosberg (eds.). POLITICAL PARTIES AND NATIONAL INTEGRATION IN TROPICAL AFRICA. U of California Press 1964.

12. Wiking C. MILITARY COUPS IN SUBSAHARAN AFRICA: HOW TO JUSTIFY ILLEGAL ASSUMPTION OF POWER. Uppsala, Sweden: Scandinavian Institute of African Studies 1983

13. WEST AFRICA (magazine): Sep 5-11, 1988, p 1648; Dec 16-22, 1991, p 2115, Mar 16-22, 1992, p 444, May 18-24, 1992, p 840

14. Ayittey George B. AFRICA BETRAYED. St. Martins Press, New York 1992

15. Onwumechili Chuka. AFRICAN DEMOCRATIZATION AND MILITARY COUPS. Preager, Connecticut 1998

16. Liddell Hart. STRATEGY. Meridian 1991; Faber and Faber Ltd. 1954, 1967

17. MacDonald BS: MILITARY SPENDING IN DEVELOPING COUNTRIES. HOW MUCH IS TOO MUCH? 1997 ISBN 0-88629-314-6 Varleton University Press

18. Karnow S. VIETNAM - A HISTORY. Penguin 1991

19. Ford RE: "TET 1968 - UNDERSTANDING THE SURPRISE". Frank Cass London 1995

20. McNamara RS. IN RETROSPECT: THE TRAGEDY AND LESSONS OF VIETNAM. Times Books, 1995.

CHAPTER X:

1. See Hakan Wiberg" The Security of Small Nations: Challenges and Defences" Journal of Peace Research, Vol.24, No. 4, 1987. p.339. For a deeper analysis and semantic discussion on this, see B.Buzan People, States and Fear: The National Security Problem in International Relations. (Sussex: Wheatsheaf Books Ltd., 1983) p.6. This is well illustrated at the International Institute for Strategic Studies 1980 Annual Conference. See the works of these scholars in the amended printed Papers Presented at the I.I.S.S. Annual Conference in Stressa. (London: Adelphi Papers, no.166; 1980).

2. See "Born-Again Diplomacy" in Neswatch (Lagos) October 29,1990. This author had an Interview with M.A Vogt, one of Nigerian's leading analyst on strategic studies on July 13 1993, and two top military officers, who prefer not to be quoted, said that "Nigeria's unwillingness to assert its leadership has engaged the attention of the politically - aware section of the Nigerian community for a long time. They look at their population, economic potential and large market and see themselves at the vanguard of African and sub-regional emancipation. However because of the countries non-aggressive and subdued approach to border conflicts, especially with Cameroon and Equitoria Guinea when twenty Nigerians were massacred, earning for itself the derogatory label of sleeping giant. Now is pay-day, the initiative is that "we are ready to collect our own".

3. "When Nigeria speaks" West Africa April 4, 1988, also"Giant In the Sun", The African Guardian (Lagos) October 15, 1987. p.7.

4. As pointed out by Dr. Theo-Ben Gurirab, the UN General Assembly President: "It is perhaps a fortuitous but fitting coincidence of history that at the century's end, the secretary-general of the UN and both the president and vice president of the General Assembly are sons of Africa,". Nigeria's objective in ensuring a lasting peace and stability in a fellow African country, donated to S'Leone five thousand bags of rice and a consignment of medicine to former combatants of the Revolutionary United Front (RUF) and Armed Forces Revolutionary Council (AFRC) in Sierra Leone (News Agency of Nigeria. The election of Nigeria's ambassador as vice president was to demonstrate the UN's solidarity with the country, return to democracy after many years of isolation caused by military rule. (News Agency of Nigeria (NAN) Wednesday, September 15, 1999)

5. See Aderemi Ajibewa "Regional Security in West Africa: A Comparative Study with special reference to the OAU Peacekeeping in Chad and the ECOMOG in Liberia". Unpublished Ph.D. Thesis, University of Lancaster 1994, also Aderemi Ajibewa, "Regional Security Problems and Needs" Quarterly Journal of Administration Vol. 24, Nos 1 & 2.

6. C. Clapham, Third World Politics:An Introduction.(London: Croom Helm, 1985) p.1.

7. The literature on this subject is extensive, see Caroline Thomas, In Search of Security The Third World in International Relations (Great Britain: WheatSheaf Books Ltd. 1987), p. 35; Michael Zimmerman, "The two big issues in the world after the reduced threat of nuclear war are poverty in Third world and the global environment" Newsweek International, Jan 1, 1990 and Zdenek Cervenka, The Unfinished Quest for Unity: Africa and the OAU. (London: Friedman Publ., 1977) and B. Buzan, People, States and Fear: The National Security Problem in International Relations. (Sussex: Wheatsheaf Books Ltd., 1983) p.245

8. Among the general literature are C. Clapham, Third World Politics (London: Croom Helm, 1985), Gerald A.Heeger, The Politics of Underdevelopment (London: St. Martins Press, Inc., 1974); See the works of the following: I.William Zartman, Ripe For Resolution Conflict and Intervention in Africa.(Oxford: Oxford University Press, 1985). Chapter 1, Aristide Zolberg, "The Structure of Political Conflict in the New States of Tropical Africa" American Political Science Review, LX11, 1, 1968, and those of Christopher Bertram, Jusuf Wanandi, Stanley Hoffman, Udo Steinbach and others gave us a sound discourse on the Third-World conflicts and International Security, see (London: Adelphi Papers, No.166; 1980).

9 Barry Buzan, People, States and Fear: An Agenda for International Security Studies in the Post-cold War Era. (London : Harvester Publ. 1991). p.188.

10. Works in this direction include, Ralph Onwuka and A.Sesay (eds), The Future of Regionalism (London: Macmillan, 1980), David Mitrany, A Working Peace System (Chicago: Quadrage Books, 1966), W.H.Riker, The Political Theory of Coalition (New Haven: New York Press, 1962). Others are Carol Lancaster, "The Lagos Three: Economic Regionalism in Sub-Saharan Africa," in John Harbeson and Donald Rothchild (eds), Africa in World Politics (Boulder: Westview, 1991) pp. 249-267 and

J. Ravenhill, "Regional Integration and Development in Africa: Lessons from the EAC. Journal of Commonwealth and Comparative Politics. 17 (3), 1979).

11. For an elaboration of obstacle to regional integration at the continental level in Africa, see R.I Onwuka and A.Sesay (eds) op.cit p.2.

12. Interview on the 20 Sept 1994 with Prof. Amadu Sesay, who has done extensive work on socio-economic integration in West Africa, and on Nigeria's leadership role, West Africa, 17-23 February 1992.

13. Interview with Margaret Vogt, see Newswatch, October 29, 1990. Infact, Cote d'Ivoire supported Biafra during the Nigeria's civil war and gave Ojukwu a home after the war.

14. See Aderemi Ajibewa, "Regional Security in an Expanded ASEAN: A New Framework", Pacifica Review, Vol.10, No 2, June 1998, p. 129, and G.Boyd (ed), Regionalism and Global Security (Lexington: Lexington Press, 1984) and Leslie H. Brown, "Regional Collaboration Resolving Third World Conflicts" Survival May-June, 1986, pp. 210-211.

15. Mohammed Ayoob, "Regional Security and the Third World" in M.Ayoob (ed), Regional Security, Third World and World Order (London: Croom Helm Ltd, 1986) pp.3-4.

16. Tom Imobigbe, "Ecowas Defence Pact and Regionalism in Africa" in R.Onwuka and A.Sesay (eds) The Future of Regionalism in Africa (London: Macmillan Press, 1985)p.117.

17. Robin Luckham, 'Security and Disarmament in Africa' in Alternatives: A Journal of World Policy (New Brunswick) 9, 2, Fall 1983, p.205.

18. The concept of interest is notoriously slippery. See T.B.Millar, "Conflict and Intervention" in M. Ayoob (ed), Conflict and Intervention in the Third World. (London: Croomwell Limited, 1975. p.5.

19. Barry Buzan op.cit. p.253.

20. See I.W.Zartman, "Ideology and National Interest" in Vernon Mckay (ed), African Diplomacy: Studies in the Determinant of Foreign Policy. (New York: Fredrick Praeger, 1966)

21. See Aderemi Ajibewa "Regional Security in West Africa: A Comparative Study with special reference to the OAU Peacekeeping in Chad and the ECOMOG in Liberia". Unpublished Ph.D. Thesis, University of Lancaster 1994, pp. 352-3.

22. F.S. Northedge and M. Donelan (eds), op.cit p. 244.

23. See Robinson, op.cit. p. 188 and G.R. Berridge, International Politics: States, Power and Conflict Since 1945.(Sussex: Wheafsheaf Bks, 1987) p. 136.

Nigeria, the mover of the intervention initiative, as stated earlier, is indisputable primus inter pares in Black Africa, successive Nigerian leaders have been very careful to draw a distinction between domination and leadership, prefering to play leadership as to gain good level of relations in the sub-region. The Liberian civil war provided an opportunity to play the leadership role.

24. For details of the report by William Keelings, see Financial Times (London) 21 June 1991. The Nigerian Government issued a press statement denying the claim, see West Africa 5-11 August 1991 also Newswatch December 7, 1992. From the tone of

the Security Council Resolution 788, although championed by Nigeria, it was, however quite clear that countries in the region, especially Nigeria, will continue to finance the peacekeeping mission in Liberia. I interviewed many military officers between 20- 26 June, 1993.

Since I took an undertaking not to disclose the name of this source, confidentiality prevents me from naming most of the staff interviewed on 23 -26 June 1993 at Abuja and ECOWAS Secretariat respectively.

25.Eyo Ate, "NATO Powers, African Security and the Tripoli Summit" Nigerian Forum (NIIA, Lagos) Oct. 1982, p. 791.

26. The "maximalist" school of thought in Nigeria's foreign and defence policy calculations feel Nigeria should become very active in monitoring trouble spots in the sub-region, or a "big brother" in a coalition. While the "minimalists", have seen some limitations on the Nigerian state which are its structural and technological underdevelopment. Interview with Margaret Vogt, Jinmi Adisa and Nwokedi in Lagos, Ibadan and Ife respectively. For more detail on the former, see Eyo Ate, NATO Powers, African Security and the Tripoli Summit" Nigerian Forum (NIIA, Lagos) October 1982. p.791 and the latter's view Celestine Bassey "Nigeria's Defence Policy in a future Continental Order" Nigerian Forum (NIIA,Lagos) Vol. 13, No.2, 1987. This author had informal interview, discussion with other military officers in Lagos and Abuja.

27. N.Nnadozie Nwosu, "African Border Wars, the Cameroun Provocation and Nigeria's Restraint: A Commentary", Nigerian Forum Lagos :N.I.I.A., Dec. 1982 pp. 923-24.

28. For more details on the economic position of Nigeria in the negotiation of Lome I and the establishment of ECOWAS, see Aderemi Ajibewa, "Nigeria and the EEC" and Aaron.T.Gana, "Nigeria, West Africa and the ECOWAS" in A.B.Akinyemi et.al.(eds), Nigeria Since Independence: The First 25 Years.(Lagos: Heineman Educational Books Ltd., 1989).

29. See Jinmi Adisa, "The Politics of Regional Military Cooperation: The Case of ECOMOG", in M.A. Vogt (ed), The Liberian Crisis and ECOMOG. (Lagos:Gabumo Publ. Ltd.1992) p. 210. For an analysis of the Nigerian economic assistance in terms of grants, concessionary prices for African States before the establishment of ECOWAS, see O. Aluko, 'Oil at Concessionary Prices for Africa: A Case Study of Nigerian decision-making" African Affairs Vol.75, No. 301, October 1976, p.430.

30. Aderemi Ajibewa, "The Third Republic and Nigeria's Foreign Policy Option" in B.A. Ojo (ed), Nigeria Third Republic: The Problems and Prospect of Political Transition to Civil Rule (Nova Science Publ. Inc., 1998), Chapter 5.

31. New African January 1994.

32. See Jullyette Ukabiala,"Defence Ministry plans to Recycle Used Shells" The Guardian, Lagos, Sept. 10, 1987. pp.1 & 2.33. For a brief reason given for the action, See also Byron Tarr " The Response of External Powers to ECOWAS' ECOMOG Initiative", a contribution to ECOMOG: A Preliminary Assessment of Conflict Resolution in Africa (Unpublished manuscript, 1993) pp.31-32.

34. Official Journal of ECOWAS, Vol.17, June 1990, p.24. The Chadian war caused Prof. Bolaji Akinyemi, then External Affairs Minister, to shuttle to France in search

of peace for the war-torn Chad because the war has always spill over to Nigeria in form of refugees and destitutes. In addition, to have peace and security in the sub-region, Nigeria under Major-General Muhamad Buhari hosted a summit with his counterparts from Ghana, Togo, and

Benin Republic after the three extradiction treaties aimed at raising security and peace by checking trafficking in arms and ammunition, currency, drugs, narcotics and psychotropic substances were signed.

35. The African Guardian (Lagos) April 29, 1991. p.13
36. Quoted from S.Byron Tarr, op cit. p.23.

CHAPTER XI:

* Kelechi Kalu has published several articles and book chapters on Nigerian Foreign Policy, Third World Studies, Political Economy of Ethnicity in Nigeria and The Political Economy of State Reconstitution inAfrica. He is the author of Economic Development and Nigerian Foreign Policy (New York: The Edwin Mellen Press, 2000). He is an Associate Professor in the Department of Political Science at The University of Northern Colorado, Greeley, Colorado.

1. In Theory of International Politics, (New York: Random House, 1979), pp.91-92, Kenneth Waltz argues that for constructing a sensible theory that richly describes the motivations and actions of states within the constraining structure of the international system characterized by anarchy, one has to assume that "survival is a prerequisite to achieving any goals that states may have." This assumption makes it possible to analyze the behavior of states in trade and or other cooperative policies as if such policies are premised on the security need of states.

2. Stephen Krasner, "Realism, Imperialism, and Democracy: A Response to Gilbert," Political Theory, vol. 20 No. 1, (February 1992): 38-52, p.39.

3. Robert O. Keohane, "Realism, Neorealism and the Study of World Politics," in Robert Keohane, editor, Neorealism and its Critics. (New York: Columbia University Press, 1986), p. 7.

4. Ibid., p. 11.

5. Kenneth Waltz, op. cit.

6. Ibid.

7. See Robert O. Keohane, "Institutional Theory and the Realist Challenge after the Cold War," in David A.Baldwin, editor, Neorealism and Neoliberalism: The Contemporary Debate. (New York: Columbia University Press, 1993), p. 271.

8. Ibid. In Complex Interdependence, Robert Keohane and Joseph S. Nye argue that international organizations have been very important in helping states develop coalitions in world politics in such issue-areas as the 1972 Stockholm Environmental Conference, the 1974 World Food Conference, and the 1975 United Nations special session; and, to discuss a New International Economic Order and the continuing functions of the IMF and GATT in the management of money and trade. (New York:

HarperCollins Publishers, 1989), pp. 35-36. For a counter argument on the effectiveness of international organization and cooperation, see Joseph M. Grieco, Cooperation among Nations: Europe, America, and Non-Tariff Barriers to Trade. (Ithaca & London: Cornell University Press, 1990).

9. See David A. Baldwin, (1993), p.272. The concept of international regimes as used here is the same as Stephen Krasner's. Krasner defines international regimes "... as sets of implicit or explicit principles, norms rules, and decision-making procedures around which actors expectations converge in a given area of international relations." See Stephen D. Krasner, editor, International Regimes. (Ithaca & London: Cornell University Press, 1983), p. 2.

10. Robert O. Keohane, After Hegemony: Cooperation and Discord in the World Political Economy.(Princeton, New Jersey: Princeton University Press, 1984), p. 84. Keohane defines discord "as the situation in which governments regard each others' policies as hindering the attainment of their goals, and hold each other responsible for these constraints,"(p.52) and cooperation is a situation that allows "... intergovernmental cooperation [to] take place when the policies actually followed by one government are regarded by its partners as facilitating realization of their own objectives, as the result of a process of policy coordination," (p.51-52).

11. Classical Realists such as Thomas Hobbes and Hans Morgenthau assume that some individuals naturally lust for power, and thus the fundamental purpose of statecraft must be the acquisition of sufficient power to prevent other states from dominating one’s state. Neorealists such as Kenneth Waltz, John Mearsheimer and Joseph Grieco argue that while states acquire more power for survival and security, it is not the individual leader’s lust for power that results in their behavior. Rather, it is the absence of a world government that lead states to sort out their security needs through unilateral military and economic policies. Thus, irrespective of the nature of a given state, neorealists argue that similarly placed states in the international system will tend to behave in a similar manner due to the effect of anarchy.

12. Kenneth Waltz, (1979), pp. 105-107. Also, see Joseph M. Grieco, (1990), pp. 3-10. Realists and liberals share the view that the fear of cheating impedes cooperation among states. Grieco criticizes liberals for believing that only the fear of cheating inhibits agreements from which both sides would gain. According to Grieco, state "A" as a "defensive positionalist" may also fear that state "B" may have greater relative gain that could compromise "A's" security.

13. Robert Jervis, "Cooperation Under the Security Dilemma," World Politics, Vol. 30 (January 1978), p. 167.

14. See David A. Baldwin, (1993), op. cit., p. 274.

15. See Akinyemi, A. B., et. al. (1983). Readings and Documents on ECOWAS, (Lagos: Nigerian Institute of International Affairs), pp. 671.

16. Ibid., p. 686.

17. Ibid.

18. See Kelechi Kalu, Economic Development and Nigerian Foreign Policy, op. cit.

19. Some might argue that Nigeria's population and Gross National Product (GNP), both of which are estimated at 55-75% of ECOWAS total makes Nigeria a core state and

therefore an effective underwriter of the community's collective interest. I disagree. Raw materials are generally irrelevant until they have been transformed into useable products. See Clement Adibe, "ECOWAS in Comparative Perspective," in Timothy M. Shaw and Julius Emeka Okolo, editors, The Political Economy of Foreign Policy in ECOWAS. (New York: St. Martins Press, 1994), pp. 194.

20. See West Africa (28 May-3 June 1990): 883 and Clement Adibe, op. cit., p. 195.

21. Aaron T. Gana, "Nigeria, West Africa and the Economic Community of West African States," in A. B. Akinyemi, S. O. Agbi and A. O. Otubanjo, editors, Nigeria Since Independence: The First 25 Years (Volume X : International Relations) (Ibadan: Heinemann, 1989), p. 121.

CHAPTER XIII:

Adelman, I and Morris C.T. Society, Politics, and Economic Development Baltimore: Johns Hopkins University Press. 1967.

Afigbo, A.E. "Federal Character: Its Meaning and History". in Ekeh P and Osaghae, E.E (ed) Federal Character and Federalism in Nigeria. Ibadan: Heineman Educational Books, 1989.

Agbese P.O. "Ethnic conflicts and Hometown Associations: An analysis of the experience of the Agila Development Association. Africa Today April-June 1996 Vol 43 No. 2.

Alesina, A., and E. Spolaore. Public Goods and Ethnic Divisions. World Bank, Washington, DC. 1997.

Ayida, A.A. 1990. "The Rise and Fall of Nigeria." Lagos - Malthouse Publishing Press Ltd.

Awolowo, OJ: The Peoples Republic

Azikiwe, N. Inaugaural Address

Bardhan, P. "Method of Madness? A Political Economy Analysis of the Ethnic Conflicts in Less Developed Countries." World Development Vol 25 No. 9 p.1997

Barro, R. "Determinants of Economic Growth: A Cross-Country Empirical Study," NBER Working Paper No. 5698. 1996.

Coates, S and Loury, G.C. "Will Affirmative Action Eliminate Negative Stereotypes?" American Economic Review.1993

Collier, P. "The Political Economy of Ethnicity." Paper presented at the Annual Bank Conference on Development Economics. Washington DC. April 1998.

Cronje, S. The World and Nigeria. London: Sidgwick and Jackson 1972.

Cross M. 1978: "Colonialism & Ethnicity: A Theory and Comparative Case Study." Journal of Ethnic and Racial Studies Vol 1, 1978.

Ekeh, P.P & Osaghae E.E (ed). Federal Character and Federalism in Nigeria. Ibadan: Heineman Educational Books. 1989.

Easterly, W., and R. Levine. "Africa's Growth Tragedy." Quarterly Journal of Economics. 1998.

Emretiyoma, K. "Exorcising the Ethnic Demon" in the Vanguard Newspaper, Nov 10, 1999

Fukuyama, F. Trust: The Social Virtues and The Creation of Prosperity. NY: The Free Press. 1995.

Gboyega, A. "The Public Service and Federal Character" in Ekeh P and Osaghae, E.E (ed) Federal Character and Federalism in Nigeria. Ibadan: Heineman Educational Books, 1989.

Geller, D.S.; J. D. Singer. Nations at war: A Scientific Study of International Conflict. Cambridge: Cambridge University Press. 1998.

Graf WD. The Nigerian State: The Political Economy, State Class and Political System in the Post-Colonial Era. London: James Currey 1988.

Gurr T.R. "Minorities at Risk: A Global View of Ethnopolitical Conflict". United States Institute of Peace, Washington DC, 1993.

Harris, JR. 1997. Africa and Southeast Asian Development Since 1960: Are there Lessons that Can be Learned? Mimeo. Boston University.

Herbst, J.: "Is Nigeria a Viable State?" The Washington Quarterly Spring 1996 Vol. 19.

Horowitz, D.L 1998. Structure and Strategy in Ethnic Conflict. Paper presented at the Annual Bank Conference on Development Economics. Washington DC. April 1998.

Horowitz D.L. Ethnic Groups in Conflict Berkeley. University of California Press, 1985.

Holden, M (Jnr). Continuity and Disruption: Essays in Public Administration. Pittsburgh: University of Pittsburgh Press. 1996

Huag, M. R. "Social and Cultural Pluralism as a Concept in Social System Analysis," American Journal of Sociology 73 (November, 1967)

Jalai, R. "Preferential Policies and the Movement of Disadvantages: The Case of Scheduled Castes in India." Journal of Ethnic and Racial Studies Vol 16 No. 1 January 1997.

Lederach JP Building Peace: Sustainable Reconciliation in Divided Societies. Washington D.C. United States Institute of Peace Press. 1997

Lian, B, JR Oneal. "Cultural Diversity and Economic Development: A cross-national Study of 98 countries, 1960-1985". Economic Development and Cultural Change, 1997

Loury GC (Paper on Racial Income Differences) (19XX)

Maier K. Into The House of Their Ancestors: Inside the New Africa. New York: John Wiley and Sons.. 1998

Maynes, CW. Containing Conflicts. Foreign Policy, Spring 1993 No. 90.

Marx, A.W. Making Race and Nation: A Comparison of the United States, South Africa, and Brazil. Cambridge: Cambridge University Press. 1997.

McDonough P. Barnes SH. The Cultural Dynamics of Democratization in Spain London: Cornell University Press 1998.

Mohammed-Salih, M.A.; Markakis, J. Ethnicity and The State in Eastern Africa. Uppsala: Nordiska

Morris-Jones,W.H & Austin D. (ed.) Soldiers and Oil London: London: Frank Cass, 1978.

Nnoli, O. Ethnic Politics in Nigeria. Enugu: Fourth Dimension Publishers. 1978.

Osaghae E.E. "Managing Multiple Minority Problems in a Divided Society: The Nigerian Experience." Journal of Modern African Studies 36

Orizu, N. Without Bitterness ******* 1944.

Paden, JN. Ahmadu Bello Sarduana of Sokoto London: Hodder and Stoughton1986.

Pfaltzgraff RL, and Richard H. Shultz (ed.) Ethnic Conflict and Regional Stability: Implications for US Policy and Army Roles and Missions. US Army War College. 1993.

Post K, Vickers M. Structure and Conflict in Nigeria 1960-1966. London: Heineman Educational Books 1973.

Putnam Robert. Making Democracy Work: Civic Traditions in Modern Italy. Princeton: Princeton University Press. 1993.

Renolds, L.G. Economic Growth in the Third World, 1850 – 1980. New Haven, CT: Yale University Press. 1985.

Rodrick, D. "Where Did All the Growth Go? External Shocks, Social Conflict, and Growth Collapses". NBER Working Paper 6350, 1998.

Sachs, J, and A. Warner. "Sources of Slow Growth in Africa". Harvard Institute for International Development. 1997.

Sanda, A. O. (ed). Ethnic Relations In Nigeria. Ibadan: Department of Sociology, University of Ibadan, 1976.

Soynika, W. "Of Faith and Culture" Post Express December 1, 1999

Soyinka, W "The Federal Quest" West Africa Review 1.1. 1999

Toyo, E " The Minority Question and the Common Good". The Guardian November 4, 1999.

Uhuo, J. The Era of Ethnic Clashes in The Vanguard Newspaper, Nov 10, 1999

Utomi, P. " Minority Question and the Common Good". The Guardian November 4, 1999.

Central Bank of Nigeria. Annual Report, 1990

Central Bank of Nigerial. Statistical Bulletin Vol 6, No. 2, December 1995.

Federal Office of Statistics: Digest of Statistics December 1996 FOS Lagos, Nigeria.

Federal Office of Statistics: Review of the Nigerian Economy July 1998.

Federal Republic of Nigeria Gazette No. 70 Vol 83 Federal Character Commission Establishment December 1966.

"Cautious, Pace: After Nile 12 Dust." The Guardian December 12, 1999.

The London Independent Observer December 11, 1999.

The Vanguard Newspaper November 3, 1999

"The Northern Governors Urge Strict Federal Character Compliance" The Guardian November 1, 1999.

"Five Die as OPC, Ijaw Youths Clash" The Vanguard Newspaper November 1, 1999.

This account is in the Guardian of December 12 1999.

At the time of writing many more States in the North – Kano, Sokoto, Borno - have declared their intention to adopt Sharia. The government of the eastern State of Cross River has threatened to declare the state a "Christian State" and the Christian Association of Nigeria (CAN) has threatened to go to court to challenge the constitutionality of the adoption of Sharia. CAN has also threatened civil disobedience.

These conflicts in the first Republic led to a disastrous civil war between 1967-1970 in which about one million people lost their lives. This section relies heavily on Afigbo A.E. (1987)

On derivation, Aboyade (1979) had this to say: "The derivation principle has little or no place in a cohesive fiscal system for national or social development." Put differently, a country trying to forge a national character, unity and identity. There has been a slight amendment to this. Thirteen percent of Federally collected revenues is now set aside for the Niger Delta and Oil Producing Areas.

CONTRIBUTORS

Dr. Olayiwola Abegunrin: Olayiwola Abegunrin is a professor of international relations at the department of political science, Howard University, Washington Dc. Formerly the acting head of department of International Relations, University of Ife (now Obafemi Awolowo University)Nigeria, Dr. Abegunrin holds a PhD in International Relations, History and Political Economy from Howard University, Washington DC. His research and publications focus on international relations, African Politics, Political Economy and US foreign policy towards Africa. He is the author of *Nigeria and the Struggle for Liberation of Zimbabwe: A Study of Foreign Policy Decision-Making of An Emerging Nation* (Stockholm, Sweden: Bethany Books, 1993); Co-author of *U.S. Foreign Policy Towards Southern Africa: Andrew Young And Beyond* (London: Macmillan Press, joint publication with St.Martin's Press, New York, 1987) and three other published books. His articles have appeared in scholarly and internationally recognized journals, including, *International Affairs*(London), *Scandinavian Journal of Development Alternatives* (Stockholm, Sweden);*Journal of African Studies*(UCLA), and many others.

Dr. Remi Ajibewa: Dr. Aderemi Ajibewa graduated with a PhD degree in Politics & International Relations from the Lancaster University, U.K. His research interest include: Regional Security Issues, US Foreign Policy, Comparative Politics, International Relations, Peace & Conflict Analysis/Resolution. Aderemi Ajibewa is currently a Researcher/Community Organizer at the Minnesota Association of Community Organization for Reform Now (MN ACORN). His research and teaching career has been international in scope. He has worked in many areas and developed expertise in many sub-fields of international politics including, non profit organizations and teaching at Universities in Asia, Africa, Europe and the US. He was recently co-ordinator of International Studies program at the University Malaysia Sarawak. In his long career as a university professor, he has taught at the University of Ife, Nigeria, Sussex University, Brighton, Edge Hill College, Ormskirk, U.K and the University Malaysia Sarawak, Malaysia.. He won the prestigious British Airways fellowship in 1989 and the Lancaster University Senate Award. At the Univ. Malaysia Sarawak, he was given an award for "excellent teaching" in 1996. He has been a visiting scholar and lecturer in Singapore,

Brunei and the United States. His views have appeared in several authoritative journals and books such as " Destiny of the Colored Peoples of the US Politically Considered", Nigeria and the European Community in Macmillan Ltd.,1990, Indigenous Technology and Industrialization in Developing Countries: Nigeria As a Case Study, Journal of Third World Science, Technology and Development (Frank Cass, London 1990), The Civil War in Zaire (now Democratic Republic of Congo), Africa Update, (US) Fall, 1997, A Framework for Internal Regional Conflict Resolution in Southeast Asia Context, The Indonesian Quarterly, South East Asian Security Issues, UNIMAS Today,(Malaysia) 1997, The Civil War in Chad, International Security Digest (London) Vol. 2, No.6, 1995, Regional Security Problems and Needs, The Quarterly Journal of Administration Vol. XXIV, Oct. 89/Jan. 90, The Organization of African Unity and the Quest for An African High Command Nigerian Forum, Vol. 8, 1988, Two Party System is Ideal. A Commissioned Paper for the Federal Government of Nigeria Political Bureau on Nigeria: In Search of a New Political Order Vol. 1, 1987, Regional Peace - Keeping in West Africa: Learning and Lessons for Southeast Asia The Indonesian Quarterly Fourth Quarter, 1998, to mention a few.

Dr. Victor Edo-Aikhiobare: Edo-Aikhionbare is an Associate Professor and head of the department of political science at Salt Lake Community College, Salt Lake City, Utah. His research interests are in democratic governance, legal and constitutional systems, and international law and politics. His publications have appeared in the National Social Science Journal, U.S. Encyclopedia of International Relations, Focus, and others.

Adeolu Esho Esq: Adeolu Samson Esho graduated from the University of Ife, Ile-Ife (now Obafemi Awolowo University) with a BSc degree in Social Science majoring in Political Science in 1984 and an MSc degree in International Relations in 1986. Adeolu, as one of the multitude of Nigerian youths dreamt big dreams including becoming either a diplomat or a professor of political science but had to adjust his ambition midway as a result of the uncertainty of the Nigerian situation and the shear luck of working in a computer management consultancy company in Lagos as a deputy manager, administration. Here he developed an interest in computers and found a new career. This new interest took him to London, England, where he studied for and obtained a masters degree in information systems engineering at Southbank University. He had to undergo a one year study to show competence for the MSc program by obtaining a post graduate diploma in information systems engineering. Adeolu moved to the USA where he worked as a systems engineer with a systems integrator headquartered in Dallas, Texas and later with Compucom in Silicon valley, California. He hold the Microsoft Certified Systems Engineer (MCSE), the Novell Certified Engineer (CNE), Compaq ASE, HP STAR Network Connectivity Professional and the Intel Systems Integrator certifications among others. Adeolu is now based in Irvine, California with his wife and two children. Though now officially known as a Systems Engineer, Adeolu's primary constituency remain political science and he does not shy away from discussion in this area whenever it arises. He is an executive board member of the Council for African Affairs (CAA) and the Nigerian Democratic Leadership Forum (NDLF).

Kelechi Kalu: Kelechi Kalu received his Ph.D. in 1997 from the Graduate School of International Studies, University of Denver, Denver, Colorado. He has published several articles and book chapters on Nigerian Foreign Policy, Third world Studies, Political Economy of Ethnicity in Nigeria and The

Political Economy of State Reconstitution in Africa. His is the author of The Political Economy of Foreign (Forthcoming, 1999). Kelechi serves as Program Chair, International Studies Association of the Southwestern Social Science Association. He teaches in the Department of Political Science at The University of Northern Colorado, Greeley, Colorado.

Zephyrinus Okonkwo: Dr. Zephyrinus C. Okonkwo was born in Amuzi-Ikenanzizi in the Obowo Local Government- Imo State Nigeria. He attended St. Joseph's School Achara, St. Teresa's School Ikenanzizi, and Sacred Heart School Umunkpeyi. (His father was a teacher!). He attended the University of Lagos from 1975-1978 (for the NCE -program in Mathematics and Chemistry), and served in the National Youth Service Corps at Government Secondary School Bama-Borno State (1978-1979) where he taught Physics and Mathematics. He taught in Imo State for one year before returning to the University of Lagos for B.Sc.In Mathematics/Education and graduated with First Class Honors in 1982. In the fall of 1982, he started the new M.Phil program in Engineering Analysis in the Faculty of Engineering University of Lagos, and earned the Master of Philosophy in Engineering Analysis in 1985. In 1990, Dr. Okonkwo started the Ph.D. program in Mathematics at the University of Texas at Arlington and graduated with the Ph.D. in spring 1994. Dr. Okonkwo has presented several scholarly papers at conferences. His main research focus is in the area of Differential Equations and Optimal Control Theory. Some of his latest publications include: Admissibility and Optimal Control for Difference Equations. (Dyn Systems and Applications Vol. 4 (1996)), Ito-Type Stochastic Functional Differential Equations with Abstract Volterra Operators and Their Control (Dynamic Systems and Applications Vol. 6 (1997)); Approximation Procedures for an LQ- Optimal Control Problem (Libertas Mathematica, Vol. XVIII (1998)); Stochastic Functional Differential Equations with Abstract Volterra Operators 1: Existence of Solutions- (Volterra Equations and Applications -Gordon & Breach, 1999), and Curriculum Innovations and Emerging Careers in the Mathematical Sciences-Technology Education Review, Vol. 1 (2) (1998). Other research interests include mathematics and Science Education, and economic development. He is a reviewer for the Mathematical Reviews and a Consulting Editor for Technology Education Review- a referred journal. Dr. Okonkwo formerly a tenured Associate Professor of Mathematics at Alabama State University, is currently at Albany State University, Albany, Georgia. He is married to Maryjane Okonkwo. They have four children.

Mark Okoronkwo: An international civil servant, Mark is currently the Claims Officer of a UN Peacekeeping Mission on the Golan Height, between Syria and Israel. He holds a B.A degree in Business Administration. He is married and has 4 children.

Nowamagbe A Omoigui: Dr. Nowamagbe Austin Omoigui is an Associate Professor of Medicine and Chief of Cardiology at the University of South Carolina in Columbia, SC, USA. He is a Board Certified Internist and Cardiovascular Disease Expert with a Masters Degree in Public Health (University of Illinois).

He attended Federal Government College, Warri; Kings College, Lagos and the University of Ibadan, Ibadan, Nigeria, before proceeding to the US for advanced postgraduate studies. Before then, he had been a youth corper at the Brigade of Guards, Nigerian Army after which he underwent additional training at the University of Benin Teaching Hospital. He was recipient of the prestigious NYSC Presidential National Certificate of Honor in 1983. In the US he trained in Internal Medicine at the University of Rochester affiliated hospitals and Cook County Hospital, Chicago, Illinois, before proceeding to Stanford University Medical Center, Palo Alto, CA, for fellowship in Cardiology and Health Policy. At Stanford, he was the recipient of the prestigious Timothy Beckett and Hewlett Packard Awards. He subsequently attended the Cleveland Clinic, Cleveland, Ohio where he acquired skills in advanced interventional cardiology. Dr. Omoigui is an amateur military strategist and foreign policy analyst both of which he pursues as hobbies.

Tope Omoniyi: Dr. Tope Omoniyi, formerly a Senior Lecturer at the Centre for Applied Linguistic Research, School of English Language Education, Thames Valley University, London, United Kingdom, is currently a senior lecturer in sociolinguistic at the Department of English Language and Linguistics at Roehampton Institute, London. His research and teaching and research interests include issues relating to language and identity, language, ethnicity and citizenship; language and hybrid identities especially in cross-border contexts; mediated discourse and identity; refugee studies; and language in national development. Published works include "My blood, my nation: Ethnicity and nationality as alternative and hierarchical identities in African Borderlands" ITL Review of Applied Linguistics 1997: 117-118, p.27-50; Rural Communities across International Boundaries: Implications for Language and Ethnicity in Afro-Asian Perspective, In J.A. Fishman (ed.) Language and Ethnic Identity in Disciplinary and Regional Perspective. New York: OUP 1999.

Adegboyega Somide: Adegboyega A. Somide is a Ph.D. candidate in political science at the Rockefelller College of Public Affairs and Policy, State University of New York at Albany. His current research interests include ethnic relations in South Africa and Nigeria and the role of regional organizations in managing internal conflicts in Africa.

Bamidele A Ojo: Dr. Ojo is a professor of political and international studies at the School of political and International Studies, Fairleigh Dickinson University in New Jersey, USA. He is also the executive- director of the Council For Africanaffairs, a non-profit research and educational foundation on African affairs. Bamidele received his BS in Political Science, Msc in International Relations and Diploma in French from the University of Ife in Nigeria. He also received an Mphil in African Studies and a Phd in Political science from the Centre d'etudes d'afrique noire, Instititut d'etudes politiques,

Universite de Bordeaux 1. France. And an LLM International Law from the University of Nottingham, England. Dr. Ojo also received other degrees including a DELF in French from the Universite de Clemont ferrand, France, DIHL, International Humanitarian Law, Wegimont, Belgium. He has published extensively in comparative politics, international law, African studies and human rights. Among his publications are: Human Rights and the New World Order: The Questions of Universality, Acceptability and Human Diversity(Commack, NY: Nova 1997);(editor) Nigeria's Third Republic: The Problems and Prospects of Political Transition To Civil Rule (Commack, NY: Nova, 1998); (editor) Contemporary African Politics: A Comparative Study of Political Transition To Democratic Legitimacy(Lanham: MD: UPA, 1999) and he is currently working on Globalization: In Context and Viewed From Below and Amidst the Decay : Issues, Problems and Politics In Contemporary African Politics. Bamidele is also actively engaged in encouraging Nigerians abroad to get involve in salvaging Nigeria from its current malaise. " We can write, we can profess, we can condemn but we can also impact more when we are involved".

Kasirim Nwuke: Kasirim holds a PhD and teaches economics at Wellesley College, Wellesley, MA and a Research Fellow at the African Studies Center, Boston University,Boston, MA.

INDEX

F